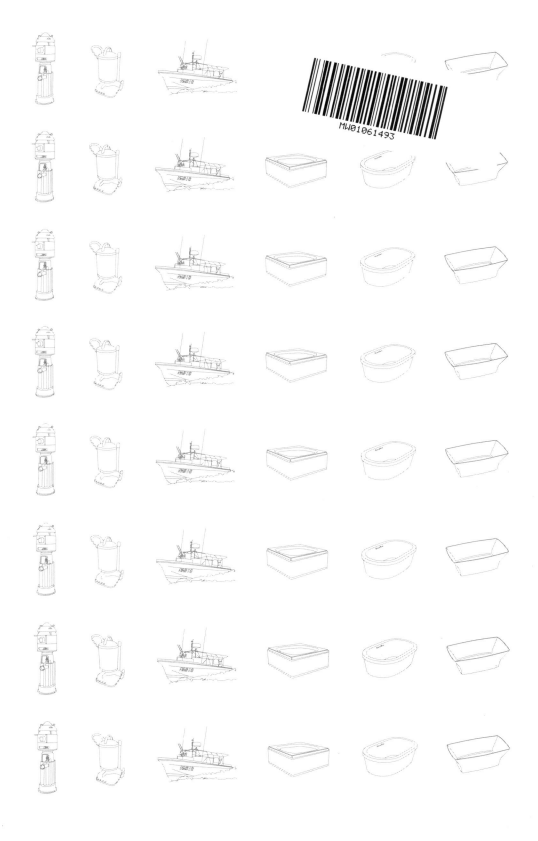

SPIRIT, WIND & WATER

The Untold Story of the Jacuzzi Family

Remo Jacuzzi

WELCOME RAIN PUBLISHERS
NEW YORK

Dedication

To Paula, the love of my life and mother of our six children, I dedicate this book. Her support throughout the sometimes hard, but mostly wonderful times of our fifty years of marriage also made possible the publication of *Spirit, Wind & Water*.

The book relates how we first met in 1951, in a high school math class, and married six years later. Paula had the good fortune over the years to know many of my Jacuzzi aunts and uncles, and her talent for remembering their many stories and numerous family events enabled me to portray my family in a warmer and more complete manner than I could ever have managed by myself.

Acknowledgments

High on the list of people I must acknowledge for their help and encouragement with the project of writing this history of the Jacuzzi family are the three youngest children of my grandparents Giovanni and Teresa Jacuzzi. These ladies, my aunts Cirilla, Stella, and Gilia, literally poured out their hearts with their recollections of their young years growing up in Italy and then of the Jacuzzi families' lives in the United States. They very much wished for a true history of the events that shaped theirs and the family's lives and accomplishments. Hopefully this book, *Spirit, Wind & Water* accomplishes their objectives.

My oldest brother, Virgil, who was born in Italy in 1919, and my cousin Lola Jacuzzi Fenolio, born in California, also in 1919, and my sister Jaconda Jacuzzi Hawkins, born in 1923 in California, provided much information about their own young lives and those of the family as they grew up in California. They, being a number of years my senior, provided both their written and verbal recollections, which helped give body to the descriptions of the Jacuzzi family's early years in the United States. Also a great help with this project were my brother Dante; my cousins Leo Bianchi, Lydia Benassini Negherbon, and Tullio Jacuzzi; Granucia Jacuzzi, my cousin Aldo's wife; my maternal cousin Federico DeCesero; my wife, Paula; and especially my sister Rachel, who added her valuable recollections and suggestions. I also thank the many other Jacuzzi family members who generously contributed photographs of their branches of the family. I am most appreciative to these and other family members who provided help and encouragement.

In addition to family contributions I must acknowledge the help and materials provided by friends and ex-Jacuzzi employees, including Janet Gregor, Lovetta Loveless, Don Roescheise, Bill Hartman, Tim Grissom, Phillips Kauke, Nell Lyford, and Inez Marchetti. Their assistance has also proven invaluable.

ACKNOWLEDGMENTS

My acknowledgments would not be complete if I did not also recognize my parents Valeriano and Giuseppina Jacuzzi. While they both passed on before I started this project, they were instrumental in instilling in me a love of family and family unity that I hope is conveyed by *Spirit, Wind & Water*.

Contents

The Giovanni and Teresa Jacuzzi Family Tree

*The 13 children born to Giovanni and Teresa Jacuzzi were:

Rachele (Rachel), son, born November 11, 1886
married Olympia Calugi
children: Giordano (Gordon)

Valeriano (Valerio), son, born December 16, 1887
married Giuseppina Piucco
children: Virgil, Dante, Jaconda, Teresa, Mary, Flora, Remo, Rachel

Francesco (Frank), son, born March 12, 1889
married Rena Villata
children: Giocondo, Ugo

Giuseppe (Joseph), son, born February 5, 1891
married Rena Beggio
children: Aldo

Gelindo, son, born January 31, 1894
married Rosie Meinero
children: Lola, Olga, Tullio, Rodolfo, Daniele

Giocondo, son, born July 5, 1895
married Mary Guarneri
children: Anna

Felicita, daughter, born May 15, 1897
married Luigi Lanza
children: John

Angelina, daughter, born November 23, 1899
married Peter Tunesi
children: Doris, Edith

Ancilla, daughter, born November 8, 1901
married Peter Bianchi
children: Leo, John

Candido, son, born February 24, 1903
married Inez Ranieri
children: Alba, John, Irene, Kenneth

Cirilla, daughter, born March 13, 1905
married Joseph Benassini
children: Harold, Lydia, Norma

Stella, daughter, born April 3, 1907
married Rino Marin
children: Silviano, George

Gilia, daughter, born September 15, 1908
married Jack Peruzzo
children: Nilda, Esther, Peter

Original Jacuzzi Family

Stella (Jacuzzi) Marin
1907-2003

Candido Jacuzzi
1903-1986

Gilia (Jacuzzi) Peruzzo
1908-

Valeriano Jacuzzi
1887-1973

Felicita (Jacuzzi) Lanza
1897-1978

Giocondo Jacuzzi
1895-1921

Angelina (Jacuzzi) Tunesi
1899-1990

Francesco Jacuzzi
1889-1973

Teresa (Arman) Jacuzzi
1865-1943

Giovanni Jacuzzi
1855-1929

Rachele Jacuzzi
1886-1937

Ancilla (Jacuzzi) Bianchi
1901-1949

Giuseppi Jacuzzi
1891-1965

Cirilla (Jacuzzi) Benassini
1905-2000

Gelindo Jacuzzi
1894-1950

Preface

Reflections

"Il passato è un futuro; e il futuro è un mistero."
"The past is a future; the future is a mystery."
—Stella Jacuzzi Marin, twelfth child of my grandparents,
Giovanni and Teresa Jacuzzi

For me, a Jacuzzi is a person, not a machine. A Jacuzzi is a member of my family.

In early 1982, I had just made a tough decision, one that would take my life in a completely new direction. After having oriented my education and my life to work for Jacuzzi Brothers, Inc., the family business founded by my father and his six brothers, and after having worked for the company for more than twenty-three years, I left Jacuzzi Brothers to start my own business.

Incorporated under the laws of the State of California in 1920, Jacuzzi Brothers was originally a family partnership formed in 1915, the year some of the Jacuzzi sons joined together to operate an airplane propeller manufacturing company in Berkeley.

Many of the company's products were highly successful and its business decisions sound, which, in turn, provided the resources and direction to grow the business into a worldwide enterprise. Other products and decisions, however, resulted in heartache and financial loss for the Jacuzzi family.

By 1979, after some troublesome years and an acrimonious lawsuit, the majority of the family ownership decided to sell the company to a growing conglomerate.

I worked a couple of years after the sale for Jacuzzi Brothers, Inc., but

I found working for the nonfamily business was no longer the same. It didn't provide the feeling of working for myself that I had when the business was owned by our family.

The original Jacuzzi family consisted of my grandparents, Giovanni and Teresa, and their seven sons and six daughters, who, between the years of 1907 and 1920, all immigrated to California from northern Italy. For the most part, the majority of the extended Jacuzzi family worked for the family business.

I would say that Jacuzzi Brothers was the central unifying element that kept our large family as close as we were over the years, but this is not to imply that all family members were always in agreement in all decisions that were made.

About Our Family Name

People are often surprised to learn that Jacuzzi is not an Italian or Japanese word for "swirling water." It is, instead, our family's ancestral name.

I am sometimes asked about the spelling of our name, especially by those who are familiar with the Italian language. Since the Italian alphabet does not include the letters *J, K, W, X,* and *Y,* some wonder why our name is not spelled I-A-C-U-Z-Z-I, in accordance with modern-day Italian.

The explanation lies in the evolution of my forefathers' language. Italy was not declared an official kingdom until 1861, and even then it was not the unified country we know today. The people who inhabited this vast peninsula spoke in numerous languages and hundreds of dialects, most of which were rooted in Latin.

The language (or dialect, if you prefer) of my Jacuzzi ancestors was Friulano, which does include the letter *J.* Family records on churches, cornerstones, and memorial plaques (some dating as far back as 1528) show at least six different renderings, including: Jacucio, Jacucivs, Jacuzzo, Jacuz, Iacuzzi, and Jacuzzi. However, the earliest of our family's records list our surname just as we spell it today, Jacuzzi.

With the unification of Italy, the official national language was based on the Tuscan dialect and alphabet used by Italy's great poet, Dante Alighieri, author of *The Divine Comedy.* After unification, although the

Italian government strongly encouraged the adoption of the Tuscan alphabet and language, the majority of dialects continued to be spoken, often influencing the official language.

Spirit, Wind & Water

I believe hard work is the most important element in success. Neither heritage nor receiving some help with a business endeavor has anywhere the same value as one's own ability to put his or her nose to the grindstone.

I offer my own ancestors as proof, for while Jacuzzi may be a household word today, it was a name barely recognized beyond a few small towns in northern Italy just three generations ago. We did not begin as wealthy people, but we were a people rich in spirit.

Some might say that the greatness of the Jacuzzi family began in 1907, when my father and one of his younger brothers immigrated to the United States in search of a better life, or in 1915, when some of the brothers left their imprint on the up-and-coming aviation industry by producing a revolutionary propeller design.

Others could cite the time in 1920, when the brothers developed the first totally enclosed cabin, high-wing monoplane, or in 1926, when they invented the deep-well injector pump, or even in 1954, when Jacuzzi Brothers, by then a booming corporation, introduced the portable hydromassage.

Certainly, all of these achievements in wind and water were great.

And although the Jacuzzi Brothers company became an important unifying element, the story of my family embraces much more. It is an extremely powerful one involving love of God, love of family, family unity and discord, poverty and wealth, hard work, overcoming catastrophes and setbacks and triumphs.

Indeed, I, and all of the family members, know the true secret behind the evolution of Jacuzzi from a surname to a brand name. If our family is to be deemed in any way *great* or *successful,* that honor must be made retroactive to at least the generation of my grandparents, Giovanni and Teresa Jacuzzi. They, our family pillars, personified initiative, courage, tenacity, and loyalty, and they passed those character qualities on to their children and grandchildren.

Giovanni and Teresa understood the spiritual side of our world, and they taught those universal truths to their children and grandchildren. Were it not for their moral and spiritual training, their children might have given up on their enterprises when times of disaster and setback came. But the family legacy—and a strong bond of unity—did not accommodate surrender.

Therefore, my story of the Jacuzzi family—a narrative formed out of spirit, wind and water—begins with Giovanni and Teresa.

ITALY AND AMERICA

Giovanni and Teresa Arman Jacuzzi – 1912

*Parish of the Holy Cross and the Blessed Virgin Mary
of the Rosary – Casarsa*

Chapter 1

Giovanni and Teresa

"Oggi, dobbiamo ricordarli con onore."

"Today, we should remember them with honor."

—Lola Jacuzzi Fenolio, Giovanni and Teresa Jacuzzi's first grandchild

My grandparents, parents, uncles, and aunts did not set out to attain worldwide fame; that came as a by-product of their collective ambition. The Jacuzzi family simply worked to improve the quality of life, both for themselves and for those whose existence was as ordinary as their own. They had ideas and ingenuity and offered one another mutual support in putting those ideas to work. Still, I doubt that any of my ancestors knew how widely accepted and popular their innovations would become. Certainly in the middle of the nineteenth century, my family's ambitions did not extend beyond the small Italian towns in which they lived and worked.

My grandfather, Giovanni, the youngest of three children, was born to Francesco Jacuzzi and Maria Angela Paron Jacuzzi in Casarsa della Delizia, a small town in the northeastern province of Udine, Italy, on October 5, 1855. His father and his mother, who went by her middle name of Angela, named my grandfather after his paternal grandfather by giving him the name of Giovanni Battista, or, in English, John the Baptist. This obviously was a favored family name, for my grandfather had an uncle who was also named Giovanni Battista Jacuzzi. My family called this uncle *Barba Titta*, or Uncle Titta.

Giovanni was a handsome boy with curly blond hair and bright blue eyes. He was of average stature—slender and full grown at five feet,

3

eight inches—but strong and wiry. From an early age, he carried himself erectly, with an alert and energetic demeanor.

Giovanni's father, Francesco, my great-grandfather, was a gifted woodworker. While many in the region were farmers, he earned his living making furniture, doors, and cabinets. He passed this skill on to his oldest son, Luigi, and to his younger son, Giovanni, who later trained his own sons. And, eventually, Francesco's cherished woodworking tools were passed down to Giovanni. So painstakingly taught and learned, the craft proved to be invaluable to my father and his brothers many years later.

Once, when my great-grandfather was asked to make a new set of doors for the Catholic church in Casarsa, the parish priest was so pleased with the craftsmanship that he hired him to be the church sexton. In this position, Francesco was responsible for the care and upkeep of all the church property. But an incident occurred while Francesco was employed by the church that hurt him very deeply.

At the church's request, he signed some papers that made him a guarantor in a certain matter of church business. When the church was unable to meet its financial obligation, Francesco was held liable for the debt. Although he had been a devout man, Francesco grew bitter and would have little to do with the church after that. He reared his children to believe in God, pray, read the Scriptures, and observe the Ten Commandments, but, as a family, Francesco's household was wary of "organized religion."

In 1870, after Francesco's heartbreaking episode with the church, a friend offered my great-grandfather a good job: to become a conductor of horse-drawn streetcars in Trieste. He readily accepted the offer as his recently married daughter, Deosolina, had moved there. He now had the opportunity to reunite his family in a new environment.

Trieste, a large port city on the Adriatic Coast about fifty miles from Casarsa, could offer opportunities that Casarsa could not. My great-grandfather, his wife, Angela, and sons, Luigi and Giovanni, immediately moved there so Francesco could start his new job. In addition to his work as a streetcar conductor, he also kept up his carpentry trade. Luigi, who was eighteen at the time of their move, soon also gained employment as a streetcar conductor.

As there was no public schooling in Casarsa, a little instruction from the Catholic nuns was all the education Giovanni received prior to his living in Trieste. Once the family moved to Trieste, however, his mother, Angela, wanted her young son to have the advantage of a better education. She hired a special tutor to teach him reading, writing, and arithmetic. This basic education served my grandfather well, for later in life he became a successful businessman and head of a large, energetic and pioneering family.

Life in Trieste offered my grandfather other opportunities. Giovanni used to tell his children that he liked to go to the opera, plays, and the circus acts that performed there. He also mentioned seeing the Buffalo Bill show with its many horses and Indians adorned with feathers and beads, which greatly impressed him.

The Breadwinner

Within a few years, however, sorrow struck Francesco's family. First, Luigi died of pneumonia. Then Francesco's daughter, Deosolina, who was childless, became ill and died. And lastly, Francesco also died. Giovanni, who was working as a cabinetmaker, became the sole breadwinner for his mother and himself. Eventually, Giovanni also became a streetcar conductor, a job he held until a very cold winter when heavy and deep snow shut down the streetcars.

During this cold spell he went back to work in a cabinet shop, in working conditions that alternated between extreme heat and cold. He became severely ill with rheumatic fever and was unable to work for several months. Giovanni and Angela were evicted from their rented home and the landlord took them to court to recover the unpaid rent. Ironically, the opposing attorney was a man whose name was the same as that of my grandfather's—Giovanni Jacuzzi. The judge required Giovanni to repay the debt with payments of a few cents per month. When Grandfather arrived to pay the first installment, the landlord took the money and threw it away. Interpreting this action as an indication that the landlord had abandoned the claim, Giovanni never tried to pay him again.

Eventually, in 1884, after fourteen years in Trieste, nostalgia for Casarsa compelled Grandfather and his mother, Angela, to return to

Casarsa. There, near the church, Parrocchia di Santa Croce e Beata Vergine del Rosario (Parish of the Holy Cross and the Blessed Virgin Mary of the Rosary), Giovanni and his mother found a small store with an attached one-bedroom apartment. They purchased this property, opened a fruit and vegetable market in the storefront, and lived together in the rear apartment. Giovanni worked there with his mother for a short time, but as there was very little business, he traveled to Venice to try to make a living selling fish. Things did not go well there either and he returned to Casarsa. Using the woodworking skills his father taught him, he found work in a furniture and cabinet shop. During this time, Giovanni dreamed of starting his own family and built his own matrimonial bedroom furniture.

While their lives together were by no means blissful, the mother and son never succumbed to despair. Rather, they discovered that through hardship their faith in God had been strengthened. Sometimes pain can have that effect on us. In addition, Giovanni was soon to encounter a feeling he missed for a long time—joy, in the person of Teresa.

Teresa

Teresa Arman was born on October 10, 1865, the year the Italian government passed laws calling for unification of the nation. Teresa was born on a Casarsa farm that belonged to her grandfather, a wealthy and literate landowner named Osvaldo Arman. There Teresa lived with her father, Giuseppe, mother, Felicita, a sister, Antonia Margarita, but called "Margarita" for her late grandmother (Margarita Mior Arman), two brothers, Antonio and Luigi, and an uncle and his wife and their six children.

Teresa's mother Felicita was a Raffin, a family that came from the neighboring village of San Lorenzo di Arzene. The Armans were orginally from Rome, where Osvaldo Arman first worked as a street vendor selling polenta. A widower, Grandfather Arman was a true patriarch—the uncontested head of the family and holder of the purse. He was also devoutly religious.

The extended family situation in which my grandmother was reared was not uncommon. In nineteenth-century European culture, it was generally expected that when sons married, they would live and raise their families in the same home in which they themselves grew up. A daughter, on the other hand, usually would move into the family home of her husband.

This arrangement was not only customary, but it also provided a family group that, by working together, had a greater chance of success and prosperity. It was also quite an acceptable practice when Osvaldo added the dowries of his daughters-in-law to the family's communal wealth.

Like Grandfather Giovanni, Teresa's early years had been disrupted by sorrow. A brother, Luigi Arman, died as a child of heart failure. Another staggering blow came when Teresa was eleven years old—her mother severely injured her leg and died from blood poisoning. Teresa's father later remarried, but there were no children from that union.

However, my grandmother had little choice but to accept her circumstances and to adapt to her situation. Despite the crowded atmosphere of her home life and the arrival of her father's new wife, Teresa adjusted well. It may have benefited her that there was little time for mourning. The size of her grandfather's farming operation required that every member of the household work many long and hard hours.

A public school, mostly for children aged six to eight, was opened in Casarsa in 1860. Although Teresa was only five, she was enrolled there at the insistence of her father, who was functionally illiterate (even though his father could read), and wanted an educated child to assist him in his personal business and legal matters and to help assure he would not be taken advantage of. Since his other two children were too old for the school, Teresa would become the most formally educated of them.

When she was not at school or working on the farm, Teresa usually was at church in Casarsa. The Catholic Church was an important part of Teresa's life. Her deeply religious grandfather, Osvaldo, led the family in daily prayers. From the nuns, Teresa received encouragement and instruction in reading and writing and training in the catechism. The nuns also taught her how to sew.

Teresa, in turn, taught the catechism to the younger children in her church. Her admiration for these nuns and her love for the church were so great that Teresa seriously considered joining a religious order herself. But that was not to be. Teresa's frequent visits to the church in Casarsa had been noticed by a certain young man.

Married Life

With his home situated near the church, Giovanni observed the regular comings and goings of the townspeople. One girl in particular—a pretty, young brunette with wavy hair who made frequent visits to the church—soon attracted his attention. She was about five feet, two inches, and her petite size, along with her dark brown eyes and energetic manner, only added to her appeal. Giovanni had several opportunities to talk with her and her stepmother, either before or after their church visits, and finally worked up the courage to request permission to visit their home.

The initial response Giovanni received was not encouraging. While the stepmother liked him, Teresa's father had another young man in mind—someone he deemed more suitable for his daughter. Teresa's father was unconvinced that young Jacuzzi's future was bright. Giovanni had little family income to get him started, and his earning potential did not appear great. Teresa's father objected vehemently to the relationship.

But Teresa's stepmother intervened, using a logic based on custom to try to persuade him. She explained that in marrying Giovanni, Teresa would have the advantage of being the only woman of her generation in the house. This argument, together with Giovanni's persistence, won my great-grandfather over. After an engagement of one year, my grandparents were married on January 30, 1886, in the church in Casarsa. He was thirty; she, twenty.

Teresa's father's concerns were not without substance. Materially, Giovanni would bring very little into the marriage. But what he couldn't contribute in money and possessions, he made up for in diligence and initiative.

The young couple set up housekeeping in the small apartment behind the vegetable store. In keeping with the promise Giovanni had made to his mother, Angela lived with them until her death in 1891, though living conditions in the apartment were cramped. A bedsheet suspended from the ceiling divided the room where the couple and Angela slept.

The early years of their marriage, especially the first two, were difficult for Giovanni and Teresa. Money was scarce. Grandfather Giovanni used the tools he had inherited from his father and continued his cabinetmaking and carpentry trade. However, customers were often hard to find and slow to pay.

During the first year of their marriage, they had some relief when Teresa, along with her brother and sister, inherited a two-bedroom apartment in San Lorenzo di Arzene. This would be the first of three real estate legacies that the Raffin families would leave to Teresa and her siblings. Keeping their storefront property, Giovanni, Teresa, and Angela moved to the more spacious home. Its upstairs bedrooms were reached by an outside stairway.

Eleven months after their marriage, on November 11, 1886, a son, Rachele, was born. A second son, Valeriano—my father—was born on December 16, 1887. Both sons were born in the San Lorenzo apartment.

Soon after, Grandmother Teresa inherited two more parcels of property from the Raffins. These endowments were propitious, for Teresa was pregnant with their third child and they needed larger living quarters. Teresa reached an agreement with her brother and sister to sell the San Lorenzo apartment home they all owned.

Using the proceeds from the sale of the storefront property near the church, and from the sale of other properties Teresa had inherited, Teresa and Giovanni purchased property close to Casarsa within the district of the neighboring town of San Vito al Tagliamento, which they usually referred to as San Vito. Here they would build their new home. Grandmother and Grandfather held on to one piece of inherited property, approximately one acre of land the family called the *champut* or small field. The *champut* was used for raising corn and grape crops.

Although their newly purchased property technically lay within the incorporated limits of San Vito, the Jacuzzis always identified Casarsa as their home. It was much closer to their property than was the town of San Vito al Tagliamento, and most of their business was conducted in Casarsa. It seems, in the beginning, they disagreed about the size of the home, with Grandmother preferring a relatively small one. However, Giovanni's dream of having a large, substantial home eventually won out.

In early 1888, they began building the new three-story home for their growing family. Soon they encountered a major setback, for their money ran out before the house was completed. The first and second floor living quarters were finished. However, the third floor, designated as a granary for storage of the farm crops and the home's roof were not finished.

Grandfather Giovanni already had moved his family and they were occupying the main floors. Only a temporary covering protected them from the elements. With no money for construction, something had to be done. Teresa asked her father, Giuseppe, to loan them the money necessary to get the house under a roof, but he refused. Although he had consented to their marriage, Giuseppe's built-up displeasure with Giovanni and Teresa surfaced when they asked him for the loan.

Giuseppe let loose a litany of complaints. First, he considered Giovanni too proud as he didn't wear *zoccoli*, the wooden shoes of a farmer (wooden soles and leather uppers), and he didn't work in the fields like Giuseppe. The insults continued: Giovanni went to the barber every week instead of learning how to shave himself with his own razor, and his clothes were fashioned by a tailor, instead of being hand-sewn. But what bothered him most was that the couple had ignored the tradition of naming children after their grandparents.

Persisting, Teresa appealed to her father on behalf of his grandchildren. She discussed how her husband was not a farmer but a businessman, and that leather shoes and tailored clothing were more in order for him. Then, a compromise was reached regarding the naming of the children. Their next son would be named Francesco, after Giovanni's father, and the following one would be named Giuseppe, after Teresa's father. In addition, the first daughter would be named Felicita, after Teresa's mother, and the next daughter, Angela, after Giovanni's mother.

Teresa's appeal, Giuseppe's tender heart for his grandchildren, and the compromise finally overruled his resistance. Giuseppe loaned them the money and Giovanni finished the house. And soon afterward, in accordance with their promise, Giovanni and Teresa named their third son, Francesco. Uncle Francesco, or Frank, as he was called in America, was born in March 12, 1889, in the new home that now had a roof.

I often marveled at how clearly my father, Valeriano, could summon distant memories. His earliest was of the house under construction, when he was just ten months old. He remembered being carried in his mother's arms so he could watch the workers lay in the flooring boards on the second floor.

He was aware that the work was not yet completed. In particular, Pa—the name we called him, from the Italian *papa*—remembered the tapered shape of the boards. They were cut in slabs according to the natural contour of the tree. As a child's eye is often drawn to unusual colors or designs, baby Valeriano was intrigued by the alternating pattern of these boards as they were placed with the broad end of one board next to the narrow end of the board beside it.

Years later, when Pa shared this memory at a family gathering, his mother, Teresa, was amazed to learn that he had remembered something so vividly at such an early age and from such a long time ago.

While Grandfather Giovanni supported his family during the first years of his marriage as a cabinet and furniture maker, the region was poor. Business and money were scarce. He told my father, that in those early years, often he would complete a job, to be repaid with only these words, "I'll pay you later, mister, when I have some money to pay you."

Grandfather lamented the hardship of those years, and yet, his life illustrates that though times may be trying, difficulties can make us aim ever higher.

A Business Man

Have you ever heard someone say "an opportunity presented itself"? I find that phrase misleading. As a rule, opportunities never "present" themselves—enterprising people discover them. My grandfather, Giovanni Jacuzzi, was such a person, for he soon discovered some business opportunities that were much more reliable than cabinetmaking. These endeavors would improve his financial situation significantly and lay the groundwork for his family's success in business.

Although Casarsa was a small town, the main rail line connecting Venice and Vienna ran through it. A station was located in Casarsa, causing the town to be filled every day with travelers, and it was in these travelers that Giovanni first saw opportunity.

"Would they," he wondered, "be willing to pay to have their baggage carried or to have errands run?"

With nothing to lose, Giovanni took a chance and discovered that many of them were indeed willing to pay for his services, so he began working as a self-employed porter. He carried trunks, gave travel advice, and generally assisted travelers with their many questions and needs as they passed through the Casarsa station.

Furthermore, Grandfather realized many of the strangers passing through his town ran successful businesses in other cities. He started looking for opportunities to engage them in conversation, hoping to learn from their experiences and expand his own knowledge. He would often pay someone to fill in for him as porter during the lunch hour so he could eat in the *osteria* (inn) among the businessmen. There, he had even more opportunities to talk with these intriguing travelers. From Giovanni's perspective, to converse with them was to learn from them.

Eventually, Grandfather Giovanni made enough money to purchase concessions from the major Italian newspapers. These, plus other reading materials, proved to be highly marketable to the train passengers. The financial base created by this business venture, plus the many relationships he was establishing with local businessmen and land owners, as well as out-of-town travelers, opened Giovanni's eyes to another opportunity. He grew adept at arranging real estate transactions. Whenever he would hear of local property for sale, he would keep a watchful eye and listening ear for a potential buyer.

Given Giovanni's reputation for honesty and friendliness, he was able to negotiate many of these deals, thus becoming a self-made real estate broker. With virtually no overhead costs, Giovanni's commission was almost entirely profit. Even though he had very little formal education, Giovanni was becoming an astute businessman. He studied people and knew what it took to earn and keep another man's trust.

Due to Giovanni and Teresa's initiative and integrity, the future was looking brighter for their family . . . or at least more secure.

View of back side of Jacuzzi ancestral home – 1912

Jacuzzi family at their ancestral home – 1912
Back row from left: Ancilla, Felicita, Gelindo, and Giocondo, whose hat legend
"Giornalaio" translates "newspaper vendor"
Front row from left: Stella, Cirilla, Teresa with Gilia at her side, Candido,
Giovanni, and Angelina

Chapter 2

Growing Up in Casarsa

"Se la luna nuova non è fatta per il 6 di Marzo, sarà la luna di Aprile non di Marzo."

"If the new moon is not made by March 6th, it's the moon of April and not March."

—Teresa Arman Jacuzzi, my grandmother, on the thirteen new moons in each calendar year

Over the years the Jacuzzi family continued to grow in number. By the time their last child was born in 1908, Giovanni and Teresa had thirteen healthy children, seven sons and six daughters. The first six children were sons, including Rachele, born in 1886, and my father, Valeriano, 1887, both of whom were born in San Lorenzo di Arzene. All of the other children were born in their ancestral home, located in the municipality San Vito al Tagliamento near Casarsa, beginning with the next four sons: Francesco, 1889; Giuseppe, 1891; Gelindo, 1894; and Giocondo, 1895. Six daughters and one more son followed: Felicita, born in 1897; Angelina, 1899; Ancilla, 1901; son Candido, 1903; Cirilla, 1905; Stella, 1907; and Gilia, 1908.

Giovanni continued to enjoy relative success in his business ventures, enabling him to purchase several more parcels of farmland. The house, as customary in that part of the world, included the family living quarters, the connecting barn, granary, and stables.

The original 1888 three-story structure near Casarsa was built with sturdy stone and had a plastered façade and a tiled roof, while the addition made in 1905 was similar in construction but larger. The washed stones for the walls of the second addition were hauled from the nearby

Tagliamento River. There were no windows on the side of the house facing the Communale Road leading to San Vito because this part of the house was built very close to the road's property line.

The addition's third floor also was designated as a granary as in the original home, but included small fireplaces that would be needed in the family's future endeavor of raising silkworms.

The second floor of the original home and its new addition was living quarters for the family. Six bedrooms were located across the front of the house. The largest corner room was shared by the four oldest girls. Grandfather and Grandmother slept next door. The two youngest girls, Stella and Gilia, had a small bedroom in the center of the second floor. The boys slept in the other three bedrooms. My grandparents slept on a woolen mattress pad; the children had mattresses stuffed with the most tender parts of corn husks.

The new lower floor included the barn for the cows and horses. An open and gated passageway separated the barn and carpentry shop from the original first floor's living and kitchen area.

There was no plumbing; a hand pump and toilet were outside.

The Farm

Grandfather worked his railroad concessions and real estate dealings in town, and sometimes his sons helped him deliver newspapers. My grandmother Teresa and the older children managed the family farm, which consisted of the house with about one and one-half acres, plus several other land parcels in the area.

Though Giovanni was not a farmer, he felt secure in leaving the operation of their farm to Teresa, since she had grown up on the land. He did insist, however, that she not look like a peasant wife, so she never wore the apron typical of most working women. Her dresses were dark, with skirts cut just below the ankle. She liked to wear a head scarf tied around the back of her head and flat-heeled dark shoes. Giovanni always dressed in the attire of a businessman—a suit, necktie, and hat. He never worked in the fields.

The girls wore mid-calf-length dresses that had long sleeves, high necks, and buttons up the back. Hand-knitted stockings were held in place above their knees by string ties stitched at the top of the stockings.

Underskirts were made of white muslin, with some petticoats made out of the colorful skirts of old dresses. They had no coats: shawls were their only outer garment when it was cold.

The boys, unlike their father, dressed in practical, handmade clothing suitable for farm work. During the cold months, the boys and the girls wore wooden shoes during the week. They wore much nicer, handmade slippers to church. The children went barefoot in the summer.

The *zoccoli*, or wooden shoes worn by everyone except my grandfather, were described to me in great detail by my aunt Gilia. Unlike the wooden shoes seen in the Netherlands, these were made with a wooden base covered by a leather top. The wooden or lower parts of the shoes were usually bought by my grandparents, who fashioned the leather tops. Gilia said that some farm families made their own wooden sections, however. All shoes were left at the bottom of the stairs and never brought into the bedrooms.

Health Problems

Life was a daily struggle in many ways for the family. Certainly, Grandfather Giovanni and Grandmother Teresa had their share of health problems. In 1911, Grandfather had a severe case of rheumatism. His pains were so great that he couldn't tolerate the touch of his bedsheets, so Teresa hung the sheets on a wire net strung over the bed. The local physician advised Giovanni that he should go to Abano, a town near Venice with hot thermal baths. Aunt Stella remembered that either Giocondo or Gelindo accompanied their father to Abano for treatments at a special bathing center.

When they returned, Giovanni was improved, but he needed to keep his legs warm, especially when he was at rest. Teresa kept two bricks warm all day by placing them on top of their stove. In the evening, just before going to bed, Giovanni sat near the stove to rest and warm his legs with the heat from the stones and bricks that he would wrap in paper and cloth and place near his body. Although he gradually recovered, on some days Grandfather Giovanni was too sick to go to work, so Uncle Giocondo would take care of his business at the train station.

Around this same time, Grandmother Teresa lost several teeth and traveled about thirty miles to the city of Udine to consult with a dentist.

This man advised her that he wanted to remove all the roots of the missing teeth and to extract all of her remaining teeth. The dentist proposed a set of false teeth as the final remedy. Grandmother and Grandfather accepted this treatment plan, and after many trips in the horse-drawn *carretta* (buggy) to Udine, the task was accomplished.

It was a glorious day when the children gathered outside to watch for their mother's final return from the dentist. As the *carretta* turned toward their house, Grandmother smiled at them and they could all see her gleaming, new white teeth. However, this joy was short-lived, for the dentures fit uncomfortably, and Teresa was plagued with dental problems for the rest of her life.

Work Days

Their days were the days of a hardworking farm family. The younger children spent part of their days at school, where boys and girls were taught in separate classes and kept apart by a fence in the schoolyard. The Jacuzzi children walked to school in the morning, returned home for a two-hour lunch, then walked back to school for the afternoon. Teresa instructed her children to use very polite, formal language when they addressed their teacher.

Grandmother Teresa and the older children fed the animals, milked the cows, and made cheese and butter. They tended the chickens and brought in the eggs. They worked in the vegetable garden. They carried water in big buckets to the house and the garden. They made their own clothing and household items like soap.

The washing of clothes, called the *bucato*, was highly organized. At a minimum, it was a two-day process that required fair weather, although three days of good weather were certainly preferable. The *bucato* was an elaborate washing process that was typically used for the lighter-colored clothes.

First, all the best white clothes were placed in the bottom of a wooden tub, which was usually a water trough used by the cows and horses for drinking. Sheets were put in next, followed by the more grayish colored kitchen towels. All the clothes were packed down tightly and covered with a finely meshed cloth. Then, the family covered the clothes with about six inches of wood ashes. Boiling water was poured over the clothes and the tub was left to stand overnight.

In the morning, the water was drawn out by using the spigot at the tub's bottom. The chemical produced by the boiling water and ashes was potassium carbonate, or lye. The resulting soapy water from the first wash was saved to wash the colored clothes. The clothes were always scrubbed, if necessary, on a washboard before being wrung out. Finally, all of the clothes were carried to a little river in Casarsa for rinsing. When they were hauled back home and hung out to dry, the fragrance of the brightened, freshly cleaned clothes would fill the yard.

Other chores assigned to the younger children included the daily emptying of the bed chamberpots. They washed these bowls and let their mother or one of the older girls inspect each pot to make sure it was properly cleaned and there was no remaining odor. Aunt Gilia remembered this unpleasant duty very well.

The butchering of a pig involved a very long and hard workday. The event was so arduous that my aunt Stella remembered it with no fondness, but in great detail. On the day designated for the slaughter, the butcher would sometimes arrive to assist. Preparations were made for the preservation of the meat; the fat would be rendered, the bones salted, and the intestines cleaned out.

The girls always cleaned the intestines, which was a tedious job that involved scraping the inside lining with vinegar and water. The intestines were used to sack various parts of the pig's meat, which was made into *mortadella, salami, cotechini, salsiccia,* and *copacolla.* Aunt Stella recalled that the men would usually take a breakfast break while the slaughtered pig was hanging to dry under the farm's big mulberry tree in the backyard.

Workday meals were basic. Breakfast was a bowl of milk and a slice of *polenta* (a staple food of northern Italy, made from boiled cornmeal). The largest meal of the day was at noon, when the family would often share *salsiccia, polenta,* cheese, and *salami.* In the evening, they again would eat *polenta,* often in a bowl of milk, with a vegetable salad.

Hunting snails, a special treat, would occur after a heavy rainfall. The prized snails would first be fed cornmeal to flush out their bodies. They were then removed from their shells, washed, and made into an omelet. Other edible treasures found in the wild included dandelion, corn, *ardelut* (a type of lettuce, now available in America as "mache"), shoots from hops, mushrooms, and *confolon* (poppies).

Special Days

The family's combined efforts would culminate each Friday, when Teresa was taken to market in nearby San Vito by Giovanni, in his horse-drawn *carretta* (buggy). While there, she sold butter, eggs, cheese, vegetables, and occasionally young chickens. A charming and persistent saleslady, my grandmother rarely returned with any unsold goods. She and my grandfather would return by noon, often bringing back a fresh fish that was in season. Teresa also used her market money for cloth and related sewing items to cover the family's forever changing clothing needs.

Aunt Cirilla recalled a more memorable time when the *carretta* was used. She and Aunt Ancilla received permission from their parents to take the horse and buggy into town for a social event for young people. Ancilla was old enough to drive the buggy and Cirilla was thrilled she had been allowed to join her older sister. Just as the two girls were pulling up in front of the party, the horse "relieved itself." Cirilla and Ancilla were mortified by their less than dignified arrival!

The bicycle was another form of transportation for the family. Giocondo and Gelindo shared a bike on alternate days. Once, however, on Giocondo's designated day, Gelindo desperately wanted to go see a girlfriend in Valvazone. He tried to dash away with the bike, but Giocondo stopped him, and Teresa caught the two brothers arguing over it. She was very upset with their bickering, which she stopped by applying the *menescola*, a long wooden spoon used for stirring foods like *polenta*. "Sparing the rod and spoiling the child" was evidently not among her beliefs.

The family attended special showings of movies, which were viewed in a Casarsa barn that had been converted to accommodate the evening's entertainment. The movie always began with an abrupt, shrill whistle that sounded like a train whistle. A hand-cranked generator powered the projector.

On some evenings, my grandparents left the oldest children in charge and went to the opera in Udine. First, they had dinner and then went to the show. Teresa and Giovanni loved the Udine opera and looked forward to hearing it and seeing the actors who sang and performed the various stories.

Sundays also brought a welcome change from the work week. Since Giovanni preferred early mass, he would stop at the butcher's on his way home and purchase a piece of meat for the family's Sunday dinner. Teresa took the rest of the family to both early mass and vespers.

After Sunday dinner, Giovanni gave each child his or her allowance. The youngest ones got a small amount, about 5 cents; the older children were given a bit more. The neighboring farms also enjoyed the Sunday afternoon break, and men played on the side roads. The Jacuzzi children played simple games involving buttons and small stones; they walked on stilts and enjoyed *wuita wata* (blind man's bluff), *campo* (hopscotch), *sia sia saia* (rocking in a see-saw motion while holding hands and singing).

Holidays were special times. At Christmas, the children left their wooden shoes on a windowsill for gifts left by the *uccellino del bosco* (small bird of the forest). Typical gifts were chestnuts, *mandorlato torrone* (almond candy), fruit, and nuts. One Christmas, Aunt Gilia's shoe held a precious doll, but later the family pig ate the doll! This was the only "store-bought" doll Gilia ever remembered owning.

On Christmas Day, the children would go around to the neighbors' houses to offer them greetings of the day, and were usually rewarded with small coins. This same ritual would be repeated on New Year's Day.

Giovanni observed that a large family like Teresa's, working and living together, could amass wealth and prosper in a manner not possible otherwise. This was a primary motivation for him and Grandmother to have such a large family. Although Teresa initially resisted building a large home, Giovanni wanted to build a large and prosperous home, not only for themselves, but also for future Jacuzzi generations. They fully expected that at least some of their sons, following tradition, would marry and live in the home with their wives and children. This is the reason they built the first large addition to their home in 1905, the year their eleventh child, Cirilla, was born.

Work Across the Border

In the first years of the new century, my grandfather was doing increasingly better in business, and the farm, with its two horses, six to eight cows, pigs, and a yard full of chickens, was fairly productive. Still, life for the large Jacuzzi family was meager. The children were not starving, but they were often hungry. I recall my father, or Pa, telling me how he would sometimes go out in the woods and fields near their home to eat berries and grapes. Sometimes, in the early spring, he would eat the buds off certain plants because he was still hungry after a meal.

My father hesitated to say he went to bed hungry but would admit, "I could have eaten more."

Certainly there was no money in the family coffer for anything beyond the basic necessities. So, it was becoming apparent that the older boys would have to get jobs, and, in order to do that, they would have to cross the border into either Austria or Germany. Quite often representatives from various companies in these nations would visit the villages of northern Italy, looking to recruit young men for seasonal jobs.

It was, therefore, not an unusual thing when, in 1898, Rachele and Valeriano—the two oldest of the Jacuzzi sons—immigrated to Germany at the ages of twelve and eleven, respectively. By this time the boys had completed only three years of schooling. Although my uncle and father would both do and achieve much in their later lives, those three brief years would be all the formal classroom education either would receive. I have often thought of my own sons, and wondered if I could have allowed them to immigrate alone at such young ages. I am sure that need causes people to be more resourceful and courageous than they think possible at other times.

In Germany, Uncle Rachele and Pa were assigned to temporary jobs in the brick and tile yards, which were common to that region. For six months, they worked nine to ten hours a day in the brickyard. Each night, they slept on straw in a barn.

In addition to their pay, they were given as their weekly food allotment one kilo (2.2 pounds) of cheese and all the *polenta* they wanted. Pa told me that the brickyards were near woods that contained blueberries. Just as he had often foraged for extra food in Italy, he ate these wild berries to supplement his monotonous food allotment. As one might imagine, in addition to the basic food, the accommodations were primitive, and the pay meager. But it was, as the saying goes, "good, honest work."

Their jobs in the brickyard consisted mainly of "trimming." First, clay was poured into a mold, then a press was lowered to form and compact the brick. A worker then trimmed off by hand any excess clay, removed the brick from the mold, and placed it in an oven to bake and cure.

During the early years of the twentieth century, my father immigrated to Germany and Austria five different times for short-term jobs, usually leaving home in May and returning after about six months. On the first three occasions he went with Rachele, but Uncle Rachele received a bad head injury from a fall on his second trip, returned reluctantly for the third time, and then chose not to return to work there again. Uncle Francesco, or Frank, my father's next younger brother, accompanied him on the later trips.

During these years Pa and his brothers worked in brickyards near the German cities of Wiesbaden, Mainz, and Wellesberg, and also in Austria, near the town of Oberndorf. I remember him telling me that, although they were paid little, they were happy to be able to contribute to the family's income, as well as buy their own clothing and other basic necessities for themselves.

Through these jobs, my father and uncles gained valuable experience in manufacturing processes and in working and living in foreign cultures. When Pa was eighty-four years old, he recalled how kind and also foolish a young German worker had been. It seems this German had more money than Pa, and so he was always generous with his beer. The only problem was that he persisted in drinking it while they were working near the hot furnaces. Pa said his friend lasted a few days working with the furnaces until he finally had to choose between the work or the beer. The German took the latter.

The extra money was helpful to the Jacuzzi family, even if it wasn't much. Interestingly, the year of their greatest combined income was also the year of the family's greatest need. A storm severely damaged the roof of the house, and the extra money made by the two brothers working in Germany was just enough to help pay for the repairs.

My father often was reluctant to discuss those days, because he feared people wouldn't believe his stories of hardship. Still, I am thankful for the recollections and descriptions of his early life which he did share occasionally. These have made me grateful for my heritage, and I have tried to build on this legacy of endurance and tenacity.

One particular story that Pa related has helped me realize just how lean those days were for them. On the northern California ranch where I was reared, when a chicken died, we would simply throw its body into the field or toss it inside a barrel located far away from our home to let the scavenging animals eat it.

My father told me that when he was living in the work camps in Germany, he would often take an evening walk. On one of these strolls he found a chicken that had been discarded by one of the nearby farms. Finding that the chicken had not yet been picked over by scavengers nor begun to decompose, my father took it back to the camp, cleaned it, and cooked it over a campfire. For the two brothers, this meal was a special treat.

In the end, as much as my grandparents appreciated the extra money, they felt the boys were being exploited in Germany. They could no longer encourage their sons to make the journey across the border.

Farm Evenings

While the days were busy with work for the entire family, the evenings became a special time to learn and play together. Grandfather often brought a newspaper home, and he and Teresa would take turns reading it aloud to the children. Teresa was an especially avid reader. Giovanni was very interested in current events, and he liked to discuss political and other community news with his family at the end of the day.

In the depths of winter, the family would sometimes spend the coldest nights in the stables with the animals to stay warm, always singing or telling stories as they huddled together. During the summer months, the family would gather outside after supper when, Aunt Gilia told me, the family would sit "all in a row" on a long bench that her father made for them from a log. In addition to Teresa's reading from the day's newspaper, Giovanni, a great storyteller, would spin tales, most of which he made up on the spot. Often the family would sing, and sometimes they were joined by neighbors. Each day ended with the family saying prayers and the rosary together.

Giovanni and Teresa were fluent in both Italian and Latin versions of prayers. Grandfather also knew lyrical Gregorian chants. He was a spiritual man who always considered himself to be a Catholic, though his inquisitive nature led him to sometimes question the church's authority, including the insistence on the celibacy of priests. My aunts Stella, Cirilla, and Gilia remembered how freely he shared his viewpoints with them, especially during these evenings in Casarsa.

Another favorite nighttime pastime for Giovanni and Teresa was to teach their children the names of the stars and constellations, which could be so clearly seen in the crisp sky above northern Italy. Teresa was particularly astute in her knowledge of constellation patterns; she always began her discussions by asking her children to find the North Star.

Planning for their garden also would be determined on these evenings: vegetables that grow under the ground would be planted when the moon was waning; vegetables that grow above the ground would be planted when the moon was waxing. Teresa also knew the reliable and traditional way of determining when Easter would fall each year, a system that is rooted in establishing the time of the vernal equinox and the first full moon in March that follows the equinox.

The couple taught their children to learn the basics of astronomy by using riddles. For example, to remember the phases of the moon, the children learned to observe the bulge of its crescent and recite:

"*La Gobba al levante, la luna calante*;

"*La Gobba al ponente, la luna crescente.*"

"The crescent bulges toward the sunrise [east], the moon is diminishing;

"The crescent bulges toward the sunset [west], the moon is increasing."

I am grateful that this thirst to know more about our natural world and about God—the results of my grandparents' example and teaching—was clearly passed on to their children. Each of their children, including my father, chose to approach God in his or her own way, but each child learned of God and the glories of His creation because of their parents. Certainly, all of the following generations of the Jacuzzi family are fortunate to have had Giovanni and Teresa as our spiritual forebears.

Jacuzzi brothers, from left: Rachele,
Valeriano, and Frank – c.1911

Gelindo Jacuzzi
c.1918

Joseph Jacuzzi
c.1918

Giocondo Jacuzzi
c.1918

Chapter 3

America

"La necessità porta l'ingegno."
"Necessity brings forth ingenuity."
—Valeriano Jacuzzi, my father and my grandparents' second child

By the beginning of the twentieth century, the Industrial Revolution, which had already swept much of Europe, had yet to make any real inroads in Italy. The economy there was still heavily based on agriculture, and would remain so until World War II. Even for landowners, their farms yielded little more than what was needed to keep them in operation. Any real hope for financial betterment required a paying job, but these were virtually nonexistent. As a result, young men were leaving Italy by the hundreds of thousands, bound either for Germany, England, or, principally, for "the Americas" (both North and South), where job opportunities were more plentiful.

America

My father, Valeriano, after his experience of working and traveling in Germany and Austria for five summers, was eager to try to find work in America. Pa learned that his eighteen-year-old friend, Angelo Borean, was immigrating to the northwestern United States to work. Angelo planned to travel with two other teenaged boys and an older married man. Immigration records list Angelo's brother's home in Spokane, Washington, as their American destination.

Pa wanted to join them, but my grandparents were reluctant to let Pa go without any other family members.

However, Teresa and Giovanni just had been blessed with a healthy baby girl, their twelfth child, Stella. Surely, the responsibility of caring for another young child, plus Giovanni's understanding that America could provide good jobs that would, in turn, help the family, factored into my grandparents' agreeing to Pa's proposal.

Their final consent was given with one condition: Valeriano could go only if his brother, Francesco (Frank), would go with him. Uncle Frank readily agreed. So their father helped them obtain the necessary travel documents and bought them passage.

By September of 1907, all arrangements had been made, and my father, who was then nineteen, and Frank, eighteen, set out for America on September 28 on the ship, *La Provence*. Their objective was to secure railroad construction jobs they heard were available in the Pacific Northwest. Pa's hair is recorded as red on his passport, which is interesting to me, and reinforces how young he was, since I only remember him with gray hair.

They arrived in New York on October 4. From New York, they traveled with their Italian friends by train to Spokane. Neither Pa nor Uncle Frank could speak English, and both were unfamiliar with their new surroundings.

Apparently their naïveté was obvious, for Uncle Frank said that the station manager in Spokane charged them 25 cents each when he "caught" them sleeping in their seats while waiting for a train. The man convinced them that using the seats for sleeping, rather than sitting, incurred a fee!

When the two brothers arrived in Spokane, they were sent from one place to another in search of work. They went to Buenos Springs, Montana, then back to Spokane. They again went back to Montana, to the town of Taft. From there, they took a horse-drawn coach over the mountains to Grand Forks, Idaho. Here, they worked for a railroad construction crew and slept in very crowded quarters in a log cabin.

Then, upon hearing that the Canadian Pacific Railroad was hiring in the area of Rossland and Trail, British Columbia, my father and Uncle Frank set out by stagecoach in search of these jobs just across the border. They eventually found a railroad construction camp and were hired for pick-and-shovel labor. However, when payday came, the brothers grew curious when their wages were paid in U.S. currency. It was then that they learned that they never reached Canada. They were in Montana! Since they could not understand the language, they hadn't realized their mistake until payday!

From that railroad camp, they eventually traveled back to Spokane, only to return to Taft, Montana, again to work on the Milwaukee Road railroad construction crew. Using dynamite, picks, shovels, and wheelbarrows, they helped dig a tunnel through Lookout Pass. This was the longest of sixteen passages carved out of the Bitterroot Range.

Uncle Frank recalled that, even though the weather was cold, it was so hot down in the tunnel that the men worked without shirts, just pants and boots. He also said that it was a violent atmosphere: many nationalities were represented on these crews and communication was extremely difficult. Tempers often flared and the tension would sometimes erupt into fist, knife, and gun fights.

Memories of that turmoil were revived years later, in about 1950, when Pa spotted a man working in the Jacuzzi machine shop in Richmond, California. He told his son-in-law, Don DeShields, that this Jacuzzi employee was the same man who once tried to kill Pa in that tunnel by ramming a cart into him. Knowing that the incident was from the tough years of his youth, when he and his fellow immigrants were tired from the unrelenting work, and confused by the babble of unknown languages, Pa simply watched the man for a few moments as he worked in the Jacuzzi shop. Then Pa moved on. Pa was always very unassuming, and so it doesn't surprise me that he told Don that a confrontation could have been seen as an attempt to exalt himself.

I am pleased the tunnel excavated by my father, Uncle Frank, and men of many cultures and many languages is still in use. Known locally as the Taft Tunnel, it is now a 1.7-mile bicycle trail that allows cyclists to travel back and forth between Idaho and Montana. I have also learned that bike rentals are offered for a pleasant, one-way coasting excursion, something that I plan to do soon. It will be exciting to visit the tunnel where Pa and Frank worked.

After working at railroad construction for several months, the two brothers found mining jobs in Wallace, Idaho. The labor was just as demanding, but the working and living conditions were much more peaceful. However, while working there, Pa contracted typhoid fever after drinking from a polluted stream. Pa recalled that immediately after he sipped from the stream, a bystander told him he shouldn't drink the water.

"I already did," was his reply.

He was hospitalized for fifty-two days.

It was during this almost two-month ordeal that Pa developed a deep dislike for receiving flowers when he was sick or in the hospital. His hospital roommate had received a large bouquet of red roses from his employer. It greatly impressed my father, just to think that someone's boss would care enough about him to send flowers when he was ill or injured! However, the following day his roommate died. My father was so shocked and saddened by this that, even though he liked flowers, he never wanted to receive them when he was sick.

Upon his release from the hospital, Pa was still weak and unable to work. An older Italian friend gave him money for food, which was offered in the local saloons. His friend eventually returned to Italy and married. After he had a regular paycheck, my father sent money to this man each Christmas and Easter to repay his kindness. These gift checks continued for more than fifty years after the incident. Obviously, my father always felt gratitude for this act of compassion that allowed him to eat and regain his strength.

When he was finally able to work again, my father was sent to a blacksmith shop rather than being assigned a pick-and-shovel job. Hardships continued, the brothers had very little money, so they spent it sparingly, sometimes sleeping in stables on straw-filled bunk beds. Often, however, to conserve finances, they slept outdoors under the western sky, sheltered only by a bridge or a tree. Meals were lean and sometimes far between. Rarely did a day pass when someone didn't try to take advantage of the "ignorant foreigners," as they sometimes overheard themselves called. They often felt they were worse off than slaves, because even slaves were given food, clothing, and a roof over their heads.

After shivering through several months in the chilly climate of northern Montana and Idaho, the brothers returned to Spokane in December 1908, and stayed together there through New Year's Day. In early January, Pa took a train to the northern California mining town of

Kennet (which is now under the waters of Lake Shasta). This climate was more favorable and similar to the Mediterranean region back home. Shortly afterward, Frank joined him.

There they labored for several months until misfortune came once again, this time to Uncle Frank, whose hip was broken badly when he was pinned between two mining cars. His recovery took nearly a year.

Rachele

My father initiated the Jacuzzi family's immigration to America. His optimistic determination and desire for a better life convinced my grandfather to allow the journey. Along with Uncle Frank, Pa paved the way for the rest of the family's eventual settlement in the United States.

My father's initiative was a significant contribution to the eventual establishment and success of the family business. But the American side of the Jacuzzi family's story really gained speed when the oldest brother, Rachele, arrived. I've heard many family stories and have read enough of his writings to know that Uncle Rachele was a brilliant, fascinating man. I single him out now because Rachele is the one person primarily responsible for our family's name becoming so well known. Jacuzzi Brothers, Inc., was built upon his creative and engineering genius.

Although he was my godfather, I never really knew Uncle Rachele. He died when I was only nineteen months old. His passing at the age of fifty was a terrible and unexpected blow for the whole family.

Although he had only three years of formal education as a child and a few months of aeronautical study in Milan after discharge from his military service, he nonetheless became a self-taught engineer and inventor. His experiments and theories brought him into collaboration with professors at the University of California in Berkeley, California Institute of Technology, and at Mills College in Oakland. In two booklets, *Creation* and *Wind, Solar, and Geologic Power,* which he wrote under the pen names of R. J. Veltro and J. V. Raquelote, respectively, Rachele accurately described phenomena which anticipated the successful fission of atoms to produce energy. He was also one of the first writers to discuss the possibility of black holes in our solar system, the launching of satellites, and the storage of solar energy as a useful source of heat.

In *Creation*, written nine years before the use of the atomic bomb, he predicted that "any attempt to remove atomic energy will probably give us the annihilation of matter." The booklet's lyrical language also discussed the occurrence of what we now call black holes as "everything would collapse into a cold, small body of tremendous density." Rachele's comprehension of the possibility of such a phenomenon placed him among a very select group of early twentieth-century astronomers and physicists who had just begun to discuss this subject. It would be thirty-two years before American physicist John Wheeler coined the term "black hole" and fully proved the theory.

His second booklet, *Wind, Solar, and Geologic Power*, foretells, by more than twenty years, the use of satellites: "Some day we will probably be able to build an asteroid that will fly around the earth from west to east." Rachele also meticulously designed a very attractive, solar-panel-equipped private residence and believed the concept had great marketability. This proposal, too, was decades before solar heating came into common use in homes and businesses.

In 1930, Rachele filed for and was issued design patent # 82,221 covering the design of a helicopter-like aircraft he called an "aeroplane." In 1936, a German engineer, Heinrich Focke, successfully flew the "first" helicopter, which was of similar design to Uncle Rachele's.

His bright, inquisitive mind was evident when he was quite young. His mother, Teresa, once recalled a time when Rachele, then just six years old, was using a hand-pump to help her get water from their well.

"What is making the water come up?" Rachele asked. When she could not answer, he replied, "When I learn to read, I will find out and tell you."

Rachele evidently thought a great deal about the properties and uses of water. Several newspapers in 1923 featured syndicated articles on a device Rachele presented to University of California scientists that he claimed could make water burn like household gas. Others, in 1925, outlined a proposal that said, with funding assistance, he could install a 5,000 HP propeller fan on top of the Berkeley Hills that could push a column of frequently foggy air to an elevation of 9,500 feet, which would cause the moisture to condense and fall like rain.

Aunt Stella remembered the family always talked about young Rachele's excitement about reading. It was said that he was determined to read even at night, which led him to experiment with fireflies as a light source for the dark evening hours. According to family legend, by carefully holding a firefly's wings, Uncle Rachele could get a brief flash of illumination for his text. He also liked to experiment outside by fixing ropes and pulleys on a spike he had driven into one of the external rafters of the roof. When I visited the Casarsa home while Uncle Candido was living there, he showed me this spike, still embedded in the rafter.

Being the oldest son, Rachele eventually went to work with his father at the railroad station in Casarsa. At first, he merely assisted his father with the porter duties and newspaper concessions. However, the telegraph operator at the station took a special liking to Rachele and offered to train him in telegraphy. This opportunity intrigued Rachele's bright mind, so with his father's permission he accepted the gentleman's offer. For several months, Rachele concentrated heavily on his training until one day, in 1905, he was hired officially to work in the telegraph office.

During his free time, Rachele conducted yet more experiments. One involved working with a new bicycle propulsion concept that involved attaching a fin to the rear of the bicycle. The bike's conventional pedals swung the fin, producing a backward thrust of air, pushing the machine forward.

As he grew older, Rachele became aware that his theories were often too complex to be understood by the rest of the family.

However, new discoveries were put on hold, when, in 1906, at the age of nineteen, Rachele was conscripted into the Italian army. Due to his telegraphic skills, he was assigned to the communications corps. After one year of training in Florence, he was posted in Asmara, the primary city of the Italian colony of Eritrea in northern Africa.

Upon his discharge in 1910, Rachele returned home for only a brief period, because he had developed a new interest—no, a passion—for flight and airplane design, which enthralled him during his military service. Also, the newspapers brought home by Giovanni kept him abreast of the latest news in the field, and Rachele envisioned designs to advance the safety and practicality of the aviation industry.

While he painstakingly sketched his concepts on paper, Rachele knew that what he really needed was specialized study and the chance to make actual models of his designs for testing. Therefore, with his parent's assistance, he moved to Milan to study aeronautics, hoping also to find someone there who would be interested in funding some of his experiments.

Although he lived and studied in Milan for six months, he was unable to find the backing he sought. However, while there, he learned that the field of aviation was growing in southern California. Using money Valeriano and Francesco had sent to the family in Italy, Rachele immediately booked passage to America with little more than a dream and a few sketches. He left LaHavre, France, on the *S.S. Touraine* on December 10, 1910, arriving in New York on December 19. He had to sell his pocketwatch in order to pay the train fare to Los Angeles.

Brothers

When he arrived in southern California, Uncle Rachele asked Pa and Uncle Frank to move farther downstate and join him, so they gave up their mining jobs and traveled to Escondido. The three then joined forces, picking oranges for pay. Living in tents wasn't bad, since the climate was mild, but legions of flies and other pests made each mealtime a battle. Then, as Pa told me, he would roll up a newspaper into a tight wandlike torch, set fire to its end, and go about the tent burning the wings off the insects. Once they were incapacitated, he would sweep them up and throw them out. This was the only way he and his brothers could have a peaceful meal or gain any hope for a decent night's sleep.

My father and his brothers longed to reunite the family. But this was only a dream until they learned of an orange farm for sale near Escondido, California. When they saw the land, the three brothers knew their father would love it and could help make it profitable. By early 1911 Pa, Uncle Rachele, and Uncle Frank had scraped together enough money to put down a cash deposit to hold the farm for Giovanni's inspection.

Grandfather was scheduled to arrive in February. He and Rachele must have planned that Rachele would go to America first to join Pa and Uncle Frank, and that Grandfather Giovanni would follow. Perhaps Grandfather told Rachele to immediately look for land once he arrived. Now that the deposit was made, the brothers knew their father would have to sell everything in Italy—land, tools, farming equipment, and household goods—in order to purchase the orange farm and reunite the entire family in the United States.

Land

Giovanni Jacuzzi, at the age of fifty-five, sailed on February 4, 1911, on the *La Provence*, the same ship that had carried my father and Uncle Frank to America. Valeriano and Francesco now had been living in their adopted country for more than three years; Rachele had been in California a couple of months. The ship's manifest shows that Grandfather's destination was San Marcos, California, the home of his son Rachele.

Apparently, Grandfather liked what he saw, and the more he considered his sons' idea, the wiser it seemed. It was obvious that his three "American" sons did not plan to return to Italy any time soon, if ever. Weighing even heavier on his mind was the threat of war. "*It would be wonderful to protect my family from that possibility,*" I can imagine Grandfather reasoning. An immediate move to America would be the best way to ensure everyone's safety.

After a brief two weeks in America, Grandfather returned to Italy, assuring his sons that he would do everything he could to return within one year with the rest of the family. The fact that he made this decision quickly does not mean that he made it easily, for he and Grandmother had devoted themselves to making a life for their family in Italy. He was not completely sure that America could ever be their permanent home, but for the sake of his sons, and for the sake of keeping the family together, a thing most precious to him and Grandmother, he felt they had to try.

As Uncle Rachele learned more of the possibility of war in Europe, he wrote to his father, encouraging Giovanni to send his other sons to America. On October, 28, 1911, a fourth brother, Giuseppe, later known by his Anglicized name, Joseph, arrived in America. The records of his ship, *La Savoie*, show his destination was his brother Rachele's home at 110 E. 9th Street, Los Angeles, California.

The migration of the Jacuzzi family was gaining momentum.

Carving Out a Future

By mid-1911, Uncle Rachele, no doubt aided by his ever-growing capabilities with the English language, finally was able to get a job in his beloved field of aviation. He was hired by R. L. Remington of Los Angeles. Remington owned a few small planes that were used at a nearby aviation school. His company also was a maintenance and service provider for other airplane owners. Even though Rachele was only working as a mechanic, he was thrilled to be moving nearer his goal of aeronautical design and the building of aircraft.

Meanwhile, Pa and Uncle Frank worked at an oil refinery.

Like Grandfather, Uncle Rachele seemed to have an antenna with a frequency set for finding opportunities, for he was quick to act when he learned of a situation where he might test some of his flight-related ideas. Remington was having problems in the development of a propeller for a prototype plane.

Rachele designed and built a propeller for Remington that was successful: the plane flew! This success brought other propeller business, and Rachele soon realized he needed help from his brother, Valeriano. Remington readily agreed to hire Pa to work with Uncle Rachele. The two brothers worked hard at the design and production of new propellers.

The woodworking skills Uncle Rachele and Pa employed to carve and assemble these propellers had been passed down through at least three generations. Francesco Jacuzzi had used them to make doors and cabinets, and later in his work as a church sexton. He trained his son, Giovanni, who also earned a living in his early work years making cabinets and other furniture. Now, Giovanni's sons were using these skills to make airplane propellers in the New World.

Together, Pa and Uncle Rachele built various new propeller styles for Remington. They also helped in airplane remodeling and maintenance. Then, in 1912, Mr. Remington purchased a farm in Chino, which he soon hired my father, Uncle Frank, and Uncle Joseph to run. Meanwhile, Uncle Rachele continued working at the aviation company.

Brothers United

I do not know exactly how the brothers planned to buy their own farm, but I assume the deal fell through without Grandfather's backing, since he was unable to return quickly with the rest of the family. However, the brothers in America faithfully sent money back to Italy, and other members of the family continued to arrive. On December 14, 1912, two more brothers, Giocondo and Gelindo, traveled on the *La Provence* to the United States. They, too, declared the 9th Street house in Los Angeles as their destination. They joined their brothers on the Remington farm, leaving Rachele to live and work in the city. Gelindo supplemented their income by working as a chicken plucker.

By the end of the year, the six brothers then in California were experiencing mixed emotions. World War I loomed in distant northern Italy, causing grave concern for the father, mother, six sisters, and one brother left behind. Rachele and his brothers felt lucky to have found jobs in America and could take comfort in knowing that their youngest brother, Candido, was much too young to be drafted in Italy. Meanwhile, they continued to work hard and support each other, for it was now impossible to determine how much longer they would be separated from their parents and younger siblings.

I've often thought it interesting that, of my grandparents' thirteen children, the first six were boys. In retrospect, I'd even say this was an act of providence, for it was the sons who ventured to a new world and established a business around which the rest of the family would gather. Times have changed, but few women were starting businesses in those days. My grandparents later had six daughters. When my father, Valeriano, and Uncle Frank left for America, the girls all were ten years of age or younger and one, my aunt Gilia, was yet to be born.

However, I'm not suggesting that the contribution of the Jacuzzi women was any less vital to the enterprise than that of the men. Were it not for the moral support, financial assistance, and elbow grease—the women often worked in the shop during the early years—of the Jacuzzi sisters and wives, who knows if there would have ever been a Jacuzzi Brothers, Inc.?

Jacuzzi sisters, from left: Stella, Cirilla, and Gilia – 1912

Pasquetta Piucco – c.1917

Giuseppina Piucco – c.1917

Giuseppina and Valeriano Jacuzzi wedding – 1919

Chapter 4

To Live a War

*"Leggere i particolari della guerra è storia, ma vivere
una guerra è una cosa tremenda."*

"To read about the war is history, but to live a war is a terrible thing."
—Gilia Jacuzzi Peruzzo, my grandparents' thirteenth and youngest child

Italy's involvement in World War I was inevitable. Though the nation tried to remain neutral, its close proximity to the fighting, plus Austria-Hungary's threat to seize some of its borderland, destined Italy to enter the fray. The war would not devastate the Jacuzzi family, but they would be deeply affected by it in many ways.

Grandfather had returned to Italy from California in 1911. He was intent on preparing his house and property for sale or lease. He also had to sell his business interests and then make the necessary arrangements for moving the family to the United States. He needed to accomplish this as quickly as possible.

Grandfather was a reasonable man; he knew that all his tasks could take months. Still, he hoped and believed that one year or less would be sufficient. The thought of having his family all together in beautiful southern California was like a dream . . . but not an impossible one, he hoped.

As the months passed, it became obvious to Grandfather that he needed some help if he were to reach his goal. With only daughters and one young son at home, he especially felt the need for the help of a grown man. Therefore, he wrote Pa and asked him to come back to Italy long enough to assist in settling business affairs and arranging for the family's voyage. Being the second oldest son, and having already immigrated to Germany and to America, Pa seemed the best choice. The family also considered Pa's command of English to be very good. Deferring to Grandfather's wishes, Valeriano returned to Italy in January of 1913.

To some of the family, Valeriano was a stranger. One of the fondest childhood memories of my aunts Gilia and Stella, the youngest of my grandparents' children, was meeting their older brother for the first time, and savoring the pears and peaches he had brought with him from the United States. This was the first canned food they ever had seen or tasted!

For Sale

Because of his experience in selling real estate, Grandfather realized the land and home he had to offer were prime. Still, he knew that conditions were not in his favor. The threat of war was breeding an air of uncertainty; people were reluctant to make major land purchases. Grandfather understood their hesitancy. Furthermore, far from being heartbroken if the property did not sell, he would be just as content—if not more so—with leasing the land, thereby making it easier for him and Grandmother, and anyone else in the family wishing someday to return to Italy.

When it became evident that their property would be hard to sell, my father assisted Grandfather with another addition to the back of the family's home. This would provide a large kitchen and dining room, with a roof terrace. This addition also included an exterior area with rabbit hutches, a chicken roost, firewood storage, and a stable for the horses. Using a concrete block method he had learned in America, Pa helped build the back addition to the house. Although Aunt Gilia believed her father wanted to finish this addition so that eventually all his family, including his "American" sons, could possibly live together in the home, this was never to be. Within a few years, the last of the original family to live in the home would stand on its terrace for the Jacuzzi family's final Casarsa home photograph.

An interesting feature of this back terrace is that, because of the high ceilings in the new dining room and kitchen, the actual floor of the terrace was above the home's second-level flooring. The family entered the terrace by climbing through the second floor's windows. During this time, Grandfather bought a young horse and Pa trained it for farm work. Clearly, the Jacuzzi family was intent on making the house and farm appealing to potential buyers.

Several people expressed interest in purchasing the Jacuzzi house and the land parcels, but none were either able, or willing, to consummate a deal. However, after some months, a man from the Adriatic Coast offered to purchase everything—the land and buildings, farm equipment, livestock, and even the household furnishings. He made only one stipulation. If war came to Italy before the final transaction, the purchase agreement would be considered null and void.

Grandfather was relieved to have made this deal, and began working on obtaining the proper travel documents and making other necessary arrangements for getting the family to America. But he had been fighting the odds and the calendar all along. Italy was shifting fast from its long-held position of neutrality. Patriotic songs were being taught in the Jacuzzi children's school. On May 23, 1915, Italy officially entered World War I. By joining the side of the Allies, Italy defected from its partnership in the Triple Alliance—a flimsy partnership previously held with Germany and Austria-Hungary.

All passages out of the country were canceled and no new requests would be considered until the war was over. For the Jacuzzi family, this meant the purchase agreement for the sale of their property was nullified, and immigrating was postponed indefinitely.

Valeriano

Nineteen fifteen was a precarious time for families with young sons. The war intruded into the Jacuzzi household when Italy revoked peacetime conditions regarding military service and the draft, and my father, who was going to be drafted into the Italian Army, applied for and was chosen by the 4th Battalion of the Bersaglieri Corps.

The Bersaglieri were considered the elite fighting units. Where other troops marched, they were expected to run. When traveling by bicycle, they raced faster and stronger. They were expert marksmen and accepted special assignments where quick, precise maneuvering was required. It was an honor to be chosen to wear the uniform of the Bersaglieri.

From the time he was a small boy, Valeriano was a natural and fast long-distance runner, and he was strong as a result of his hard work. Unfortunately, for my father, his soldiering days didn't last long. Soon after being assigned to a unit, he was on a mission and traveling by bicycle across a bridge near Turin. Here, a group of thugs, possibly Italians jealous of his Bersaglieri status, grabbed him and beat him. At the conclusion of the fight, they threw Pa off the bridge. His head struck a rock, fracturing his skull.

Somehow, he survived, but the physicians gave little hope that he would live for long, let alone recover. My grandparents were told that his chances of living were "that of an egg being thrown against a stone wall without breaking." Nonetheless, their second oldest son stabilized, and surgeons in Turin, Italy, eventually were able to place a metal plate in his cranium.

He was hospitalized for three months, released into the care of his parents, then discharged from the army with official assurance that, due to the severity of his injury, he never again would be called for military service. In researching Italy's official military records, I learned that Valeriano Jacuzzi received the Italian National Decorative Medal for World War I.

Since Pa returned home quite feeble, the Jacuzzi children were ordered to keep very quiet. For a long time, noise bothered him, and he wore dark glasses because he was sensitive to light. He had acute headaches and his eyes were crossed. He wore a woolen hat to keep his head warm and he would wear a woolen nightcap every night of his life.

Slowly, however, with rest and the family's care, Pa recovered. His headaches lessened and his eyes returned to their normal alignment. Despite this close brush with death at the age of twenty-nine and a delicate brain operation made all the more risky given the primitive surgical techniques in 1916, Pa lived to the age of eighty-five!

Staying Alive

Survival became the family's collective ambition, for the war virtually surrounded them. Within a few feet of their front door ran the *Strada Maestra*, or "Master Road"—built for Napoleon's troops during their frequent war campaigns. To the rear of the property lay the Venice-to-Vienna railroad.

Both the road and the railway were major arteries for military transport. Often the trains were filled with wounded soldiers from various armies being taken to civilian hospitals. The Jacuzzi family had front-row seats as the troops traveled to and from the Italian front at the Isonzo River, north of Trieste and some fifty miles to the northeast of their Casarsa home.

There were long columns of marching and singing soldiers, including the Bersaglieri. Their smart uniforms were topped off by caps with dramatic flourishes of black feathers, and as they rode their bicycles in formations of six abreast, their swiftly moving units glistened in the sun as they pedaled past the house. There were also the mountain fighters, the Alpini, who were distinguished by the single feather in their felt hats. Younger children, including the Jacuzzi brood, tagged after the passing soldiers, asking for candy and bread. In the evening, they watched from their upstairs windows, when soldiers camped for the night across the road from the house. The men set up their kitchen and cooked their meals of *riso alla tureggrana* or rice with tomato sauce. Other soldiers prepared boiled meat, potatoes, and soup, which they ate with small *pagnotta* bread loaves. Coffee, wine, and canned milk made up the beverages.

War and Silk

Even though war raged around them—and eventually completely engulfed them—local families had to concentrate on the business of survival. Crops had to be planted and harvested, livestock cared for, and family members clothed and fed. During this time, my grandparents continued to engage in a business which I have always found quite fascinating. Just as they had done before the war, they raised silkworms for their cocoons, and as I learned more about this enterprise, I understood the reason they installed fireplaces in the third-floor granary when they expanded their home in Casarsa.

Silk cultivation had flourished in Europe for several centuries and had been a particularly popular cottage industry in the Italian city-states. By the early part of the twentieth century, there were many farm families in the San Vito and Casarsa area engaged in the production of silkworm cocoons. The process basically involves 1) the incubation and care of the domesticated silkworm from its egg stages through cocoon building, 2) the availability of mulberry tree leaves upon which the worms must feed, and 3) the use of steam to kill the cocoon's larvae, which allows the silk thread that formed the cocoon to unfurl without damage.

Around May, my grandparents purchased about one to two ounces of silkworm eggs. Grandmother placed these eggs within a folded cloth, which she wore at her bosom for about ten days, or until the eggs hatched.

The larvae were then taken to a large open room on the third floor, which served as the granary. There, my grandfather had prepared three layers of suspended mats that ran the length of the granary. Tender, young mulberry leaves and the tiny silkworm larvae were placed on some spread-out newspapers on each layer of mat where they were fed until they were large enough to live directly on the mats. Grandfather and Grandmother coordinated the stages of growing their silkworm with the family's ability to provide plenty of mulberry leaves.

As the silkworm grew into caterpillars, my grandparents and their children placed more and larger leaves on the mats for their feeding, until eventually entire branches would be required. The silkworm ate all the leaves right down to the bare branch. Near their maturity, they would have to be fed about every four hours. By the time the silkworm had developed an appetite that great, the children could sometimes hear them eating from the two floors below!

Sometimes, a neighbor would be enlisted to assist in the care of the silkworms. Additionally, during cold weather, fires had to be kept going in the fireplaces built into the third floor's walls, for the silkworms were very sensitive to cold.

About six weeks after hatching, the caterpillars, having grown to a length of about three inches, stopped eating. At this time, they appeared transparent. They then spun their cocoons of fine silk on spirals of straw that were placed on the mats. Each cocoon contained approximately 2,000 to 3,000 feet of silk.

Grandfather and Grandmother sold their cocoons to processors in the mill at Pordenone, where they were paid in cash, a much-needed commodity during the war years. At the mill, the workers heated the cocoons with steam to kill the larvae inside. After that, they unwound the silk from the cocoons onto spools.

My grandparents used their cash to buy items they normally couldn't afford, like fresh fruit, especially their beloved cherries and small melons. Once, they used the silkworm money to buy beautiful silk fabric from the mill, which was made into suits for Pa and Grandfather. On other occasions, they also bought silk material to make clothes for other family members.

So between farming, raising silkworms, and feeding the many hungry strangers—refugees and soldiers—who regularly appeared at the door during the war years, Grandfather and Grandmother Jacuzzi, and their eight children were all quite busy.

Interestingly, a local exclamation in the Casarsa region during this time was *Corpo di baco*! (literally, "Body of a silkworm!"), used in the sense of "Holy smokes!" or "My goodness!" It was one of the many expressions my parents passed down to their children and their children's children. My son-in-law Scott Stewart heard our family, including his wife, my daughter Loretta, saying it, and finally asked, "What is the 'Corporate e buckle' you and your family are talking about?" This gave us all a good laugh!

Undoubtedly, the Casarsa Jacuzzis were preoccupied with coping on a daily basis, they must have spent some anxious moments wondering about the five sons who were in America, for the war eventually brought an end to all overseas communication. Before Casarsa was invaded, some of the family's letters made it out of Italy and to California, but for the most part, their contents were blacked out by a censor. These letters to the brothers began with "Dear Sons," and then the entire letter was marked through, with only "your loving Mother" or "your loving Father" left intact. After the invasion, all communication stopped. Finally, after three years, letters again flowed freely between the family in Italy and the family in America.

It must have saddened my grandparents that, during the war years, a shadow fell across the Jacuzzi family name. Some of the people in and around Casarsa grew very resentful of the Jacuzzis, who had five of their sons in the United States, and Giovanni was even accused of being unpatriotic.

Some thought the boys had immigrated to avoid the war, but the Jacuzzi sons were but a few among thousands who left the country during this period, and my grandfather's two oldest boys served in the Italian military. I would like to think that the attraction of a new life in California, rather than the avoidance of military service, was the primary motive for my uncles' expatriation.

Refugees

In the fall of 1917, Italy's fortunes in the war went from bad to worse. On October 24, the German and Austrian armies broke through the front along the Isonzo River near Trieste, a position which the Italian army held since midsummer.

This break occurred in the famous Battle of Caporetto, named for the Austrian town where the battle took place (now Kobarid, Slovenia). The struggle was not limited to the namesake small town, however, since the German-Austrian drive covered a wide front, including several lightning attacks along the Isonzo River in which the Austrian and German troops routed the Italian army.

From October 24 to November 6, a period of only thirteen days, the front shifted westward nearly sixty miles, engulfing Casarsa. Killed, wounded, or missing Allied casualties, mostly Italian, totaled in the hundreds of thousands. The debacle of that retreat is memorialized in Ernest Hemingway's famed 1929 novel, *A Farewell to Arms*.

But this was not fiction for the Jacuzzis and their neighbors. Now they lived behind enemy lines.

Life had been difficult; it was about to get worse. Many people were fleeing from the region, hoping to find greater safety farther to the south. Grandfather chose to remain in Casarsa with his family, and to continue working the farm and his other businesses as long as possible.

My aunts Stella and Cirilla, recalling what life was like for the family during this time, said that the school in town was converted into a military hospital and didn't reopen as a school until 1919, so occasionally a few of the children went to their teacher's home to study. Grandmother Teresa paid the teacher with eggs and a chicken. The children had no writing paper or pencils for their lessons, but the teacher salvaged a few school books.

Often, the Jacuzzis survived only by their wits. Candido once scavenged near the rail lines and found treasures of eggs, sugar, salt, and cheese tossed out of a train in an attempt to make room for soldiers. However, there was very little soap and the family suffered the indignities of poor hygiene, with everyone suffering from lice. Sometimes, the Austrian soldiers came to the door, asking for food they wanted to send home to their families. Grandmother often tried to barter corn for soap and salt. One time, she was tricked and given sugar instead of the much more precious commodity, salt. The family salvaged blankets and capes from the road in front of the house and used this material for clothing.

During the retreat in October 1917, the road in front of the Jacuzzi house was littered with more than clothing: it also became an exodus route for the retreating Italian army and refugees. The seemingly endless rain added to the misery of the troops and displaced civilians, who were fleeing, some on foot, others in cars and trucks, and some even by horse-drawn wagons, carrying whatever possessions they could. The adults and the children cried from frustration and hunger. Aunt Gilia remembered that the Italian army was especially feared, for its troops would often be far rougher on their fellow citizens than the occupying troops that followed.

My grandparents helped as many refugees as they could by giving what food and shelter they had available. These pathetic, sad people arrived wet and dirty, and Grandfather worried each time one of them tried to make a fire in the stable to dry out their clothing.

Aunt Stella recalled: "Often our house would be full of people we didn't know. I remember one day a group of angry soldiers came in. They stuck a stiletto knife into the table and told my mother to give them something to eat *or else*. My mother told them all she could give them was some *polenta*, some homemade cheese, and a bottle of wine. At that, they were satisfied. They sent everyone else out of the room and ate."

After seeing this, my father said it would be better if we would leave too, so we got together the most important things. . . . "We loaded an old trunk and chest full of clothes and blankets, then packed some cheese, *salami*, bread, and *polenta*."

Two cows and a horse pulled the carts with their belongings, but the family did not get far. By the time they reached the town of Zoppola, about four miles from home, they found the road so clogged with refugees and soldiers that traveling any farther was either futile, impossible, or both. Grandfather decided it was best to head back home, unsure though he was of what fate might face them there. Doubt about the wisdom of their decision increased, since everyone else was leaving the region. But the family came home just in time to extinguish a fire in the stables attached to the main house, and gave thanks many times for arriving just then, because they could have easily lost everything they owned.

Under Occupation

Soon after the events of the fall of 1917, the Italian army left the region and the refugees were also gone. The future was uncertain though.

Now only German or Austrian soldiers traveled the road in front of the house. Sometimes, they were accompanied by their prisoners, most of whom were Russian. Often the soldiers' clothes were patched with paper; they wore wrapped rags for socks.

To add to the difficulties of living under an occupation, every member of the family except Teresa fell very ill with influenza, which was known locally as *febre spaniola* (Spanish fever). Some of the girls lost all of their hair and all of the family suffered from fevers and the accompanying painful symptoms of the disease.

Grandmother Teresa desperately sought a doctor, but there was no qualified one available, so a former prisoner of war, an elderly count, visited the home to advise her. The little old man instructed Teresa to wrap all of the sickest family members in cold, wet sheets, which she did. Felicita had begun her recovery by this time and she helped my grandmother carry the heavy sheets up the stairs to the beds of the suffering family members. Finally, everyone's fever subsided, and the crisis passed.

Family members regained their health, but they had no way of knowing how they would be treated by the occupying armies, or if they would be permitted to remain on their land. But Grandfather was soon assured by German officers that, if he and the family showed no fear, and that if they fed any soldiers who came up to the house, they would be kept safe. This proved to be good advice. While the soldiers weren't always kind, no real harm came to any of the family members.

As more and more patrols trudged by, some came into the house, where Grandmother offered them milk to drink. She would convince fearful soldiers that it wasn't poisoned by drinking some herself.

There were several more tense moments. Often, soldiers questioned why Valeriano was in the home, and the family had to show documents proving that Pa had been dismissed from the army due to his injury. Another time, the oldest sister, Felicita, found several live hand grenades in the yard.

The numerous land mines in the area touched the family in a tragic way when, on a Sunday afternoon right after the war, Grandfather's uncle who shared his name (and whom the family called *Barba Titta* or Uncle Titta), visited the family to alert them to be especially careful around any lumps in the ground that appeared suspicious. Returning home to nearby town of Casa Bianca, Uncle Titta was ironically killed by just such an exploding land mine.

Another time, an angry Austrian soldier demanded my grandfather's watch at gunpoint. My aunts recall Grandfather's sternest warning: "*Never* argue with a soldier, especially one who has been drinking!"

Another challenge was to protect valuable livestock. At times, the family herded the cows together in the back of the stable area, which was connected to the bottom floor of the house. They boarded over the entrance and stacked hay up high to hide the animals from the soldiers' view. Sometimes a soldier knew the cows were there, but kept the secret so he could have some food. Pa and Uncle Candido successfully hid the family's pig upstairs, but they weren't as lucky with their horses, all of which eventually were stolen.

At first, the family dug holes in the garden in an effort to hide potatoes, grain, linens, copper pots, wine—anything that the occupying armies could steal. Later, Grandfather decided to dig a larger space under the carpentry shop and use this for a more permanent and less damp storage area.

An even graver concern was for the girls of the community, who had to be hidden from the soldiers, so the Jacuzzi girls frequently remained very quiet upstairs, eating all their meals in the bedroom, until danger passed. Other times it was necessary to secrete them in isolated places, since the soldiers were less likely to find them if they were hidden in small groups. The neighbors cooperated in protecting one another during these dreadful days.

Much of the time, as my aunts Cirilla, Stella, and Gilia told me, the soldiers whom they encountered were neither angry nor dangerous. More often they were hurt, hungry, and scared. Wounded soldiers were often brought to their home on stretchers. Once a soldier came to the door seeking warmth and shelter from the torrential rain. His uniform was threadbare, almost disintegrating like tissue paper due to the soaking rains. Grandmother offered him a blanket and a meal. Another time, on a Sunday when the family attended afternoon vespers at the church, an Austrian soldier in full uniform knelt in the aisle. He prayed and cried aloud to Jesus, imploring Him to end the war soon. All he wanted, the soldier said, was to go home.

The official German and Austrian occupation lasted one year, though the two countries' control in the region lasted slightly longer. Despite the many dangers, my family was spared the tragedies so many Europeans encountered during that awful war. Each evening, my grandmother insisted the family join together in prayers for peace. The rosary often was said. I thank God for protecting them.

It is both paradoxical and heartwarming that in the middle of such atrocity there was a love story to be told . . . that of my father and mother.

Love and War

As difficult as things sometimes were in the area where my family lived, the war brought even greater hardship to those who lived in the nearby mountain villages of the Alps. Often, members of these families traveled down to the agricultural flatlands and attempted to buy food and supplies. The journey was made on foot, at night, under the cover of darkness. Usually they did not have money, so they offered bedsheets, homemade slippers, bundles of wood made up of tree branches, or whatever items they could make, barter, or part with as payment.

Once, two men from the small village of Soffranco came down from the mountains to buy food and grain from my family. Grandfather Jacuzzi made a proposal. As the men did not have money to pay for food, he asked if they might have anyone in their household who could come help with the farm and other chores, which were overwhelming his family.

Grandfather was still trying to work odd jobs and my father had not yet recovered from his injury. It also was not safe for Pa to be seen outside, where he could be taken as a prisoner or considered an Italian soldier. The youngest girls, and boy, Candido, were still too small to do heavy farm work. So, it fell on my grandmother and the oldest girls to keep the farm running.

The livestock, which numbered (in the pre-war years) as many as eight cows, two horses, two pigs, plus chickens, ducks, turkeys, rabbits, cats and dogs, were always in danger of being stolen during the war. Sunrise to sunset, chores included milking, cleaning the stables, feeding all of the animals, and planting and harvesting crops, including the family's vegetable garden. A typical day included Felicita's holding the plow, while Angelina drove the horse that pulled the plow. The silkworm crop, a very valuable asset for the family, was a time-intensive indoor project. Clearly, help was needed.

The men, distant relatives named Giovanni Battista Piucco and Antonio Piucco, replied that they had no young men available—all were off fighting in the war, but they each had a daughter they could send. So a deal was arranged for the two girls, Pascua (Pasquetta) Piucco, Antonio's daughter, and Giuseppina (Pina) Piucco, Giovanni's daughter, to come work for the Jacuzzi family. Antonio's wife Giovanna was Pina's godmother.

In exchange for their labor, Grandfather agreed to pay their families with food, grain, and other farm produce until conditions improved. Pasquetta and Pina—willing workers, strong and beautiful—were warmly welcomed into the household, and quickly became more like daughters and sisters than hired workers. My grandparents insisted that they sleep in the house with the family, and not in the hayloft, which was the normal place for hired help. Grandmother Teresa taught them many things about cooking, giving the girls many recipes and techniques they hadn't learned in their own homes.

The girls' fathers came occasionally to visit, always traveling by foot at night. During these clandestine visits, they retrieved whatever food and other material they could safely carry, concealing their sacks of goods from any Austrian and German soldiers they might meet on their return trek into the mountains.

In spite of the tensions that clouded this time, my mother, Pina, remembered a prank that she played on Candido during the war. As she, Candido and others in the family were working in the fields, Pina came across, and killed, a venomous snake. She coiled it around the water jar from which everyone felt he drank from too often during his frequent work breaks. When Candido reached for the jar, he let out a scream in fright and ran away. Candido was like a younger brother to Pina and she often cut his hair.

In the beautiful and vivacious Pina, Valeriano found the girl he wished to marry. She was tall and slender with blond hair and clear blue eyes. She was always a willing worker who brought joy to the Jacuzzi household with her happy, outgoing nature. She laughed freely, loved to sing, and made friends easily. Pina had a liking for a young man from the town of Forno di Zoldo, located near Soffranco, when she came to work for the Jacuzzi family, but as time passed she fell in love with the kind, thoughtful, and handsome Valeriano. After a period of courtship, their intention to marry was announced, and a wedding was planned.

Just as Aunt Felicita would later assist her own sisters with their wedding preparations, she worked with my mother in the sewing of her wedding dress. My grandfather helped my father build a bedroom set in the days before the wedding, which took place soon after the close of World War I. My mother's father (a widower), her two brothers, and a sister made the journey down from the mountains to attend. Many of the neighbors, glad to have something to celebrate after the gloom of war, joined the family for the wedding feast.

The devoted fifty-three-year marriage of Valeriano and Pina—my father and mother — has convinced me that love can blossom anywhere, even in the midst of great adversity.

Sadly, Pasquetta, who had come down from the Alps with my mother, worked alongside her at the farm, and had witnessed firsthand Pina's growing affection for my father, died of consumption (now more commonly called tuberculosis) on February 16, 1920, at her home in Soffranco. Though she attended Pina and Valeriano's wedding, she never shared the many happy and successful years my parents spent together.

The Jacuzzi family had grown to love Pasquetta as one of their own. With a nature similar to Pina's, she was a diligent helper and a very outgoing, friendly, and happy person. In fact there was hope that she might join the Jacuzzis in their move to the United States, and possibly even marry one of the older Jacuzzi boys. They felt they lost part of their family when she died.

My maternal grandfather, Giovanni Piucco, was killed in the early 1920s in an accident while hunting with friends in the mountains near Soffranco.

SUCCESS AND SORROW

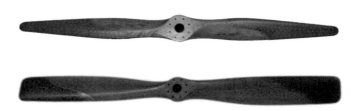

Jacuzzi toothpick propeller (top)
Jacuzzi squared tip propeller (bottom)

Rachele Jacuzzi (center) in propeller shop

Gelindo Jacuzzi (left) in propeller shop

Chapter 5

The Toothpick

"Dobbiamo essere attivi, fare lavoro utile, e vivere a lungo . . ."
"We must be active, do useful work, [and] live long . . ."
—Rachele Jacuzzi, my grandparents' first son and child

World War I brought a hefty dose of life's ironies to my family: hardship befell some members, while opportunity came to others.

My grandparents, my father and his new love, and the younger Jacuzzi children endured the war in Italy. However, during this same time, the brothers, who were in America, continued their pursuit of a better life through hard work and inventiveness. They also maintained high hopes that Grandfather would realize his plan of bringing the entire family to the United States. Indeed, hope was all they could hang onto, since the war had interrupted all communication.

Rachele continued his job repairing airplanes and building propellers, while Frank, Joseph, Giocondo, and Gelindo managed and worked the Remington family's farm. Rachele still embraced his dream, yearning to design and build airplanes, not just to repair them. His start came when he and Valeriano worked on improving the Remington propellers, before Pa left to manage the Remington farm and then returned to Italy in 1913. Uncle Rachele continued to develop new ideas and refine his sketches, certain he could make revolutionary contributions to the field of aviation.

The Toothpick

Rachele, therefore, was happy to learn that at the upcoming World's Fair, the Panama-Pacific International Exposition of 1915, a featured exhibit would showcase the latest in airplane design. There, he hoped to discover what others were doing, and to learn what opportunities might be available to him in the industry.

Most important, he wanted to contact other airplane builders and owners who might like to test his propeller designs, so he traveled from Los Angeles to San Francisco to attend the fair.

While there, he found a temporary job as a mechanic with the Christoferson Aviation Company. But the highlight of his time in the Bay Area was seeing the very latest in aviation models. At the exhibit, he met a flyer who had a prototype airplane that was not performing to expectations, so Rachele convinced him to try one of his propellers. To his delight, the pilot discovered that all Rachele had told him was true: the unique design of the propeller really did enhance engine power and flight. He quickly became one of Rachele's chief endorsers.

Uncle Rachele's propeller soon attracted the attention of several flight enthusiasts. With the American aviation industry still in its infancy, new developments and ideas were received with keen interest by airplane builders and investors.

I can see how this new propeller caught their attention. Evolved from earlier prototypes that he and Pa created for Remington, Uncle Rachele's ingeniously redesigned propeller was narrower, longer, and lower pitched. The altered propeller dynamic allowed the engine to run at increased RPM with greater power output. Because of its configuration, it was soon dubbed "The Toothpick." In both design and construction, it was superior in performance and durability to anything else available at the time, being fashioned from layers of laminated wood, usually protected by bronze sheathing at the tips. The Toothpick propeller would become the first mass-manufactured product bearing the *Jacuzzi* name. Aunt Stella remembered Rachele telling her that he actually conceived and presented this narrow propeller design years earlier, while in Milan, where his idea received a cool reception, so he was thrilled when the American aviation industry embraced its clarity and simplicity. Indeed, Uncle Rachele's life now appeared to be headed down the path he had dreamed of—focusing his mind, hands, and pioneering spirit in the field of aviation.

Some of our family records indicate that one of Rachele's first satisfied customers—the pilot he met at the World's Fair in San Francisco—was somehow affiliated with the Hall-Scott Motor Company. Soon after this successful and satisfactory use of the Toothpick propeller on the aviator's airplane, Hall-Scott asked Uncle Rachele to manufacture several more propellers for their inventory.

Hall-Scott Motor Company moved from Los Angeles to the San Francisco Bay Area, which was fast becoming a hub for aviation endeavors. For a brief time, Uncle Rachele returned to work in Los Angeles. However, since most of his orders were coming from the Bay Area, he decided to move his operation to a rented garage in East Oakland, in order to be closer to his customers. In addition to Hall-Scott, these valued customers also included the Union Gas Engine Company and the Gorham Aviation School. An importer, Mr. G. Turola, advanced Rachele the money necessary to get the new shop up and running.

Gelindo

The work load was now overwhelming Rachele and he needed help. His next older brother, my father, was in Italy, but Gelindo, although recuperating from an illness, answered the call to join him. Previously, Gelindo had been working at odd jobs in Los Angeles. He often made a few dollars with a device he had built—a portable foot-powered grinding wheel, which he set up on street corners and used to sharpen knives and scissors.

He also had a job washing dishes, but when the restaurant owner couldn't pay him in cash, he instead offered Gelindo a small building lot. At the time Gelindo didn't think the lot was worth very much so he decided to hold on to it for a while. As it turned out, Gelindo showed some business savvy, for when he did sell the lot at a later time, he made quite a profit. . . . The lot was located in Beverly Hills!

With Gelindo's move to Oakland, Rachele was glad to have some company, as well as some help. For a while, Gelindo worked the early daytime hours in a poultry house, then he would go to the propeller shop to work with Rachele in the afternoon. Uncle Gelindo was an easy-going man, who loved to recite proverbs in Italian. A visitor to the shop might find him working away, while he whistled or sang arias from operas.

Gelindo enjoyed and obviously had some skill as a boxer, so he often spent his evenings in a local gym, where he became friends with his frequent sparring partner, the rising star of boxing, Jack Dempsey.

Sharing a mutual interest in invention, and always thirsting for more technical insights, Rachele and Gelindo enjoyed visiting with astronomy and physics professors at Oakland's Mills College. They also took time off to make the winding journey up Mt. Hamilton to tour the Lick Observatory. Uncle Rachele also began to establish professional friend-ships with professors at the University of California at Berkeley.

Within a few months, propeller orders were so numerous that both brothers had to work full-time just to keep up with the demand. Building propellers was precision work, and Rachele was glad to have Gelindo's eye for detail on the job. For many years, Gelindo would have the responsibility of ensuring the balance of each propeller before it was allowed to leave the Jacuzzi Brothers' shop.

An American Wedding

The following year, on June 15, 1916, Uncle Rachele, twenty-nine, married Olympia Calugi, thirty-four. They met in Los Angeles, when he was staying in a boardinghouse run by Olympia. Rachele had been directed by a friend to this house as a good place to stay, and when he moved to San Francisco, Olympia followed him.

Unfortunately, the happy days surrounding the wedding were not to last. It is poignant to me that my godfather, a man so brilliant, so gener-ous with his ideas and his family, was, in the end, burdened with a stormy marriage, its peaceful seasons often followed by intervals of strife.

After several years of marriage, they separated for nearly a year and then filed for divorce. Much of the conflict apparently had to do with the fact that Rachele, who desperately wanted children, married Olympia thinking she was also keen to have a family. But Olympia was unable to conceive, a condition she probably knew of prior to the marriage. Before a full year passed, however, they reconciled and canceled the divorce, spending the remainder of their years together. Whether or not they were content is mere speculation. They had earlier adopted a three-year-old boy named Giordano (Gordon), in 1931.

Family Business

Though it would not become an official corporation until 1920, the founding of Jacuzzi Brothers is generally considered to have occurred in 1915. In 1917, Uncle Rachele's propellers were in such high demand that the other brothers, Joseph, Giocondo, and Frank, also joined the business.

Mr. Lee Scott visited the small East Oakland shop to see for himself how these propellers were being made. Favorably impressed with the brothers' craftsmanship, he requested they move their shop closer to the Hall-Scott Motor Company.

Mr. Scott's company used testing stands prior to shipment in order to assure the quality for each motor and propeller. After Hall-Scott tested the Jacuzzi propeller, the company asked Rachele to be the exclusive supplier of Hall-Scott's propellers. Within a few days, Mr. Scott delivered sixteen propellers that had been started in his pattern shop. The challenge was to transform these into the Jacuzzi model. The brothers were successful in producing ten Toothpicks from the sixteen originals.

Uncle Rachele considered his customer's requests to move and to be his sole supplier. Since additional shop space was needed anyway, and because it would be easier for the Hall-Scott personnel to monitor the tests being run on the propellers in the Jacuzzi shop rather than running them again in their own, Rachele agreed to the requests.

In keeping with their European traditions, the brothers all agreed it would be to their advantage to live together. So when they moved their shop to Berkeley in September 1917, the five rented a large ten-room house at 1633 Kains Avenue, within walking distance of the 1450 San Pablo Avenue shop. Olympia, Rachele's wife, handled all the cooking and housekeeping.

A typical workday in the shop might include orders taken in the morning that were calculated and drawn by Rachele, who used the metric system (not used in America), which had to be converted into English inches and feet for the final drawing and production. The laminations were carefully cut and by evening, the final propellers, ranging from six to ten feet in length—with the typical propeller measuring eight to nine feet—were glued together with 250-ton steel presses.

During this period, many other aviation enthusiasts visited the brothers' shop, either for guidance, or out of curiosity. Other times, they sought to learn how to duplicate the successful Toothpick propeller. One day, one of their customer's engineers, Mr. L. H. Parker, of Union Gas Company, came to observe. He asked Uncle Rachele if he could watch him draw a propeller design. He then asked if Rachele would sell him the plan. Rachele politely refused. But the engineer was persistent.

Another day, Parker visited and started making sketches of his own, hoping that Rachele would watch him and be drawn into giving him tips and advice for design improvement. However, Uncle Rachele was cautious. Instead of sharing his secrets for a successful product, he watched Parker and learned a few new procedural steps that he later incorporated into his own work.

By 1918, the brothers had enlarged the shop and purchased bigger equipment. They also bought an adjoining lot on San Pablo Avenue and Page Street to allow future expansion.

New Family

In addition to their work at Jacuzzi Brothers, the four unmarried brothers, Gelindo, Frank, Joseph and Giocondo, enjoyed meeting and befriending other immigrants, while strengthening their English and their knowledge of their new land. They soon met and fell in love with four charming and intelligent women.

Like Uncle Rachele, they were eager to marry their sweethearts and begin their own families. Between late 1918 and mid-1920, four Jacuzzi brothers celebrated California weddings. Uncle Gelindo married Rosie Meinero on December 14, 1918, Uncle Giocondo married Mary Guarneri on April 19, 1919, and two months after that, Uncle Frank married Rena Villata on June 21, 1919. Finally, Uncle Joseph and my second aunt Rena, Rena Beggio, were joined on June 12, 1920.

Jacuzzi Brothers, Incorporated

Since the business was growing, by 1920 it was necessary for the five brothers to establish a financial arrangement that would be equitable and agreeable to all. They decided to form a corporation and divide the company ownership into shares, with each brother receiving an equal number. Because of her active role as the manager and housekeeper of their home, the brothers further agreed that Olympia should be included, and she was given the same number of shares as the brothers.

Although other family members would receive shares at a later time, these were the original Jacuzzi Brothers shareholders: Rachele, Frank, Joseph, Gelindo, Giocondo, and Olympia. Each was allotted 6,000 shares. (My father, Valeriano, received 6,000 shares upon his return from Italy in 1921.)

The articles of incorporation, dated May 3, 1920, and filed by the Berkeley law firm of Elston Clark & Nichols, reveal the brothers' over-all business plan. They state they will "manufacture, buy, repair and deal in Airoplanes, Airoplane Propellers . . . and carry on Transportation Service by Airoplane."

The document further attests that the business planned to have a full-service automobile division. Only time would tell whether or not the shares would pay any real dividends, but if business continued to grow as it had been, the future looked promising.

A Thriving Business

The worldwide conflict that endangered some of the Jacuzzi family greatly helped others. In Italy, Grandfather and Grandmother, the eight children, and a future daughter-in-law and her distant relative continued suffering many hardships, while the five brothers in America were benefiting from a boom in their business brought about by that same war.

Declaring war on Germany, the United States officially entered World War I on April 6, 1917. Aviation historians consider World War I as a benchmark in the history and development of the industry. This was due to the technological advances and the greater dependability airplanes demonstrated during that conflict. Certainly, the Jacuzzi Toothpick represented one of the best inventions in this era.

It was an exciting time for the industry because, for the first time, the United States Army Signal Corps made strategic use of its Aeronautical Division. By May 1918, this group was reorganized and renamed the Army Air Service (later to be called the Army Air Corps and, still later, the United States Army Air Force), becoming a major portion of the nation's military strike force. Many of the airplanes used, both for training and combat, were equipped with Jacuzzi Toothpick propellers. Some of these aircraft included the Curtiss *JN4*, *Standard II*, *Thomas-Morse*, and the *Handley-Page*. It strikes me as regrettable, yet true, nonetheless, that the success of the Jacuzzi Brothers Company in those early years was due primarily to the war.

Years later, Uncle Frank, whose English name for Francesco in many ways sums up his personality, looked back on those times in the shop, when he always carried a wooden rule in his pocket, and said: "It was a damn good propeller!"

There is no arguing with him, because the Toothpick made thousands of successful flights over many thousands of miles, although I have been unable to determine exactly how many propellers were produced by the Jacuzzi Brothers Company during this time.

A Jacuzzi Toothpick is housed in the Smithsonian Institution's National Air and Space Museum. Many are presently in the hands of private collectors and in a few smaller museums. I own two Toothpicks, and one specially designed Jacuzzi propeller with squared-off tips. They are truly a concrete link to my heritage, for it is a joy to admire their smooth, finely crafted surfaces and know that my uncles worked on them.

It is also interesting for me to imagine how they may have been used, on which planes and for what duty. Uncle Gelindo's daughter, Lola Jacuzzi Fenolio, who served as Uncle Rachele's personal secretary, compiled a year-by-year synoptic chronology during her service with Jacuzzi Brothers. Lola's time line for 1918, the year the Army Air Service was formed, is as follows:

"During the year, many airplane companies sprang up with government contracts, and the Jacuzzis made thousands of propellers for them, as well as for old established companies."

For the year 1919, Cousin Lola continued: "The Jacuzzi propeller . . .

had flown the skies of most of the countries of the world and had carried the first transcontinental air mail in America."

These years were profitable for the company, but emotionally trying for the family, with the Jacuzzi brothers wondering what had become of their parents and siblings. They all longed for the war to end soon so the family could be reunited.

Jacuzzi family on the terrace of their ancestral home before leaving Italy – 1920

Jacuzzi family's first home in Berkeley, CA – recent photograph

Double wedding – Luigi and Felicita Lanza (left), Peter and Angelina Tunesi (right)

Chapter 6

Together Again for the First Time

*"Sentimmo che le forze alleate erano sbarcate a Genova e
Napoli. Non potete immaginare la nostra speranza e felicità.
Passarono vari giorni eccitanti e dopo giunse la notizia che la
pace era raggiunta con la firma dell'armistizio. Era 11 Novembre,
1918, il compleanno del fratello più anziano, Rachele. Saltammo
felici piangendo e ridendo al tempo stesso. Le campane delle
chiese suonavano. Finalmente la terribile guerra era finita."*

"We heard that the Allied forces had landed in Genova and
Naples. You can't imagine our hope and happiness. A few exciting days passed and then the news came that peace had come
with the signing of the armistice. It was November 11, 1918, my
oldest brother Rachele's birthday. We jumped in happiness and
cried and laughed all at the same time. The church bells were
ringing. Finally, the terrible war was over."

— Stella Jacuzzi Marin, the twelfth of my grandparents'
thirteen children

Soon after the Jacuzzi family learned that their liberators were in Italy,
they saw both the Allied troops and the Germans and Austrians on the
road in front of their house. The Allies came in proudly; the Germans
and Austrians fled in retreat, eager to cross the Italian border. By mid-
November 1918, the word spread rapidly through Casarsa and throughout the surrounding area that the war was finally over. The family gathered to celebrate with friends and neighbors. Grandfather Giovanni and
my father had buried a small barrel of wine months earlier, agreeing to

retrieve it only after the war was officially declared to be over. How happy they must have been to unearth and uncork that barrel!

Italy

The war prevented the family from communicating, but the silence was finally broken when my grandparents received a letter from Uncle Rachele in America. His letter traveled almost a month before reaching Casarsa. Rachele wrote about many things, detailing the new lives he and his brothers were building on the other side of the world. Rachele told of his marriage to Olympia, of Gelindo's marriage to a young lady named Rosie Meinero, and all about the manufacturing company called Jacuzzi Brothers. Throughout the New Year of 1919 and in 1920, the letters from Rachele and the other brothers were full of more exciting news. These letters announced the marriages of Giocondo, Frank, and Joseph, as well as the 1919 arrival of Gelindo's daughter, Lola, and the 1920 birth of Giocondo's daughter, Anna.

Rachele encouraged Grandfather and Pa to proceed with their earlier plan to relocate the family to the United States, since it was becoming ever more certain that he and his brothers would not be returning to Italy. America was now their home, as it would become for the entire Jacuzzi family. This second decision to leave Italy was much more difficult than the one made before the war. My aunt Cirilla recalled many tearful conversations between her parents during this time. War-torn though they were, the house and land survived the harsh years of the conflict intact. To leave now would be agony; they were not at all sure they could bring themselves to do so.

An additional hardship was the difficulty, if not impossibility, of selling or leasing the land so soon after the war. The armies had disfigured the countryside, and it was doubtful that many people could afford to buy or maintain land, since the war also ruined them financially. But two considerations caused Grandfather and Grandmother to lean toward immigration. First and foremost, they wanted to reunite the family. Second, they were concerned that their daughters, especially Felicita and Angelina, had many longtime friends and were becoming very interested in local boys, but Grandmother wanted her girls to be more than farmers' wives. Grandfather added that if one or two of his daughters married, it would be very difficult to leave them behind, and it might be equally hard to persuade any newlyweds to join the family in America. If they were to go, they must go quickly.

Numerous families who fled during the war had since returned to the area, often to find their homes severely damaged or reduced to rubble. The government instituted a rebuilding program, whereby a landowner, if able to substantiate his claim, could apply for financial reimbursement for losses sustained during the war. Regardless of whether he chose to remain or leave, Grandfather knew his home and land needed substantial repair. He inspected his property, calculated his losses, which could include damage to buildings, as well as any crops and livestock confiscated by the occupying armies, and filed his claim. It was soon approved, and the rebuilding and repair work began in earnest. At the same time, Grandfather reached several decisions: the family would move to America, but now he would attempt only to lease the Italian house. Selling it and the land was not an option.

First chosen to emigrate to California, in 1920, were their two oldest daughters, Felicita, twenty-two, and Angelina, nineteen, accompanied by their youngest son, the fifteen-year-old Candido. It must have been heartbreaking to abandon lifelong friends. Grandfather made the travel arrangements and notified his sons in America of the new arrivals. On March 6, the day of departure, Grandfather accompanied the three to Genova, where they departed on the *France*. The ship's manifest listed their destination as 1450 San Pablo Street, Berkeley, California, the address of the brothers' shop. Both Uncle Rachele's name and that of the company, Jacuzzi Brothers, are included in this document. To ease the sorrows of departure, Grandfather assured them that the family would all be together in a year. Felicita, Angelina, and Candido arrived in New York on March 14, 1920.

Within a few months, Grandfather had located a suitable tenant for the farm and house. He set aside one upstairs room, where some furniture, linens, and other household items were stored. In this way, any family members who chose to return to Italy would have a furnished place to live.

Grandfather then made an arrangement with a longtime friend to serve as the agent and manager of the property, ensuring that everything, the property as well as the financial transactions, were cared for properly.

It has always been fascinating for me to visit Casarsa and this home, which remained under the ownership of the family, and eventually the corporation, for many years, until 1975. The present owners, Rino and Silvana Bianchini, have always been very gracious when my family and I visited what is now their family home. In fact, we have developed a friendship with the Bianchini family. When their son, Emanuele, was an exchange student, he lived with my cousin, Uncle Gelindo's son, Daniele Jacuzzi, and his wife, Jean, in their California home.

The Journey

After nine months, the remaining Jacuzzi family prepared to join the rest of the family in California. Grandfather and my father decided to depart from France rather than from Genova, so the first leg of their 7,000 mile journey was by rail, then by ship to New York, followed by another overland journey to San Francisco. The group included Grandfather and Grandmother, my parents, Valeriano and Pina, my oldest brother, Virgil, a baby at the time of the voyage, and the other final members of our family born in Italy: Aunts Ancilla, Cirilla, Stella, and Gilia. These aunts, as well my father and mother, shared with me many memories of the journey, and even Virgil remembered a few incidents. From all of these, I have compiled an account of the voyage.

In mid-December 1920, farewells were made to all their friends and the only relatives they were leaving behind, Grandmother's brother and his wife, Antonio and Carolina Arman. A close friend assisted by carrying Virgil in her arms as they traveled to the train station. Though everyone cried, there was no turning back. In late afternoon, as darkness fell, they boarded the train to Milan, where they slept at a hotel.

In the morning, they boarded the train again for their next destination, Paris, where they again had another overnight stay. The following morning, as they departed Paris for the port of La Havre, they passed by the Arc de Triomphe, where a tomb for an unknown soldier had been dedicated only one month earlier.

After the nine Jacuzzis boarded their ship, the *Rochambeau*, on December 18, 1920, the steward took them to their compartments, which were comfortable and clean, with good beds. The ship's food was excellent and very filling but all of them suffered some seasickness, so on some days, the dining room was seldom visited.

The ocean passage took eleven days, during which the family enjoyed Christmas dinner, a festive meal in the dining room, served with a generous slice of cake for dessert. The next day, Virgil celebrated his first birthday on the high seas, though he fell sick that evening because so many passengers had given him candy to eat!

As the sea became calmer, the crew advised they were close to land, and on December 29, the Jacuzzi family spied the Statue of Liberty. They remembered her as "a very impressive lady who welcomed us with her torch held high."

On his earlier visit to America, Grandfather Giovanni had learned how difficult the entry process could be, thanks to the concentration camp atmosphere of Ellis Island. So this time he purchased second-class tickets, allowing them to bypass the island, where only steerage passengers were detained. After their papers were processed on the ship, the family was directed to the train depot to begin the trip to California.

Pa and Grandfather knew they should take the southern route to avoid the cold and snow of the northern winter. They traveled in Pullman cars with sleeping quarters, changing trains only once. They were in Atlanta on New Year's Day. Crossing the Mississippi River was memorable—the train was divided into sections and rolled onto a barge. After the ferrying across the river, the train was recoupled and the journey continued.

Finally, they arrived in Los Angeles, then made their way by train to San Francisco, took a ferry across the bay, and rode the electric train to Berkeley where their "American" brothers were waiting for them at the Hopkins Street stop. They took them to the house they had rented and furnished for them—a large, two-story, six-bedroom house at 2225 Byron Street in Berkeley, where Uncle Giocondo, Aunt Mary, and baby Anna, born February 20, 1920, already lived. It was January 4, 1921. The Jacuzzi family, overwhelmed with emotion, were all together again!

To be more accurate, this was the *first* meeting of the entire family. Rachele had left home before some of his siblings were born, while the brothers in America had never met Valeriano's wife, Pina, and baby, Virgil. The recent arrivals from Italy had never met Rachele's wife, Olympia, Frank's wife, Rena, Giocondo's wife, Mary, and their baby daughter, Anna, Joseph's wife, Rena, or Gelindo's wife, Rosie, and young daughter, Lola, born December 18, 1919.

The newcomers were very surprised to learn Lola's birth date, for they had thought Virgil was the first grandchild, but she had been born in California eight days before him.

More introductions were yet to come, for Felicita and Angelina, who had now been in America for almost ten months, were both engaged to be married. This development must have pleased my grandparents when they met the fiancés of Felicita and Angelina, Luigi Lanza and Peter Tunesi, respectively. Deciding to send the older daughters on first, before the final group's departure, had been a wise strategy.

America

Everything was new: the language, the currency, the neighborhood, and the house. I can hardly imagine what those first few weeks in America must have been like for my grandparents and their children. The adjustments must have been both exciting and unnerving, especially for the children. Aunt Cirilla told me that she was very sad for many days; everything was strange and unfamiliar.

The abrupt transition from a family farm in rural Italy to an American house in a bustling neighborhood was so shocking that Aunt Gilia said, "We didn't say a word and we didn't understand anything."

The house the brothers selected for their parents and sisters had been roomy, until twelve new Jacuzzis moved in. The family had to settle in quickly, for Felicita and Angelina had decided to have a double wedding just three weeks later on January 30, which happened to be the thirty-fifth anniversary of their parents, Giovanni and Teresa. The decision to proceed with the wedding so quickly was simply practical, since the house was overcrowded. The two sisters would move out after marriage, so everyone decided sooner was better than later.

Grandmother and my mother, Ma (short for the Italian *mama*) also encountered the very strong-willed woman Olympia, Rachele's wife, known for her coarse and earthy manner; however, Ma was very tolerant and welcoming to everyone and won Olympia over.

With the help of Felicita and Angelina, Grandmother Teresa and Ma attempted to organize the Byron Street household as quickly as possible.

It was soon permeated with the sweet scent of one of Grandmother's favorite dishes, baked apples, cooked in the open fireplace in the old-fashioned way.

Work and School

After the double wedding, my grandparents considered the best course for the children who remained under their roof. The youngest two, Stella, thirteen, and Gilia, twelve, were sent to Burbank Junior High School, which, due to the growing immigrant population, offered a three-month concentrated course in English, after which the two girls were placed in regular classes.

Aunt Cirilla, who was only fifteen when she arrived in Berkeley, told me that she, too, would have liked to have gone to school. However, Gelindo believed that the oldest girls should work, so he convinced my grandparents the family needed the money Cirilla's job could bring. Then, my grandparents considered sending the older children—Cirilla, Ancilla, and Candido—to a tutor, but never did. Candido, turning eighteen, joined his older brothers as an apprentice in the shop. Previously, he worked for a cabinetmaker.

Learning that sewing jobs were plentiful, Ancilla and Cirilla found work in a garment factory where, after one week of unpaid training on the machines, they were employed full-time. The girls were paid piece-work, which usually amounted to about $8.00 per week. All of their pay was turned over to their father to help support the family.

Aunts Stella and Gilia, who remained at school for three years, shared fond memories of their American school days. The teachers were kind and generous to them and they especially enjoyed the music teacher, Miss Gibson, who taught them many popular songs, such as those of Stephen Foster. Aunt Stella recalled one of her favorites from this period was "Love's Old Sweet Song," known more commonly as "Just a Song at Twilight." The lyrics dated from 1884, but the song would have been brand-new for her, as she experimented with a new language and learned new music.

The clothing the family brought from abroad worked well in the new environment. The girls felt comfortable in them at their new school, and Aunts Ancilla and Cirilla's dresses were appropriate for their new jobs, where they found themselves amid immigrants from many countries, including Mexico, Argentina, and Brazil, as well from Russia, France, Italy, and Germany.

Uncle Rachele, who had always felt responsible for all of his younger brothers and sisters, naturally assumed some of the parenting duties during his parents' first days in California, but the results were not always desirable. Once, Gilia and Stella had an organized recess at school, where the girls were required to put on gym clothes, consisting of bloomers that came just below the knee. However, the American girls liked to pull them up just above the knee, so Gilia and Stella mimicked this style. Rachele saw them one day on the playground and immediately rushed home to tell his mother that he had just seen his two sisters with their knees exposed, declaring that this was shameful and would have to be stopped.

When Grandmother Teresa talked to her daughters about Rachele's concern, they cried because they didn't want to be "different." So, Teresa reassured her son with "*non pensate, non pensate*," or "don't worry, don't worry." Wisely, she understood her daughters' need to blend in with their new environment and wasn't concerned if a little more of their legs showed for a brief time during a gym class.

Although she accommodated the younger girls, Teresa's own attire stayed conservative and always consisted of a very dark woolen dress and, usually, a woolen head scarf tied behind her head. She usually bought these scarves at Berkeley's Hink's Department Store. The style of dress was pure Casarsan, with the skirt down to her ankles.

Because her local Catholic Church had been such an anchor for her in Italy, I find it sad that Grandmother never really felt at ease in any American church. The other family members learned how to adapt to the new life, but in many ways Grandmother perceived that she was looked down upon as an immigrant. However, she continued to read her Italian Bible and study religious writing. An avid reader since childhood, she found comfort in these books during the first strange few months, and afterwards throughout her life in her new land.

Fitting In

"We were considered among the most successful people in Casarsa, and yet when we came here it was tough," said Aunt Cirilla.

Gradually, the newcomers, especially the younger generation, adjusted to living in a neighborhood. Having sidewalks, paved roads, streetcars, and nearby stores was all new to them, but they were glad to begin making friends with their neighbors, many of whom were immigrants themselves. A movie house, the Rivoli Theater, was located close by on San Pablo Avenue. Virgil remembered that Pa and Ma took him to see silent films.

For several months, Grandfather Giovanni stayed busy just getting the house in order. He bought a milk cow and some chickens, like some of his neighbors, and built a small barn behind the house. My mother was responsible for the care and milking of the cow, which she did in the new barn. Often, she tethered it with a chain and let it graze in one of the many empty lots in the area. In the basement of the house, where Grandfather made the family's wine, grapes were crushed in a large vat. Virgil remembered that, as a toddler, he used to climb up its side to look inside.

Though Grandfather enjoyed occasional visits to his sons' nearby shop, located at 1450 San Pablo Avenue, he soon grew restless and discontent. Although he was beginning to understand a little English, he was never interested in becoming fluent, so working outside of the home was not feasible. Yet Giovanni's hands and mind were idle and he needed to stay busy. Rachele, aware of Grandfather's mood and growing restiveness, asked his father to come work at the shop as often as he wanted.

Then sixty-six, he gladly went to the shop several days each week to sharpen the tools and offer any advice and help he could. While there, he also designed and built six wooden hope chests, one for each of his daughters. Pa, inspired by his father's work, built a similar chest for my mother, Pina. My grandfather surely loved staying busy, returning to the craft of his youth, while working with his sons, who as principle shareholders voted to present him with 6,000 shares in the company. With the exception of their property in Italy, Grandfather and Grandmother had all their assets in America, so they decided to buy the Byron Street home.

Finally, after years of separation and hardship, the future was looking bright. The family was together. The business was profitable. Could things get any better, or did more difficult days lie ahead?

Giocondo Jacuzzi – c.1920

Jacuzzi J-5 Mosquito
airplane – 1919

Jacuzzi J-7 *monoplane in
Yosemite – 1921
From left: Giocondo Jacuzzi, John
Kauke, Duncan McLeish, and
pilot Bud Coffee
(Courtesy of the Oakland Museum of
California, Herrington-Olson
Collection)*

Chapter 7

Giocondo

"Lavorammo per riunire la famiglia in America cosicché potessimo essere tutti riuniti, e, nonostante ciò, Dio ne prese uno."

"We strove to reunite the family in America so we could all be together and, yet, God took one."
—Teresa Arman Jacuzzi, my Grandmother

Amid life's uncertainties, a test of our mettle is how we respond to change. If change is for the better, can we accept the blessing without becoming conceited? Or, if things turn out for the worse, can we avoid growing bitter? And in the face of tragic loss, can we go on?

My family soon had to struggle with this last question.

New Heights

While the end of World War I lifted the spirits of America, it inevitably brought hardship to some of our nation's industries. Jacuzzi Brothers, so dependent on contracts with companies associated with the war effort, faced a severe downturn in business.

The demand for their propellers in the civilian market was substantially less than the war needs of the military. The industry also was developing a new type of propeller, one made entirely of metal. Rachele and his brothers experimented with this approach but found they could not economically produce metal models. After the war ended in late 1918, the brothers undertook airplane maintenance and repair work in order to keep their business in operation.

Uncle Rachele foresaw the competitive changes in the propeller business and began experimenting with new aviation ideas. He wanted to build more than just propellers. His desire was for the company to build airplanes!

During the company's earlier period of growth in Berkeley, the brothers had a larger building erected on the site of their San Pablo Avenue shop. This additional space provided enough room for them to build a prototype monoplane that Rachele had designed. The plane was a sleek, small one-seater, powered by a rebuilt Ford Model T automobile engine. The brothers designated this plane their model J-5 and called it *The Mosquito* because of its tiny size. Although the engine provided limited power and was very heavy, the small plane flew successfully on each of several test flights, with Gelindo as one of the pilots. Spurred on by their success, the brothers decided to build a larger version.

The *J-7*

Building an airplane in 1920 from scratch was a formidable task, especially one like the new model, which was much larger than the previous one. Uncle Rachele served as chief engineer for the project, while all of the brothers worked on the execution of his design. John H. Kauke, who was called "Jack," had worked in the shop during the war as a propeller inspector for the government's Air Service, and was hired as the plane's project manager. Jack Kauke went to the University of California at Berkeley in 1912 to start his studies in aeronautical engineering but after one semester transferred to Stanford University, where he earned his degree. As project manager, Jack assisted Rachele with engineering and production of the *J-7* and was also responsible for promoting the airplane, communicating with potential customers and raising funds for the company's growth. Uncle Rachele and the brothers obviously were impressed by him and held his engineering expertise and communication skills in high regard.

Eventually, the job became a family affair. In the evenings, the wives and sisters of the brothers joined them in the shop. The ladies' job was to stretch and stitch unbleached muslin over the wings and tail section using fine French seams, then doping the fabric several times with shellac until the surfaces were drum-tight and hard.

An issue of *The Injector*, a Jacuzzi corporate publication, reviewed the history of this project and listed the *J-7*'s specifications:

Overall length	29 ft.
Span	52 ft.
Height (to top of radiator)	10 ft., 6 in.
Propeller	8 ft., 2 in.
Wing area (including center section)	400 sq. ft.
Weight, empty	1,800 lbs.
Fuel capacity (2 wing tanks)	80 gals.
Oil capacity (tank in wing)	4 gals.
Fuel consumption per hour	8 to 9 gals.
Radius of action	900 to 1,000 miles
Speed, at half-throttle	100 mph
Speed, at three-quarters-throttle	125 mph
Minimum landing speed (full load)	45 mph
Approximate ceiling	22,000 ft.
Engine	L-6 Hall-Scott, capable of developing over 200 hp

The airplane was designed to seat seven, including the pilot, with the seats arranged in three rows. The pilot and one passenger, or a co-pilot, sat in the front, with three passengers in the middle row, and two passengers in the back. Large windows along the sides gave passengers an unobstructed outside view—a first for commercial aviation. The wings ran across the top toward the front of the cabin.

In an article John Kauke wrote for the February 7, 1921, issue of the *Aerial Age Weekly*, he pointed out that one of the most noticeable features of the *J-7* was its cabin design. The fuselage merged with the central section of the plane's body and the plywood roof of the central section was also the ceiling of the passenger compartment, an innovation that made the plane appear small for its interior capacity.

There was no other commercial craft like it. The *East Bay Magazine* of December 1966 declared that the plane's design "was to the aircraft of that era what the Lear jet is today." *Aerial Age Weekly* magazine in May 1921 offered some contemporary perspective on the advanced technology of the Jacuzzi Monoplane:

. . . a particularly striking feature of the flight from a passenger-carrying standpoint was the relative comfort enjoyed by pilot and passengers in the Jacuzzi plane as compared to the ordinary cockpit job. The sedan-like cabin of the Jacuzzi plane made it possible for the pilot to wear nothing more than the clothes which one would wear were he to drive to Reno in a car.

"The Jacuzzi Monoplane," as it was often referred to in news and magazine articles, officially was called the *J-7*, which identified its builders and its seating capacity. The aircraft was distinctive and achieved pioneering status. It was the first high-wing monoplane with a totally enclosed, multi-passenger cabin, to be designed, built, and flown in America.

A letter dated November 22, 1920, from Jacuzzi Brothers, Inc., to Colonel Jordan, Assistant Postmaster in San Francisco, describes the performance detail, specifications, and anti-fire-hazard features of the plane and stated the following report of a test flight flown by pilot G. V. Greg of Alameda:

> In a flight from Redwood City to Oakland while passing behind the Hayward Hills, the monoplane carrying five people encountered a north wind full of air pockets which was one of the roughest ever experienced on the Coast. The plane came thru this in perfect condition and made a safe landing at Durant Field thus showing exceptional strength of construction and excellent maneuverability.

The letter then made the following offer:

> Should the officials of the Post Office Department be interested in giving us a trial order for a single machine of this type we could furnish one complete for fourteen thousand dollars. ($14,000 was worth approximately $150,000 in today's value.)

The brothers had ambitious plans for the new plane. They were not the only ones who were betting on its success. Aunt Cirilla remembered that her parents, the sisters, and the spouses were all engaged: "With this project, the entire hope of the family was resting."

In February 1921, Jacuzzi Brothers, Inc., publicly announced its intention to open a ninety-mile passenger service route that would connect San Francisco, Oakland, Richmond, and Sacramento. Their one-of-a-kind monoplane, rivaling the railroad in comfort and besting it in speed, would provide a revolutionary new service within the Bay Area and even in the Yosemite Valley.

Test Flights

Although amateur pilots like Gelindo had flown *The Mosquito*, the larger and more complex *J-7* required a professional pilot at the controls. Mike Brown, a proven military pilot and a flight instructor from Mather Field in Sacramento, was hired for some initial test flight.

One of the earliest tests was conducted with the cooperation of the U.S. Air Mail Service when one of their in-service airplanes, a DeHavilland, flew alongside the *J-7* on a 374-air-mile round-trip flight from the Marina Air Field in San Francisco to Reno, Nevada. It was after this flight, requiring the plane to reach 14,000 feet to cross the Sierra Nevada Mountains, that the Jacuzzi Monoplane began receiving very positive reviews in newspapers and aviation magazines.

Just how many test flights were completed is uncertain, but one of particular importance occurred in April 1921, as reported in the summer 1968 issue of the *American Aviation Historical Society Journal* records, ". . . In April 1921, Mike Brown flew Mr. & Mrs. C. H. Caldwell, of San Francisco, over the Sierra Nevada Mountains and into Reno, Nevada."

The account continues with details of the flight, as reported in the *Gridley Herald* of April 18, 1921:

> The Jacuzzi Brothers' monoplane landed after becoming lost during a snow storm over the Sierra Nevada Mountains and circling over the Upper Sacramento River Valley fog for nearly three hours. Mr. & Mrs. C. H. Caldwell, with pilot Mike Brown left Reno at 7:00 a.m. after a successful flight there from San Francisco. With their fuel nearly depleted and suffering from the cold and dampness, they finally located Friesley Field and

landed. After refueling both the airplane and human body, they resumed their flight to San Francisco.

Other veteran military pilots, including Lieutenants George B. Gray, Daniel Davidson, and Frank Clark, flew more tests. Even after these test flights, all of which were free from incident or mechanical troubles, the brothers still were not fully satisfied with their plane's performance. Air speed thus far had averaged only 90 mph, a statistic they felt could be improved by making some modifications. Under Uncle Rachele's supervision, they primarily concentrated on reducing the weight of the airplane. This included hollowing out some of the steel bolts which held the wing struts to the landing gear assembly. Also, some of the wooden beam which connected the two wing assemblies, located directly above the cockpit, was cut away. This alteration lightened the plane while also increasing the pilot's field of vision. The rudder also was redesigned. The aircraft's average speed was increased to 105 mph.

Mike Brown flew the modified *J-7* from Oakland's Durant Field to Woodland, California. Carrying a 1,500-pound load, the plane was caught in a heavy deluge of wind and rain on its return trip. It weathered the severe storm with no difficulty. Others tests followed and pilots continued to praise its performance and craftsmanship.

John "Jack" Kauke

During the early part of July 1921 things were indeed looking bright for the Jacuzzi *J-7* airplane project. The airplane was receiving a great deal of positive press and Jack Kauke had located a potential investor by the name of Mr. Salisbury, an oil man from Alameda, who wanted to acquire stock in the company and assist in development of an airline service between the San Francisco Bay Area and Yosemite Valley.

Thanks to Kauke's habit of keeping a daily journal of his life, usually documented with letters to his family, we are able to have a fairly clear picture of the *J-7*'s flight between Oakland and Yosemite that was to take place on July 12, 1921. He had made arrangements with Mr. Lewis, the Yosemite Park superintendent, and with Mr. Mather, the National Director of Parks who was in Yosemite at the time, to view the airplane as he had requested permission to provide regular service into Yosemite.

Excerpts of Jack Kauke's letter to his family written on Monday evening, July 11, 1921 provides a picture of what was being anticipated with this July 12, 1921, flight.

Dear family:

Yesterday passed without my getting off any letter to you. This was brot about by the fact that we were flying the plane to acquaint a new pilot with it who is going to pilot it into Yosemite tomorrow afternoon. He has been into the Yosemite 7 times by airplane which is more than any other man living. He is sure he can put the ship down in the Valley without any trouble of any kind. Mather, the National Director of Parks is in the Yosemite and this trip is as a demonstration for his benefit in order to obtain his sanction of a regular service into the valley. We are taking in as passengers a Mr. and Mrs. Salisbury of Alameda with their two boys, one 15 and the other 10. Possibly there will be one other passenger besides the pilot but that is not fully settled. There will be a lot of write-ups about the trip as it will be something of an epoch-making event. The man whom we are taking with his family is paying all the expenses of the trip besides buying stock in our company. He is in the oil business and seems to have a good deal of money. Things are coming our way now pretty fast and I really think we will be able to put over some of the things we have been working on so long in the very near future. "Aviation" the most conservative and authoritative publication of its kind in America, as well as the most widely read, published a picture I sent them of our ship in their last issue. They have also advised me that another better picture I sent them more recently will appear on the cover in an early issue. . . .

Lovingly, Jack

By July 12, 1921, the *J-7* was ready to fly again, this time to be piloted by Harold L. "Bud" Coffee of Modesto, California, a former first lieutenant in the United States Air Service, the man referred to in Jack Kauke's letter of July 11, 1921, to his family. Coffee told the brothers that he would probably buy a smaller version of the *J-7* if he enjoyed this trip. The son of a prominent Modesto family and a renowned World War I flight leader, he was a beloved figure in Modesto. During the war, he served as an instructor at Rockwell Field in San Diego. While there, he trained many pilots who would go on to achieve fame overseas.

Coffee also was known for his daring exploits after the war. He flew nonstop all night from Cheyenne, Wyoming, to San Francisco, bringing eager newspaper editors photographs of the Dempsey-Carpentier boxing match. Recognized as the first pilot to fly into Yosemite Valley, he pioneered in other aviation endeavors, like achieving the first night landing in California and the first mail delivery from Modesto to San Francisco.

Besides pilot Bud Coffee, there were three passengers on the *J-7* flight: Giocondo Jacuzzi, A. Duncan McLeish, a former Army pilot and the Jacuzzi Brothers' attorney, and Jack Kauke. For some reason at the last minute, the Salisbury family did not go and Mr. Kauke took their place so the plane would have more passengers. Based on Kauke's July 12, 1921, letter, it also appears that Giocondo Jacuzzi and A. Duncan McLeish could have been last-minute additions to the passenger list.

Tragedy

The four men took off from Durant Field in Oakland, bound for Yosemite National Park, some 150 miles away. The trip was a smooth one and the plane again performed even better because of its alterations. As planned, the plane's air speed averaged 105 mph and the outward bound journey set a record time of two hours for the Oakland to Yosemite National Park flight.

The following letter that Kauke wrote to his family en route to Yosemite on this historic flight provides a clear picture of his observations. The letter was started at 5:30 p.m., July 12, 1921, at 8,000 feet elevation above the San Joaquin Valley.

> Dear Family:
>
> This I dare say is the first letter you have received written on paper supported by nothing but the air we breathe.
>
> We left Oakland just an hour ago and are now entering the foothills of the Sierra Nevada Mountains. The scene is beautiful and inspiring. It makes one feel that he has awakened from a long sleep to find himself a character in one of H.G. Wells fascinating stories.

There are four of us on board; "Bud" Coffee is pilot, and the passengers include, besides your son, Giocondo Jacuzzi and A. Duncan McLeish who was a pilot with the British during the war. "Bud" and "Mac" are in the front seat where they take turns at the dual control and exchange comments on the way "she" handles etc. I have the whole second seat to myself which gives me lots of room to stretch in as the seat can hold three easily. Giocondo is in the rear seat 5:45 P.M. We are passing over a big brush fire on the banks of the Tuolomme River.

There is just enough breeze in the cabin to keep the air fresh and the temperature could not be more perfect. The motor keeps up a continued healthy purr which is sweet music to our ears. We are still climbing and must be 10,000 ft. by this time as the oak-covered foothills look very flat.

6:00 P.M. We are now "in" the hills with the Yosemite in plain view except for a blue veil of smoke that makes wonderful lavenders and purples in the evening sun. There are some very large firs to our left with great bellows of smoke over them.

The long evening shadows make the landscape very beautiful. The plane rides with far less jar or undulation than a car on a smooth road even tho we are over the hills where "bumpy air" is to be expected. My writing would be better if I had something flatter than my knee to write on. Our pilots are smoking cigarettes now which they much enjoy. The San Joaquin Valley is far to our rear and looks like an ocean of golden water. Tall pines reach up toward us their 100 or 150 ft. of height looking like an inch or less.

We are following the Merced River roughly. I say roughly as we do not need to circle the hills as it does.

8:15 P.M. I am in a Redwood Cabin in the Yosemite. We are all here, we are all fed and the ship is in perfect condition. 2hrs & 10 mins elapsed from the time we left Oakland till we touched ground in Yosemite. A perfect and wonderful exhibition of man's latest marvel.

Lovingly, Jack

The airplane flew nicely into Yosemite Valley and landed in a meadow. Upon arrival, Jack called his wife, Ruth, who was expecting their second son in a couple of months. She didn't know he had gone on the flight, became frightened, and asked him to take the train back to Berkeley the next day.

Kauke spent the next day showing off the airplane and talking to officials. Coffee and a group of mechanics worked on the *J-7*, carefully checking it over for its return trip. The following day, July 14, the four men prepared to depart Yosemite for the return flight to Oakland, with the park superintendent, some rangers, and a group of visitors seeing them off. Uncle Giocondo promised them that the Jacuzzi airplane would establish yet another record on the return trip, and the plane, the largest ever to land in the park, lifted off at 7:07 a.m. as recorded in Kauke's log book.

Upon nearing Modesto, it was reported the pilot wanted to impress his girlfriend who lived there by "buzzing" his hometown. The daughter of a local judge, she was actually waiting for him at the airfield, since the couple had evidently discussed the plane's landing there for a breakfast break. I am uncertain whether Coffee shared these tentative plans in advance with Uncle Giocondo, but I doubt he did, since Giocondo had announced that morning that they intended to set another flight record.

Then, tragedy struck, shortly after 8:10 a.m. according to Kauke's log book entry of the time recorded upon reaching Modesto. While approaching Modesto from the east at approximately 4,000 feet, the *J-7* suddenly came apart and plunged toward the ground. An experienced Army Air Service sergeant, out for an early game of tennis, was an eyewitness to the accident. As it hit the earth, the plane narrowly missed two boys in a horse and buggy. All four men aboard the craft were killed instantly.

There were several opinions as to what caused the crash, but possibly the most credible, judging from eyewitness accounts and findings made in a military report by First Lieutenant Frank D. Hacket dated August 9, 1921, and endorsed by Air Officer H. H. Arnold, both of the Mather Air Force Base, is wing failure. Detailed inspection of the wings indicated both wings, first the left and then the right, failed close to the fuselage. It was theorized that while the wings were built along the lines of usual wooden wing construction, they were not sufficiently braced to take care of the twisting forces that took place during flight. It appeared that the front spar of the left wing broke first, causing it to torque toward the back and break away clear of the airplane. The plane then went into a steep dive. At about 2,000 feet, the right wing also broke away due to the extra strain. The *J-7* plummeted to the ground within seconds. Although the eye bolts that held the struts to the wings had been weakened by having been drilled to hollow them to reduce weight and had broken, it appeared that they probably broke as a consequence of the failure of the wings.

It should be noted that one common account as to why the plane crashed was that the pilot had carelessly flown into a 73,000-volt Sierra & San Francisco Electric Company power line. This story was popularized by the fact that several witnesses on the ground claimed to have seen electrical sparks just before the crash. The confusion is easy to understand as one of the wings did hit the power line as it fell, but this was after it had already separated from the plane.

Aftermath

A coroner's inquest was convened on the night of the accident. The jury agreed that the cause of all four deaths was the "shock and hemorrhage" from the accident. Uncle Rachele was a witness at the inquest. During his testimony, he stated that the pilot had tested the *J-7* in Oakland less than a week earlier. He added that Coffee had asked several times to fly the plane on a longer trip.

The *Modesto Morning Herald* of Friday, July 15, 1921, covered the inquest and reported that Rachele Jacuzzi stated that the accident could have been caused by an engine explosion or by a "heavy strain upon the wings, causing them to crack and crumble." The newspaper added that Rachele answered all of the jury's questions "quickly and without hesitation," also observing that "he appeared to be all wrought-up over the terrible accident."

Jack Kauke's funeral was held in Oakland and his ashes were sent for burial to Wooster, Ohio, where he was born on August 15, 1894; Duncan McLeish's funeral and burial took place in San Mateo. Considering that our family lived in Berkeley, I have sometimes wondered why Uncle Giocondo was buried the day after the accident in Modesto, the site of the crash.

Based on my interviews with family members, I believe this decision was the result of several factors. First, the family was devastated, confused, and fearful. A government investigation was launched because initial reports mistakenly stated that the airplane was a military one. It was also reported that the pilot's father requested a government probe. In an era of unregulated aviation, this official investigation by the War Department's Air Service must have been especially unnerving and difficult in the family's time of sorrow.

In this time of extreme grief and shock, the family did not have a priest who could offer them solace and guidance, since they had not established a close relationship with a Berkeley church. This lack of a strong link to a neighborhood church probably also contributed to their willingness to keep Giocondo's body in Modesto for burial.

The final decision regarding burial arrangements fell to Grandfather, Uncle Rachele, and Mary, Giocondo's widow. Aunt Mary had some family members living in Modesto. This was an extremely difficult time for everyone, but most of all for Uncle Rachele, who though numbed by despair, on that day and the ones to follow had to fulfill his obligations as an owner and designer of the airplane. From the moment he learned of the accident from a telephone call placed by a United Press reporter, he was utterly distraught, convinced as he was that his modifications had caused the plane to crash. He, Grandfather, Aunt Mary, and Mary's father rushed to Modesto in Uncle Rachele's automobile. Later that same evening, Rachele and the others had to go through the wrenching experience of the coroner's inquest.

Once they were in Modesto, he and the other family members probably decided that the wisest course was to bury Giocondo there and to do this as quickly as possible.

Given the communication and transportation of that day, making last-minute travel arrangements for the rest of the Jacuzzi family to travel to Modesto was not easy or inexpensive. So, it is not surprising that only Grandfather, Uncle Rachele, Mary, some of Mary's family, and my parents attended the funeral.

My brother Virgil, about seventeen months old, was also present, and one of his earliest American memories was of the beautiful flowers in the Modesto flower shop, where my parents stopped with him prior to the Catholic church service.

Newspaper accounts report that various city and county officials also attended.

Giocondo was laid to rest in St. Stanislaus Cemetery. On the day after his funeral, the *Modesto Morning Herald* ran a photograph of the four men and the ill-fated *J-7*. Taken at Yosemite Valley after the plane landed there, the photograph was one of several developed from a camera found in the wreckage.

Hundreds mourned Harold Bud Coffee on Saturday, July 16, 1921, at the largest military funeral in the history of Stanislaus County. The funeral was conducted at the Modesto Lodge of Elks. The AERO Club of San Francisco, of which he was a member, sent a floral piece in the form of a large propeller, fashioned entirely of white carnations. The Modesto airport was later renamed Coffee Field.

Uncle Rachele was interviewed by the same Modesto newspaper after his return to Berkeley. Its edition of July 18 headlines the story with "Jacuzzis to Remain in Aviation Business." The report included Rachele's statement concerning the company's future:

> "The policy of the company will not be changed. We will work for the development of commercial aviation," said Jacuzzi, evidently suffering from the strain of the tragedy.

Grandfather and Grandmother had been in America for just six months and already they had buried a son. Grandmother grieved so deeply for her son, the first child she had lost, that she stopped talking for a time and Grandfather begged Rachele and his brothers to pursue some other line of work. Aviation was just too dangerous.

Giocondo

Uncle Giocondo, at about five feet, nine inches, was one of the tallest brothers. He also was a dreamer like the older Rachele, but unlike all the other brothers, he was always more interested in the arts than in industry and mechanical inventions. Of all the brothers, he was probably the most reluctant to leave Italy, having always believed that his mother country's cultural environment could provide him with more opportunities to study and develop his talents. His true loves were oil painting and the playing of musical instruments, especially the guitar, zither, and flute, and in Casarsa, he studied with several music teachers. As a result, he could read and play music very well. His early aspiration was to become a self-supporting artist and to attend art school.

After coming to America, Giocondo left his brothers in Southern California while they were working on the Remington farm. They didn't know where he was until he contacted them with a postcard several days later, informing them he had arrived safely in Pueblo, Colorado. He wanted to attend art school. The brothers saw Giocondo's passion and talent for art, so, for a while, they supported him—both financially and emotionally.

However, when the propeller business grew too demanding, Giocondo returned to California to work alongside his brothers in the shop, though he still took some evening art classes. Giocondo and Mary Guarneri were married on April 19, 1919. They had a daughter, Anna, born February 20, 1920.

Unfortunately, Giocondo was never able to further pursue his real dream of becoming a professional artist. My sister Rachel Jacuzzi Bruce has one of Uncle Giocondo's portrait paintings in her home. It is a very good likeness of our father, Valeriano, when he was a young man. It is mounted in a wooden frame that Pa handcrafted.

He was a few weeks past his twenty-sixth birthday when he died. Uncle Frank, who had married Rena Villata in 1919, had a son born less than eight weeks after the plane crash. The baby was named after Giocondo. Several years later, on May 5, 1923, my oldest sister was born and was given the name Jaconda, after Uncle Giocondo. The spelling of her name with a *J* reflects the Friulano dialect, which uses *J* in place of the *Gi* in standard Italian. My brother Dante was born on July 1, 1921, just thirteen days before the tragic accident.

Final Thoughts

Uncle Giocondo's name is taken from *giocondezza*, which means "to be happy." But the sudden death of this wonderfully talented and creative brother triggered a period of deep sadness for the Jacuzzi family.

I know the events of that day must have also haunted the Kauke family, since John Kauke had been intimately involved in the *J-7*'s production. Kauke's leather-covered notebook was recovered at the crash scene. He used this as a log book for the flight, taking note of times and speed. His July 14, 1921, entry noted that he disapproved of Bud Coffee's desire to stop in Modesto, for the original plan was to see what type of time could be achieved by flying a nonstop return to Oakland. He used his diary to scribble a note to Coffee in which he asked him not to stop in Modesto, saying: "Mather asked that we make it non-stop to Berkeley or San Francisco & wire him the time. If we come down at Modesto it will look wrong." Mr. Mather, the National Director of Parks, had asked Kauke to wire him the flight time of their expected nonstop return flight.

This was the final journal entry, made in the last airplane produced by Jacuzzi Brothers, Inc.

John Kauke's son, Phillips Kauke, who was born two months after the death of his father, recalled that Uncle Rachele came to visit his mother, his older brother, and him around 1928 when they were living in Lindsey, California. He recalled that Rachele was driving a new Ford Model A and he took them all to the Visalia, California, airport for a ride in a tri-motor Ford airplane. Evidently Uncle Rachele remained a good friend of John Kauke's family, as he would naturally do, since I have heard over the years many stories of his kindness and love of children.

STARTING OVER

Steam driven rotor – c.1922

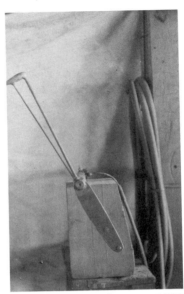

Prototype gas turbine – c.1922

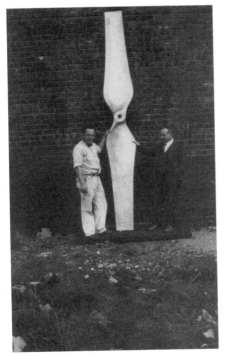

*Candido and Rachele Jacuzzi
with Frostifugo propeller*

*Frostifugo – electric motor
powered – c.1924*

Chapter 8

New Beginnings

"Non tutte le rose sono rosse o bianche, ma tutte hanno le spine."
"Not all the roses are red or white, but all have thorns."
—Gilia Jacuzzi Peruzzo, thirteenth and last child of my grandparents,
Giovanni and Teresa Jacuzzi

Grief compounded with uncertainty made life especially bleak. In addition to the heartbreak of Giocondo's death, the brothers now faced debts from the loss of an expensive airplane and the costs they had incurred to build the plane. They were forced to abandon long-held dreams, leaving them uncertain about the future of the company.

I'm inspired by the fact that my relatives did not allow themselves to be paralyzed by these circumstances—tragic as they were. It is true that the years immediately following the accident were gloomy, but it is equally true that the family, and the company, never gave in to despair.

Coping

Honoring their parents' wishes, the Jacuzzi brothers laid aside their aspirations of manufacturing airplanes and operating an airline business. They began experimenting with new concepts and pursuing other endeavors. Uncle Rachele's head still was full of ideas, and much of his time was devoted to research. The hope and belief of the family was that Rachele would come upon some new discovery or invention that would revive the success of Jacuzzi Brothers, Inc.

Meanwhile, Pa and Uncles Frank, Joseph, Gelindo, and Candido worked at whatever odd jobs they could bring into the shop. They were still receiving occasional orders for airplane propellers, though not many. They also took in various types of mechanical work, like airplane remodeling, engine repair, and auto body repair. In addition, they manufactured a wide variety of items, including radio cabinets, grape crushers, radiator fans, oil burners, and truck bodies. The brothers did anything within their abilities to keep the company afloat.

One day, several months after the monoplane accident, Grandfather and the brothers were in the shop. A stranger came in. He asked if he could purchase the *J-7* accident debris, which the brothers had stored in the shop. He offered them $50 for the bits and pieces of the aircraft, and they accepted. My father later said that the man was driving the biggest car he had ever seen. Pa always suspected the mysterious buyer was associated with Lockheed.

Their enormous debt drove the brothers to sell the airplane remnants and take in odd jobs. The development costs of the *J-7* airplane and the lean months after its loss made it necessary for the company to take out additional bank loans. There were also lawsuits and threats of lawsuits against the company by the survivors of the men who died. The total damages paid to those families is unknown, except that John Kauke's wife received a $2,000 payment shortly after his death. In an attempt to raise cash, the brothers sold some company shares, which were later redeemed. They also rented out part of the shop to other tenants, but there was hardly enough work and money coming in to meet payroll, let alone pay off debts and cover any litigation costs.

As things worsened financially and tough months were looking more like years, some of the brothers temporarily left the employment of the company. They were not giving up on Jacuzzi Brothers, Inc., but during this period it was impossible for the company to support all of them. The company had to regain its footing, and that meant downsizing. Things eventually got so tight that, for a while, only Rachele and Joseph worked in the shop. Once again the sisters played a vital role, often paying the interest on the loans to keep the creditors at bay.

Frank, the first to leave, went to work in 1921 at the Sunset Lumber Company. One year later, Joseph found work for a while at Building Fixtures Company, then he returned to the shop. By 1923, Pa and Uncle Candido also were working for Building Fixtures Company. The money they earned, in addition to providing a living for themselves, also helped finance some of Uncle Rachele's experiments. Even if they weren't working at Jacuzzi Brothers all day, every day, they still were there in spirit.

Experiments

With aeronautical research available to him in the early 1920s, Uncle Rachele was unable to obtain detailed information about a primary concern of his: What precisely happens to air when it flows around streamlined forms? He also was curious about the reaction of an airstream discharged from a nozzle perpendicular to or at an angle onto a surface.

In their own experiment, he and the brothers installed a flat coil of pipe over a gas burner. One end of the coil was connected to a water tap regulated by a valve, while the other end of the coil was coupled to a flexible length of hose with a discharge nozzle. When Rachele heated the pipe coil, and allowed water to enter, he discovered that, depending on the size of the nozzle, the heat intensity of the flame, and the rate of the water flow, a variable jet of steam could be produced and discharged through the nozzle.

While experimenting with the steam jet and the forces it exerted, Uncle Rachele and his brothers came up with the idea of using the reactive force of the nozzle jet to drive a rotating arm. To test this concept, they directed a flow of steam through a hollow rotating arm with a nozzle at its tip, oriented at right angles to the arm. They found that when a flow of steam was directed through the arm, it would rotate rapidly at a rate dependent upon the pressure of the steam. This principle would later be used in their work with the *Frostifugo*.

During these experiments, Uncle Rachele and his brothers also developed the idea of using the reactive force of a gas jet to drive a rotating arm. To test this concept, they built a rotating hollow arm that allowed a supply of gasoline to be fed through its hub to a combustion chamber installed at right angles to the tip of the arm. Rachele used a pitot-type entrance for the combustion chamber's air entry and a discharge nozzle for the escaping flame.

The brothers made this apparatus work by preheating the combustion chamber with a torch, lighting the gasoline at the nozzle, and giving it a swift start by hand. To their delight, they produced a blue flame which escaped, kicking the arm around at breakneck speed, and producing a continuous circle of fire about five feet in diameter.

These experiments continued off and on at the shop.

On December 17, 1922, Uncle Rachele fascinated a group of San Francisco reporters with a practical demonstration of the potential use of gas turbines in aircraft, during which he announced that the device would become "a means to make an airplane fly without motors." To be sure, the gadget was crude—a rotating arm formed with a piece of pipe, a blow-torch-lit combustion chamber, with an air entry and a nozzle. Still, he proved his point and made the desired impression. When the torch was lit and gas was released into it, the device spun at an estimated 10,000 rpm. The following day's *San Francisco Examiner* featured the headline: "Planes to Fly With Power But No Engine; Gas Turbine Invented by East Bay Man."

This was yet another discovery Uncle Rachele made in his experiments with the thermodynamics of fluids. Along the way, however, he was learning a valuable lesson: his research could have practical applications far beyond the field of aviation.

Frostifugo

One of the more interesting of Uncle Rachele's developments was an apparatus he called the *Frostifugo*. Ironically, this received more attention than some of his flight-related designs, even though it was of little success.

Having worked in some of the Southern California citrus orchards, Rachele was keenly aware of the dangers frost posed to the livelihood of citrus growers. One frigid night could destroy years of hard work. The use of smudge pots was common, as the thick smoke they produced was helpful in protecting the citrus crop. Another means of increasing the ground-level temperature is to use a propeller to create a wind current over the trees which would mix the warmer higher elevation air above the citrus trees with the colder, lower air to effectively raise the air temperature above freezing. Rachele believed his *Frostifugo*, or Frost Machine, would provide greater protection than either the smudge pots or a wind propeller system.

The *Frostifugo* consisted of a special steam-driven propeller and a steam boiler fashioned from an oil burner, a coiled two-inch diameter pipe, and a Penberthy injector. Uncle Rachele and the brothers first used these components in 1922, while conducting their aerodynamic experiments with steam.

In 1923, the brothers showed their concept to Mr. R. S. Reems, who believed enough in the principle—and in Rachele—to invest money. The brothers wanted to build a large unit to blow steam and air over orchards, which they believed would be much more effective than their wind propellers. They already were producing some wind propeller systems to help with frost prevention for several clients, including Pacific Car and Equipment Company in San Francisco, Mr. C. R. Towt, and other individuals.

The first *Frostifugo* consisted of a water boiler made up of forty feet of two-inch pipe formed into a cylindrical coil and a Ray oil burner that heated the coiled pipe which converted water as it flowed through it into steam. Part of the boiler's pressurized steam was discharged through both tips of a hollow steel seven-foot propeller in a manner which used reactive force to turn the propeller at high speed. For safety, a heavy wooden guard was built surrounding the propeller. Another portion of the pressurized steam was directed to a Penberthy injector, which drew makeup water from a barrel and injected it into the boiler system. Basically a Penberthy injector consists of a nozzle that directs a pressurized flow of steam into a venturi tube, which causes a suction to be created in the annular space between the nozzle and venturi. This suction was used to draw and inject makeup water into the boiler.

Although numerous modifications and adjustments had to be made before the device operated, the brothers gained much practical information from this experience. For example, as the oil burned and produced the flame around the open coil, an enormous current of flowing air occurred. This required extra oil consumption. Rachele also learned that the heat of the flame and the passage of the water through the coil, if not adjusted, could cause dangerous coil distortions.

The brothers' first attempt at using the Penberthy injector was to operate it as originally designed for use in a steam-boiler system. This proved to be unworkable because of the many variables that had to be simultaneously controlled.

They learned that in order to have more reliability and control, they would need to convert the Penberthy injector from using pressurized steam to using pressurized water to draw makeup water into the system. In order to accomplish this conversion, they had to significantly redesign the Penberthy injector. (This first conception of a water-driven injector would later lead to their development of the world-famous Jacuzzi jet pump.)

Financial backing continued also to challenge them. One day, immediately after he saw a demonstration of the *Frostifugo*, Mr. Reems told them he would no longer provide any monetary assistance. Nevertheless, by 1924, Uncle Rachele had found another investor, Mr. C. Smith.

Smith's money enabled them to build a refined machine that, when attached to a water supply, would heat the water into steam which, when directed through the hollowed blades of the propeller and through the nozzles at its tips, would turn the propeller at high speed, blowing a strong, steam-laden current of air. The brothers were confident this process would assist in frost protection.

However, before the enterprise could really get started and marketed on a large scale, the brothers needed to test the machine one final time. During this final trial, everything was functioning well, with the propeller spinning at a greater speed than ever before. Suddenly, the blades broke off at the hub's welding. One of the blades disappeared in the ground and the other sank halfway into the upper part of the wooden guard.

The resulting disappointment marked the end of this version of the *Frostifugo*. Eventually, the design was altered to a large-scale propeller driven by an electric motor. This unit, also marketed under the name *Frostifugo*, was much more successful than its predecessor and many of these wind propellers were sold to orchard owners.

Back to the Shop

Still trying to bring back their business, the brothers designed and built oil burners for small furnaces. They sold a few of these. Always drawn to aviation parts, they continued to conduct experiments with the manufacture of steel airplane propellers, but they still were not able to economically produce metal models comparable to their groundbreaking wooden Toothpick design.

Uncle Rachele also continued his experiments that built on his earlier work with his redesigned Penberthy injector. In these tests, he and the brothers used the same aerodynamic and hydraulic principals they observed earlier in their pursuit of aviation and development of the early *Frostifugo*. In their quest for the jet nozzle and venturi design that could best produce the most vacuum and strongest fluid flow, they directed the flow of steam through a nozzle put between two foils placed side-by-side to simulate a venturi. Rachele observed the flow of steam by using colored smoke from a burning stick placed adjacent to the nozzle. In this way, he determined which nozzle designs and foil (or venturi) shapes produced the most vacuum and most forceful air flow with the least amount of fluid turbulence. After many experiments, trials and errors, the brothers realized they could build a water-driven injector that would be decisively superior to their previously modified Penberthy injector.

A small prototype injector was built that used pressurized water. The suction side was connected to a sealed milk bottle partially filled with water. When the pressurized water circulated through the injector, the bottle's cold water started to boil, since the vacuum produced by the injector had reduced the air pressure inside the bottle to below the water's vapor pressure.

These steam and water experiments were interesting, but their practical uses were as elusive as the steam vapor that filled the shop.

So, starting over did not seem to be going well. They were making different products, but none of them caught on. Jacuzzi Brothers seemed nearer to closing than ever. But what the brothers could not see was this: They really were on the brink of new and larger success. Little by little, and through both successful experiments and failed applications, Uncle Rachele was nearing a discovery that would affect nearly every rural home in the civilized world.

Valeriano and Giuseppina Jacuzzi Ranch – c.1928

Gelindo and Rosie Jacuzzi Ranch – c.1928

Jacuzzi family gathering at Valeriano and Giuseppina's Ranch – 1930s

Chapter 9

Return to the Land

"Ti ho detto che non voglio niente altro che Italiano parlato a questa tavola!"
"I told you I don't want anything but Italian spoken at this table!"
—Gelindo Jacuzzi, my grandparents' fifth son and child

Although thirteen of Giovanni and Teresa's children were born, reared, and worked on the family farm in northern Italy, only two of them, Uncle Gelindo and my father, Valeriano, returned to agriculture in America. Though they would have preferred to continue working with their brothers in the Jacuzzi Brothers company, without sufficient work for them all and families to feed, Uncle Gelindo and Pa ended up, in the early 1920s, buying adjoining farms.

Their Jacuzzi Brothers, Inc., stock had little value. Their propeller work had dried up. Building airplanes was no longer possible. The large *Frostifugo* machine had not been successful. The other experiments in the shop, although interesting, didn't appear to have practical applications. Even so, neither Uncle Gelindo nor Pa would have ever considered selling their ownership in the company when they bought their farms, or ranches, as everyone in our family always called them. They both felt the company was part of their family and hoped that one day they could return to work with their brothers. For now, they would work the land.

Uncle Gelindo's Ranch

In 1922, a Berkeley neighbor told Aunt Rosie and Uncle Gelindo, who was then working in a cannery, about an eighty-two-acre parcel of land. The neighbor had inherited the land and since his three sons were not interested in farming, he wanted to sell it. He asked Gelindo if he knew of someone who might be interested. Gelindo decided to look at the farm himself, as he knew of the dire financial situation of the company and realized he would need employment soon. Uncle Gelindo and Aunt Rosie, who is my godmother, made the then three-hour, forty-mile trip to Antioch to see the farm. They found the property to be landlocked, basically a hay field with access only by way of the Southern Pacific Railroad right of way. It had no house, no buildings, no well for water, no electricity, no roads, no nothing!

Gelindo, who had experimented with commercial fertilizers in Italy, decided he could make the farm profitable. Aunt Rosie, who had no farming background, was at first reluctant and questioned the advisability of the move. She finally deferred to her husband and said that since she married him "for better or worse," she would do her part to make the farm succeed.

Gelindo first had to build their home on the raw property. He bought an old house in Berkeley, dismantled it, hauled the lumber to the ranch and built a shell. Having used all their savings for this project, Uncle Gelindo and Aunt Rosie borrowed $75 dollars to buy a cow and some barley seed, and used the leftover funds to rent a seed spreader.

When Gelindo and Rosie moved into the home in 1923, with their two small daughters, Lola, who was three, and Olga, one, the inside of the home consisted of two-by-four frames dividing the rooms. They had a wood stove for cooking and heating. Their bathroom was an "outhouse," complete with an old Montgomery Ward catalog. The family coped for several years with no electric power.

Water was a more urgent matter. For at least six months, the only source of water came from their neighbors, the Enos family, whose well was located about a quarter of a mile away. Gelindo carried water by wagon in a barrel to their home. The children were bathed in a large galvanized tub in the kitchen and water was warmed on the stove or over an open outdoor fire. Aunt Rosie washed clothes using a washboard and tub.

When a well was dug in late 1923, a hand pump was installed, and the children, when old enough, took turns laboriously working the handle up and down. Later, a windmill provided plenty of water if the wind blew, and none if it didn't. Eventually, an elevated redwood tank was added. The windmill pumped water directly into this tank, so stored water was always available. After several years, indoor plumbing was installed.

Gelindo and Rosie's first year on their ranch was a near disaster. They had hoped the barley crop would bring in enough money to keep them going. However, there was hardly any rain that year and, consequently, no grain to harvest. In addition, their milk cow died. Through these adversities, somehow, they survived. Uncle Gelindo used to comment that his son, Tullio, born thirteen months after moving to the ranch, was their "first crop." Their last two children also were born on the ranch: Rodolfo or Rudy, in 1926, and Daniele, who arrived in 1928.

Old and New Ways

Like my parents, Aunt Rosie and Uncle Gelindo taught by using the Ten Commandments. Not regular churchgoers, they nevertheless stressed the principles of good Christian living, sound morals, and high standards. Nostalgia for the Old Country also ran high, and Cousin Lola remembers her parents fondly reminiscing about Italy. When the children were young, only Italian was spoken at home, but after starting school, they all learned English. Gradually, Uncle Gelindo and Aunt Rosie learned to speak some English, and the family would find itself speaking English more and more frequently at home. Slowly, like all of the brothers' families, they were becoming more American. There were times when Gelindo became upset with these English conversations, as Lola recalled one time when the family was talking excitedly in English at dinner.

Uncle Gelindo hit the table with his fist and said: "I told you I don't want anything but Italian spoken at this table!"

The family all started laughing and questioned why he had told them this in English! From this point on, Lola felt something had changed. "Ma and Pa dedicated much effort to teach us about Italy and the Italian language, but the day had come when being a part of America was becoming reality," she recalled.

When Uncle Rachele visited Uncle Gelindo and Aunt Rosie in the mid-1930s, he asked Lola to help him with some of his English writings. It was during these ranch visits that the first drafts of his booklets foretelling so many significant scientific events were dictated to Lola, who, by then, as Uncle Rachele and her father had noticed, was very fluent in both written and spoken English. She took down all of Uncle Rachele's writings in shorthand, which she later typed for his review.

My Family's Ranch

Two years after moving his family to their ranch, Uncle Gelindo mentioned to my father that the 161-acre Burns ranch next to theirs was for sale. At that time, Pa was still working at the Building Fixture Cabinet Shop in Berkeley. There was no longer enough work at Jacuzzi Brothers, Inc., for him to support his family, which then included three children and a fourth on the way.

Pa decided to investigate. Soon after viewing the property, my parents, Valeriano and Giuseppina, bought it on October 18, 1924, from Herman and Catherine Burns. My mother was not enthusiastic about moving to the country, but like Rosie, she went along with her husband's desire to do so. My sister Teresa was born eleven days later on October 29. She originally was given the name Mary Teresa, as Maria (Mary) was my mother's mother's name, but at Grandmother Teresa's request, her name was changed to Teresa Mary.

Grandfather Giovanni encouraged them to buy the ranch and provided a $2,000 loan for the down payment. Pa negotiated a payment schedule with Mr. Burns that divided the $4,000 balance into $500 yearly installments at six percent interest.

My older brothers, Virgil and Dante, and older sisters, Jaconda and Teresa, shared their vivid recollections of their early life on the ranch, without which the story of our farm's early years would have been virtually impossible for me to reconstruct. The property consisted mostly of rolling hills and a few buildings that had been abandoned for several years. About twelve large eucalyptus trees surrounded a run-down, four-room home with a small, unfinished basement hewn out of sandstone bedrock. It was built on a slope, so the entry to the basement was at the side of the house. All of the walls, inside and out, were of single, vertical, board-and-batten construction. Although the knotholes were covered with scraps of tin, the house still was quite drafty. Also included was a two-hole outhouse complete with a Montgomery Ward catalog. I distinctly remember a crescent moon cut out in the door.

There were some farm buildings, an old hay and animal barn, and an eighty-five-foot-deep, three-foot diameter, hand-dug water well, lined with bricks. There was a windmill with a wooden tower that didn't work. Old implements, junk, and broken bits of glass were everywhere, which were collected and hauled away to help fill in the washed out areas of our access road bed. The nails and small pieces of metal and glass that would surface from the soil for years afterwards were always picked up and discarded. The access road to the ranch was basically two ruts in the dirt of a sixteen-foot-wide, one-half-mile-long right of way that crossed a creek and the Southern Pacific Railroad track to Neroly Road, which ran parallel with the track. When my parents bought the farm, they also bought the property with this right of way from our neighbors, the Lindseys, which made our access road a private one. Neroly Road at the time was also a dirt road.

Virgil remembered that, even though the ranch was purchased in October 1924, the family didn't move there until about five months later in early 1925. He further recalled accompanying our parents on day trips to the ranch. During these work days, they undertook repairs, cleaned the house, and generally made the ranch more livable prior to the move. He also credited Uncle Rachele for his generosity, since Jacuzzi Brothers loaned Pa a little extra money during that time to help with these repairs.

Our parents didn't own a car at the time, so they took the train to the ranch. They left the Berkeley train station early in the morning and were dropped off at the end of the our private road. They returned at night on Southern Pacific "Owl," which came by the ranch at 8:00 p.m. every day. My father would stand on the tracks and wave a lantern to signal the Owl to stop.

Moving to Our Ranch

By early spring 1925, Pa felt the family could make the move. All of their household belongings were loaded on a Model T Ford flatbed truck. The family consisted of Ma, Pa, Virgil, Dante, born July 1, 1921, Jaconda, born March 5, 1923, and baby Teresa, born October 29, 1924. Uncle Candido drove all of them to the ranch in a large touring sedan.

Like Uncle Gelindo's ranch, our place had no indoor plumbing. One of Virgil's first chores was to hand-pump water from the well and pour it into an old wine barrel that Pa elevated on a stand outside the kitchen. The barrel was connected to the pipes in the firebox of the wood stove and was the family's source of hot water. All water for drinking, dishwashing, and bathing was pumped by hand and carried inside by bucket.

A couple of years later, the windmill was repaired and it produced water for an overhead redwood tank. When the tank was full, the surplus water supplied a reservoir that was 30 x 30 and 4 feet deep. The reservoir, built with sandstone rock and lined with plaster, in turn, provided water for livestock and irrigation.

Pa bought his first car soon after the family arrived at the ranch. It was a 1916 touring Model T Ford, constantly in need of repairs, which Pa always did himself, with Virgil's assistance. The car had no working headlights, so when they drove it at night, as he did when he was returning from an evening visit to Uncle Gelindo's ranch, they hung a kerosene lantern from the radiator cap. Pa used horses to plow the fields until he bought a Holt tractor in 1926.

That same year, Pa and Ma decided to move the old house, so that a new home could be built on the same site. During the construction, the family cooked and ate their meals in a 12 x 20-foot, one-room redwood barn. In its new location, the old house was used for sleeping and storage.

My sister Mary was born on the afternoon of November 25, 1926, in the original but relocated house. My mother was finally able to name a child after her mother, Maria, and her given name was Mary. The day was cold and rainy. The little house's roof leaked and the children helped by placing cans and buckets around to catch the water. The doctor couldn't get to the ranch because the road was impassible by car due to flooding at the creek. Pa used a horse and buggy to get Aunt Rosie and Uncle Gelindo, so they could assist in the delivery, along with Aunt Rena, Joseph's wife, who was also present. The children stayed in the next room until after baby Mary was born. Aunt Rena recalled that there was so much water leaking through the roof, she had to sleep under the table to keep dry. When the doctor arrived at the ranch a few days later, he proclaimed that everyone was doing fine.

Grandfather Giovanni and Grandmother Teresa, whom the family always called "Nonno and "Nonna," the Italian equivalent of grandfather and grandmother, respectively, often visited the ranches and would stay with both families for several days at a time. Our Nonno always had a glass of wine with his milk and coffee at breakfast. Virgil remembered that when he was about six years old, he and Grandfather walked completely around the ranch. During this walk, Grandfather named the knoll at the southwest corner of our ranch Monte Cappelo (Mount Hat) because of its shape. Pa named our ranch the Delizia Ranch, as a nod to the full name of his boyhood town, Casarsa della Delizia.

Our new four-bedroom stucco home was completed in 1927. It had one bath, a living room, a large dining room and kitchen area, and a covered porch outside the living room and kitchen. The home was built by Bill Thutt, a builder from Antioch. Aunt Ancilla's husband, Pete Bianchi, who had a plastering and stucco business in Cupertino, plastered the interior and exterior walls, and installed the concrete floors of the house's covered porches and some exterior concrete walkways.

The full basement of our family's new home had to be dynamited and dug by hand out of sandstone bedrock. Pa hauled the sandstone off to improve the roadbed to our ranch's entry road. The basement had a concrete floor and saw many uses over the years. It was used to store our wine and vinegar as well as barley and wheat, before we built our granary. My mother also used it to store her annual canning and preserving. It also was a convenient and cool place in which she could hang her aging homemade cheese, *salami*, and other sausages.

In 1928, Grandfather Giovanni became quite ill. My father and mother wanted to visit him in Berkeley every weekend. The family needed a better car in order to undertake these trips, so Pa bought a 1925 Model T for $300. Our family's first car, the 1916 Model T Ford, sat unused for several years and rusted. When he was older, Virgil devoted many hours trying to get the old engine to start, but finally he gave up, and the car was hauled away.

My sister Flora was born in the new four-room house on September 20, 1929. Flora was named after the subject of one of my parents' favorite Italian songs, *Tu sei mia dolce Flora,* or "You are my sweet

Flora" in English. Jaconda recalls Flora as a persistent toddler who, when she wanted Ma to nurse her, would pull a chair to wherever our mother happened to be in the house.

Through the years, the home would be the site of many family gatherings, including Jaconda's September 27, 1942, wedding reception, a large and festive event attended by friends and most of the Jacuzzi family.

School Days

In 1926, Virgil and Cousin Lola became the first Jacuzzi children to begin their formal schooling in America. Thanks to the intervention of Uncle Gelindo, they were able to attend the Antioch schools, which were considered better, although our ranches were located in the Brentwood school district. On the first day, they sat at adjoining desks. Neither child spoke English. The teacher, hearing them speak only Italian, moved them to opposite corners of the classroom, forcing them to learn English very fast!

Virgil recalled that, much to his dismay, one of our neighbors, Mrs. Enos, told Ma that Virgil should wear long, black stockings and short pants to school. He did so almost until the end of grammar school, even though all of his friends wore long pants, so occasionally, on the way to school, he would switch into an old pair of corduroy pants that he had hidden in the tractor barn. When our mother discovered this and realized how miserable he was, she relented and allowed him to dress like the other American boys.

Virgil eventually erased this original image by going on to great success as a tackle on the football field, and he was named in later years to the Antioch High School "All Antioch High" team. Virgil was offered a scholarship to play football at the University of California-Davis; however, he wasn't able to take advantage of this opportunity since he started working full-time for Jacuzzi Brothers right out of high school. After World War II and his honorable discharge from the Navy, he did complete college, obtaining degrees in both electrical and mechanical engineering.

All of us, my brothers and sisters and my cousins on the adjoining ranch, attended Antioch schools. It seems like a story made for a grandfather to tell his grandchildren, but it's true that most of the children in our family did at least some homework by coal oil lamps, since our ranch didn't get electricity until 1946 when World War II was over. I was ten. Jaconda remembers that the family got its first telephone and battery-operated radio when she was a teenager. She also remembers how wonderful the spring season was at the ranch, for she loved to walk to the hills and gather armloads of wild flowers, including blue bells, daisies, lupins, and Indian paintbrushes.

Just as they did for me, the Antioch schools hold very special memories for Jaconda. Her future husband's father, Wayne Hawkins, taught her history and social studies and was her favorite teacher. She met the young man who would become her husband, Bob Hawkins, during her senior year.

Farm Animals and Crops

Our farm animals usually consisted of four or five milk cows, our two horses Nellie and Mollie, one or two pigs, one hundred and fifty or more laying chickens, usually raised from purchased chicks, Muscovy ducks, rabbits, and occasionally broods of turkeys and geese. Also included were guinea fowl, which ate the bugs around the barnyard and were good sentries, one hundred or more free-flying pigeons that would nest in nesting boxes we placed under the eaves of our barns, and several beautiful peacocks.

We also had several cats and a pair of dogs. We named the male dog "Pronto" and the female "Milecca," Italian words that translate as "fast" and "licks me" in English, the same names the Jacuzzi family gave their dogs in Italy.

In the early years, our family's main source of income was from our hay and grain crops. Crops and seasonal income varied in reliability; both were dependent on the rainfall. Pa tried other crops and vegetables to supplement our main ones, including beans, onions, artichokes, and strawberries. Pa followed the teachings and methods of his mother, Teresa, and planted crops according to the cycles of the moon.

Like Aunt Rosie on the adjoining farm—and Grandmother Teresa before them, Ma contributed to the family's income by selling eggs, cheese, and occasionally rabbits and chickens in town. The goal, however, was for our family to be self-sufficient as far as food needs. We butchered at least one hog yearly, had our own milk, butter, cheese, eggs, chickens, rabbits, fruits, and many types of vegetables, leaving only bread, flour, salt, pepper, oil, and a few other items to be purchased. Ma used hanging shelves downstairs in the making of her delicious cheese. She used the same recipe and cheese-making process that she had learned while growing up in the Italian Alps.

Our family had pigs that we raised to be butchered and processed into cuts of meat, plus pressed *prosciutto* ham and different sausages, such as *salsiccia, salami,* and *cotechino.* We rendered the lard and bottled it for cooking and to make soap. Mr. Coleman, a butcher from Brentwood, would usually butcher the pig, although sometimes this became a family effort, with Uncle Gelindo and Aunt Rosie, Uncle Jack Peruzzo, or other relatives helping.

As with most northern Italian families, our family ate *polenta* regularly, especially during the first years on the ranch, and it was a real treat when Ma baked biscuits. About the only occasion Pa splurged was the day he paid the taxes; our family had T-bone steaks for dinner that night. Steaks on tax day is still our family's time-honored tradition.

During the first year, with starter cuttings from neighbors, Pa planted our vineyard with Carignane grapes. He planted them with a 10 x 10-foot spacing between the vines and a perfect north-south, east-west alignment. Even though the vines were not irrigated, the average 12-inch-per-year rainfall produced fairly good crops.

Later, Matero and Zinfandel grapes were added. The vineyard required a lot of handwork, and all of the older children helped. During Easter vacation, this would consist of hoeing the weeds from around the vines and picking up and burning the brush after the pruning was completed. As we got older, Pa taught all of his sons and my sister Teresa, who was interested in learning, how to prune. Another task needed to prevent the growth of damaging mildew was to periodically blow sulfur dust on the vines from the early stages of their growth in the spring to harvest time. This was normally done using a backpack sulfur tank with a lever-operated bellow and a hose to direct the sulfur dust onto the vines. In the early years, my parents usually did this in the calm, windless early morning, before the children would awaken.

Some years the grapes would be shipped back East, while in others, they would be sold in the Bay Area. My sister Teresa told me of a time when she and our father took a pickup truck full of grapes into Berkeley to sell. On the way back to the ranch that evening, they had a flat tire. They had no spare, but they had an ample supply of empty gunny sacks, which Pa stuffed into the tire, and they were able to drive home safely.

During the worst Depression years, Pa was forced to store unsold grapes in the Jacuzzi Brothers shop in Berkeley. Then some of the brothers and our other relatives pitched in to help sell the grapes. They sold for $30 to $35 per ton, delivered, in those times. Our crop yielded about thirty tons each year.

It was during this time, in about 1934, that Uncle Candido visited the ranch in his new maroon Ford coupe. The purpose of the visit was to see if Pa wanted to trade his company shares in exchange for the ranch "start-up" loan the company had given him. But Pa was insistent that he wanted to continue to have a stake in the company, so he refused this offer.

Pa told Uncle Candido that during World War I, while Pa was serving in the Italian military, and when Pa was working before, during, and after the war to help the family survive in Italy, the other older brothers were in America, making money from the company's Toothpick years. He did not question their doing so. In fact, he was thrilled with the company's successful development of the propeller product that he and Uncle Rachele had begun in 1911. Nor did Pa question the path he chose during the war years, for he knew that Grandfather and Grandmother desperately needed an older son with them during that time. Pa wanted to stay invested in the company, for he always believed in its viability, and he always hoped to return to work with his brothers. Evidently, Uncle Candido understood the logic of this reasoning, for the exchange of Pa's shares was never mentioned again.

Special Days

On Christmas at the ranch, our family had a tree with ornaments and decorative, never-lighted candles. Santa would bring candy, nuts, fruit, and usually a gift of clothing. On New Year's Day, the first child to visit Ma and Pa in their bedroom got a little bit more money than did the others. Ma and Pa always gave each child, no matter how late his or her arrival for the traditional New Year's greeting, a small bag of candy and a few coins.

Easter was celebrated with a special feast, which might include a leg of lamb, *spaghetti,* or *ravioli.* Making *crostoli, biscotti,* and *amaretti* cookies was a family tradition at Easter.

Many of these holidays, like birthdays, were often celebrated with Uncle Gelindo's family. Gifts were not usually given on birthdays in the early ranch years.

Pa drove our family to Mass almost every Sunday. Our family attended St. Anthony's Catholic Church in Oakley, where my younger sister, Rachel, and I also went to catechism. The older children attended catechism classes at Holy Rosary Church in Antioch. Pa read his prayer book every evening. In good weather, he prayed and read while sitting under our fig tree beside the house. Ma also ended her day with her prayer book, preferring to read it in the solitude of her bedroom.

Remo and Rachel

In the 1930s, Jacuzzi Brothers, like the entire nation, was struggling to recover from the Depression, but things were starting to look up for the company. During these hard times mixed with hope, I was born, in the new ranch house, on January 6, 1936. I am named after Remo (Remus), one of the founders of Rome (the other being Romulus), and Cesare for Caesar, the Roman emperor. The local doctor, Dr. Johnson, made it to the ranch in time for my delivery. He spent some time sleeping on our couch while Ma was in labor.

I was told by my brothers and sisters that Virgil was very excited to finally have another brother, since he and Dante had been outnumbered by four sisters, but until he returned that day from school, he had been unaware of Ma's pregnancy. He showed his enthusiasm by bringing his greyhound, Jackie, into Ma's bedroom, so both he and the dog could meet me, but Jackie's presence in the house, especially in the bedroom with a newborn baby, was not welcomed by my parents.

I must note that, although we had always had dogs and cats as pets, Ma did not like animals to come into the house. Much like Virgil and his dog, Mary was fond of her cat. Around the time of my birth, one particularly thrilling day for Mary was the one on which her cat had kittens in

Mary's underwear drawer. This was a birthing event that did not bring joy to my parents!

Three years later, an arrival did bring much joy to my parents, to me and my older brothers and sisters. On March 19, 1939, my baby sister, Rachel, was born in the Antioch Hospital. Rachel was originally given the name Joanne Jennette; the name Joanne, or Giovanna, was chosen in memory of my mother's oldest sister, who raised her. A few days later, at the request of the family, her given name was changed to Rachel, in memory of Uncle Rachele. Virgil, their first child, had been born in the Casarsa home during the first part of my parents' marriage, a time that included a world war, immigration, and life in a new land, and now, twenty years later, Rachel, their eighth and last child, was born in an American hospital.

My Ranch Memories

One of my earliest memories is of the ranch's original four-room board-and-batten house, which Ma and Pa had moved in 1926 to make way for our family's building a new home. I recall that we used the old house to store many things. It housed our empty grape boxes, an intricately crafted, hand-crank-operated grain cleaner to clean weed seeds out of our barley and wheat seed grain, an egg incubator, and a few other pieces of equipment.

The old structure was supported on redwood block foundation piers that provided a small crawl space under the house where odds and ends were kept. One of these items was an old, abandoned still that my brother Dante built and used during his college days at the University of California at Berkeley to make homemade *grappa*, or distilled wine. Eventually, someone saw it and reported it to the Feds, who came and confiscated it. This encounter with the authorities worried my father for a while, but nothing ever came of it.

We tore down the old house around 1941, to make room for a new 28 x 40-foot granary building, where we always stored our barley and wheat crop several months after harvest so it could be sold when the price was better. Until the early 1950s, our grain crop was always harvested in sacks, which we manually picked up in our farm wagon from the field where the combine had dropped them. The job was much easier when all the handling became mechanized and could be done in bulk. While the later grain combine-harvesters were quite mechanized, needing few operators, the earlier versions required many teams of horses to pull them and a large crew of workers, whom my mother was required to feed. For one of these noontime meals, she worked hard to provide a special *polenta* and tripe meal, which the older workers loved, but the young ones were wary of. She didn't know that tripe was not a commonly eaten food.

Our cinderblock granary building also served as a grand dining hall on two happy occasions. The first was the reception for my sister Teresa's wedding to Don DeShields on April 26, 1946. Then, on June 12, 1949, my sister Mary married Jim Cline, and they also held their reception in the granary building. Most of the Jacuzzi family attended both weddings.

Two additional bedrooms were added to our home in 1945. These had a covered porch area with a good view toward the north and the San Joaquin River. The two-car garage that was added below the bedrooms connected with the basement. This addition was built by Aunt Cirilla's husband, Joe Benassini, who was a homebuilder in Oakland before he went to work for Jacuzzi Brothers. Just as he did for the original structure, Uncle Pete Bianchi did the cement work and plastering in these new rooms.

My School Years

I started the first grade at Antioch's Elementary School in 1941, when I was five years old. My parents had a time with me for a few weeks, as I did not want to go. Having been reared on the ranch, I hardly knew anyone at school, except for a few children who lived near us. Eventually, I made some friends, got used to school, and ended up enjoying it. One of my grammar school friends was Romano Marchetti, whose mother, Inez Marchetti, was a very close friend of my mother's.

Like my brothers and sisters, I had to walk the half mile to and from the bus stop for the seven-mile trip to and from school in Antioch. Even today, every time I taste Muscat grapes, I recall my first day at school, and the box lunch with Muscat grapes my mother had prepared for me.

I always did fairly well academically, although I rarely worked very hard on homework assignments through high school. In grammar school and junior high, I couldn't take part in afterschool activities because I had to take the school bus home. Then, in my first year of high school, I wanted to play football. So, in order to play fullback at Antioch High School, I hitchhiked home every afternoon. A bit later, when I was fourteen, I was able to get a license to drive a car since we lived on a farm. From then on, I drove our ranch's 1950 Ford pickup to school until my high school graduation in 1953.

During my high school summers, I used to have a great time with my friend, John Valenci, from Pasadena, who would spend the summers working on our ranch. John's parents and my father were from the same region of northern Italy. In addition to our shared ranch work, we hunted a lot of jackrabbit and birds together. Every summer we would spend a week's vacation in Yosemite National Park, where we stayed in a nice tent accommodation run by the Curry Company.

The best moment of my school years, however, was meeting Miss Paula Putnam in an algebra class. Paula, who became my high school sweetheart, was a very pretty and popular girl. She was an Antioch High School cheerleader who didn't mind dating a guy who drove a 1950 Ford farm pickup. Today, I am blessed to still have that sweetheart—as my wife and the mother of our six children.

Jacuzzi Jet Pumps – three sizes – c.1928

Model T Ford pickup used to sell and deliver Jet Pumps

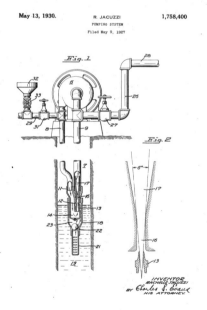

Rachele Jacuzzi Jet Pump patent

Jacuzzi Jet Pump water system, c.1949. Both parallel pipe and inner-pipe with plumbing shown.

Chapter 10

The Jet Pump

"Sì, loro avevano il potere, ma Rachele aveva la chiave."
"Yes, they had the power, but Rachele had the key!"
—Cirilla Jacuzzi Benassini, eleventh child of my grandparents

By the mid-1920s, while Pa and Uncle Gelindo were struggling to make a living on the ranches, Uncle Rachele's experiments were taking him down a path of discovery. With the early steam-powered *Frostifugo*, his experiments concentrated on the action of steam as it was forced through a Penberthy injector at various pressures. However, using a steam-driven injector for pumping water was unsatisfactory, so Rachele experimented with a pressurized water injector. Although he tested his theories with patience and determination, he could not envision the practical application of his experiments.

Grandfather Giovanni led him to the answer. After the tragic events surrounding Uncle Giocondo's death and the frustrating months of trying to get the company back on its feet, Uncle Rachele and Grandfather found great solace in each other's company. Struggling with depression, Rachele found relief by taking Grandfather for leisurely drives in the country. Sensing that part of his son's problem was rooted in a growing frustration over what seemed to be useless experiments, Grandfather tried to direct Uncle Rachele's thoughts and efforts toward something more fruitful. It was never Grandfather Giovanni's style to intrude on Rachele's work, but he liked to make suggestions based on his own experience and observations.

During one of their drives, Grandfather casually suggested to Rachele that if he really wanted to create something to help people, he should consider the difficulties of California's farmers. Why not invent a method for the farmers in the arid regions—like the one they were driving through at that very moment—to irrigate their land?

The problem these farmers faced was not a lack of water, but that most of it was simply too deep underground to be of practical use. If the water table was deeper than fifteen feet or so, as it generally was, a surface-mounted centrifugal pump was useless for pumping water out of the well.

For pumping deeper water, piston pumps comprised of a vertical reciprocating piston in a cylinder with a check valve were attached to the bottom of the well pipe and connected with a rod to a surface hand-operated lever or windmill. These types of reciprocating pumps with moving well parts were costly to acquire, install, and maintain. They also provided low water flow. The windmills obviously did not work without wind.

In the early days of our ranch, the windmill that was installed over our eighty-five-foot-deep hand-dug well was designed to use either the windmill to power the reciprocating rod to the cylinder, or if the wind was not blowing, the windmill could be disengaged and a hand lever substituted for power.

Uncle Rachele's many experiments and observations began to converge on one of his findings, that water under pressure reacted similarly to steam under pressure. His earlier experiment with the milk bottle showed that using an injector with pressurized water caused a lowering of pressure in the bottle to a point that the bottle's cold water would boil. If his hunches proved correct, Rachele reasoned that it might be possible to use water under pressure to pump more water up a pipe column to a centrifugal pump at the well's surface.

Rachele sensed that there were practical applications and purposes for his work, but what were they?

Breakthrough Experiments

In early 1926, Rachele pondered his many past experiments and his father's suggestion of helping the California farmers by devising an efficient means of pumping water. He soon theorized that a combination of a centrifugal pump installed at the surface of a well, plumbed with two parallel pipes to an injector with a check valve located below water level, could be used to efficiently pump a stream of water from depths of one hundred or more feet belowground. His thought was that the centrifugal pump's pressurized water would drive water down one well pipe through the injector's nozzle and venturi, creating a suction, which would draw in water from the well and force it up the second pipe into the suction of the centrifugal pump at the surface. Here, a portion of the pumped water would again circulate down into the injector to pump more water, and the excess water could be used for irrigation or for the home.

After unsuccessfully trying to locate an electric-motor-driven one-horsepower centrifugal pump with the right performance characteristics, he decided to build one that tested to his expectations.

Next, Uncle Rachele designed an injector for the needed well pipe sizes, with proper nozzle and venturi components for the well's water depth. Since steam and water are both fluids, he knew he could use and rely on knowledge he gained from his experiments with steam flow and from his design and tests of his first prototype water-driven injector. Once he was satisfied with his calculations, he designed and built the components of his new injector and began testing his new combination centrifugal pump and injector product.

The initial tests clearly proved Rachele's theory, and, believing that he created a one-of-a-kind product, he named the device the "Jet Pump." In reality, the jet jump was composed of two pumps—a centrifugal pump at the top of the well and an injector at the bottom of the well. His new device was indeed unique, for it used no moving parts inside the well. An added bonus of the Jet Pump was that it could be incorporated with a water pressure tank equipped with a pressure switch that allowed the system to stop and start automatically. The Jet Pump would later accommodate what became known as a "Jacuzzi Jet Charger, air volume control." This device was designed especially to maintain the proper air cushion in the pressure tank to assure the successful operation of the automatic water system.

Satisfied that Jacuzzi Brothers had a viable product, Rachele and his brothers sought a customer who would be willing to have a Jet Pump installed on his well.

Upon learning that the Philadelphia Quartz Company in West Berkeley was drilling a new well on its property, the brothers contacted the owners of that company with a proposition: If they would allow the Jacuzzis to install a Jet Pump on the new well, the company would be under no obligation to pay for it, unless the pump performed at pre-arranged standards. The owners agreed to this proposal and a date was set for the installation of the Jacuzzi Brothers' first Jet Pump.

Uncle Rachele and the brothers built and installed a completely automatic pressure system. They mounted the pump and motor on a steel channel base and fastened this to the top of a horizontal, 60 gallon pressure tank partially filled with air and equipped with a pressure switch that allowed the pump to stop and start as water was drawn from the tank. The pump's discharge was connected to the tank.

When the big day arrived, a crowd gathered to witness this innovative method for pumping water. Though the pump didn't quite reach the company's flow requirements, its owners were sufficiently impressed to ask that a Jet Pump be placed on another of their wells to replace an inefficient windmill. Encouraged by this partial success, the Jacuzzi brothers decided to immediately build ten more Jet Pump systems.

Sales

All of the brothers had their own strengths and distinct talents. Candido, the youngest Jacuzzi brother, also known as C.J., had persuasiveness and skill in salesmanship. Initially, all the brothers worked at selling the pumps, but in 1926, C.J. was the only brother given this as a full-time assignment. Aunt Gilia's husband, Jack Peruzzo, joined this sales effort. Their task was complicated by the fact that they would be selling not only a new product, but also a new concept.

Most of Candido's sales trips in those early days followed a familiar routine. He began his morning by filling the Model T Ford pickup with pumps and even tying some to its bumper. He also made sure he had a few grape crushers, another Jacuzzi Brothers' product that continued to enjoy small sales. He drove out to a rural area. Since he did not speak English very well, he looked for mailboxes that displayed Italian names and, finding one, he drove onto the farm and asked if he could give a brief explanation of the Jet Pump.

After the ten pumps were sold, Candido began to call on some pump dealers, and once again he was handicapped by his broken English.

One dealer told him, "Go home and learn to speak American, then come back and try to sell me your pumps."

Though offended by the man's rudeness, Candido worked hard to improve his English. He found that by listening to customers' suggestions, and even their complaints, Jacuzzi Brothers, Inc., could improve its product and increase its sales.

Going Regional

Since Uncle Candido's first successful contacts were with Italian-American farmers, the earliest injector pumps were bought by farmers with names like Prochietto, Maggi, Massa, and DeMartini, who conveyed their enthusiasm for the product to friends and other farmers. Such word-of-mouth endorsements proved invaluable and the company soon sold forty more pumps.

In addition to individual farmers on small farms, the company now had customers like the Calistoga Creamery, Toscana Bakery, and Mueller Brothers. Demand now grew for larger pumps, so Uncle Rachele designed units with two, three, and five horsepower. This Jacuzzi Brothers' expansion of the Jet Pump line filled greater and greater pumping requirements. Smaller units of one-third and one-half horsepower were also built.

The first dealers secured for resale of Jacuzzi Jet Pumps included Turner in Modesto, Mauzy in Walnut Creek, Stockton Hardware in Stockton, Mission Hardware in Sonoma, and Smith-Hayward. These seasoned pump dealers immediately recognized the merits of a pumping system that required no moving parts within the well. The fact that the pump required minimum maintenance after installation was another plus.

Gradually, as sales climbed, it seemed the company could be catching its second wind. Between 1927 and 1930, some more of the brothers and other family members were employed, and additional salesmen were hired. Pa and Uncle Gelindo helped in whatever ways they could, but working to make their ranches profitable remained their primary concern.

With increased Jet Pump sales, the company faced many decisions. These start-up years were critical, for it was then that Jacuzzi Brothers' reputation as a pump manufacturer would be made or broken. By 1928, a dealer network had been established from San Diego to Klamath Falls, Oregon.

Yet, there were obstacles. Other pump manufacturers often tried to dissuade dealers from carrying the Jacuzzi pumps, claiming that the Jet Pump was an unreliable, unproven product. As a countermeasure, Jacuzzi Brothers salesmen often extended the Jet Pump's warranty for four years beyond installation.

Slowly, the company grew. During the late 1920s, the propeller business was temporarily revived and Louis Ansani, the husband of Uncle Candido's sister-in-law, was hired in 1928.

In 1929, Uncle Rachele became interested in developing a turbine pump so the company could offer pumps with greater flow, and some experimental units were installed in the California towns of Concord, Hayward, and Vallejo.

During the same year, working with faculty member Professor Milikan, Rachele and his brothers designed and produced a special twenty-three-foot-diameter, four-blade propeller for the wind tunnel at California Institute of Technology (Caltech) in Pasadena.

In the late twenties, the brothers applied for a patent for the Jacuzzi Jet Pump, which they received in 1930, and in the same year they decided to display their invention at the California State Fair in Sacramento. The entire Jacuzzi family was thrilled at the outcome: The Jet Pump was awarded a Gold Medal for "Meritorious Invention" from the California Agricultural Society, making it the first-place winner in the category designed for "inventions releasing availability and lowering the cost of water." This single award gave the company and its product an official stamp of approval. Now poised to support the California agricultural industry—the nation's leading food supplier—Jacuzzi Brothers, Inc., was reborn.

Pushing on through the Depression

Thanks to publicity received from its Gold Medal award, the company was soon asked to install a Jacuzzi injector pump at the Oakland Baseball Park. This one pump replaced three competitive units from other manufacturers and was considered an engineering feat: the single five-horsepower Jacuzzi unit pumped water from a depth of 60 feet into an automatic pressure system. The country, however, was in the throes of the Great Depression, so by the early 1930s, pump sales slumped and the propeller business dwindled to practically nothing. The brothers were forced to extend bank loans and begin laying off employees. Their patent for the injector pump remained unprotected due to lack of funds, so it was not surprising when one of their laid-off employees, Fred Carpenter—originally hired in 1930 to help Uncle Rachele design a turbine unit—started the first competitive injector pump firm, Advance Pump Company, and later formed the Berkeley Pump Company.

Once again, the brothers experimented with various products, one of which was a wine filter, which they added to their product line to meet the needs of wineries.

By 1934, Mr. C. Smith, who, since the *Frostifugo* era, had been a financial backer of the company, was no longer able to continue his support. He called in a loan and agreed to settle it for $9,000, and Aunt Felicita's husband, Luigi Lanza, and Aunt Angelina's husband, Peter Tunesi, volunteered to loan the company money. Eventually, the company's bank extended credit, but it put the brothers on notice that the loan must be paid off in regular installments. Although pump sales were sluggish during the worst years of the Depression, sales continued, and the company survived the hard times.

Building on the regional dealer network established along the West Coast, Uncle Candido made his first sales trip to Texas in 1935. He lined up several dealers there.

Sorrow and Shame

During this time of business revival and endurance, my family's personal story was quite different in nature. In 1929, my grandfather became gravely ill; he lay in bed for days and said the rosary over and over. He fervently recited the Lord's Prayer. On March 19, 1929, he died. For several months, Grandfather Giovanni had battled dropsy, now known as edema, which surrounded his heart with fluids. In those days, there was no cure for the disease. Once again, my family faced the loss of a beloved family member.

Grandmother Teresa buried her husband in San Pablo's St. Joseph's Cemetery. She laid her husband to rest in a nation she still considered somewhat foreign. I am told that she was almost inconsolable. She often turned to Uncle Rachele for solace. Interestingly, the tactic Rachele generally used to cheer his mother was the same his father had used on him just a few years earlier—a drive in the country, often to either our ranch or Uncle Gelindo's.

In the late 1920s, Grandfather, before his death, and Grandmother had asked several family members to return with them to live in Italy, but no one wanted to, for Jacuzzi children were being born and going to California schools, and their parents were working there as their lives were taking root in their adopted nation. Thus, with returning no longer an option, Grandmother and Grandfather agreed to sell their home and properties in Italy to Jacuzzi Brothers. In exchange, the brothers offered Giovanni $3,000, which was to be paid in small installments over time. This was in addition to the 6,000 company shares the brothers had given him soon after his arrival in America, which were also considered part of the payment. Thus, at the time of Grandfather's death, the corporation owned the Casarsa ancestral home and agricultural properties.

Against the backdrop of the Great Depression, sales were off, but the family obviously had great hopes for the company. However, some of the brothers grew frustrated with Rachele. An inventor and tinkerer at heart, he simply could not lay aside his drive to discover. As in his youth, this zest for questions and answers took him down paths that were not always easily followed by others.

In conjunction with his widening interests, Uncle Rachele was pursuing increasingly ambitious experiments. One of these involved the design, building, and installation of giant windmills to drive turbine pumps. His brothers understood that the company could have a future in turbine pumps, but unlike most of Rachele's experiments, this prototypical windmill work was done on a large and fairly expensive scale.

He installed one of these towers in a cemetery and another on Uncle Gelindo's Antioch ranch in 1932. The windmill-driven turbine prototype installed on Gelindo's ranch towered thirty feet. It featured a three-blade propeller, with a diameter of twenty-six feet. Its turbine pump produced up to ten horsepower; it pumped three hundred gallons of water per minute from a depth of seventy feet.

Uncle Rachele's concepts and theories became ever more complex, as he pondered such matters as solar energy, solar-paneled homes, nuclear fission, and helicopter flight, not to mention harnessing both the wind and ocean as power sources.

The other brothers working for the company, namely Joseph, Candido, and Frank, harbored more practical plans. Seeing that their company had a viable and increasingly popular product in the Jet Pump, they felt that Rachele should channel his creativity as well as the company's resources into further development and improvement of that product.

This frustration came to a head in mid-1937, when, according to corporate documents, the company was reorganized. In reality, what happened was that Rachele was deposed. Since its incorporation, Rachele had been the president of Jacuzzi Brothers; he was, after all, the founder and creative genius. However, upon arriving at work one morning, Rachele found that his desk and all of his possessions had been moved out of his office. His desk had been placed in a back corner of the shop. He was stunned and heartbroken by his brothers' treatment.

It appears that the motive for deposing Rachele was triggered by his wanting to invest $2,000 in a prototype windmill to generate electrical energy, which Candido opposed.

This swift and secretive move caused a great emotional shock wave throughout the family. Soon thereafter, Joseph was elected president and Candido became the general manager. When Pa found out later about the action that Uncle Candido and the other brothers had taken, he was quite upset. Pa's feelings were shared by many family members, including, of course, my grandmother.

Immediately following his being stripped of authority, Uncle Rachele talked to my grandmother at great length; he questioned why his brothers would want to "put me in the corner." In his confusion over his brothers' actions, he told his mother that, if he chose to do so, he could ruin the company. Aunt Gilia recalled that Rachele also visited her soon after the event. Initially, she thought he simply had come to her home to see her new baby, Esther Delia Peruzzo, born on July 6, 1937. But she soon sensed there was another motive behind his visit. Gilia said Rachele clearly was upset about something, and since it was in the middle of the afternoon, when her brother would normally be at work, she asked him why he was there. He said he wanted to see Esther. So Gilia woke up the newborn and put her in his arms.

As Rachele gently held Esther, Gilia noticed tears in his eyes.

"What is wrong?" she asked.

"Wrong? Very wrong!" Rachele answered. "Gilia, you have everything to make you and Jack happy. I have nothing, nothing! They have taken everything from me and put me in a corner without any money to carry on with my work." He took out his handkerchief and began to cry. Gilia was stunned by this news and did not know how to console him.

However, since he was such an honorable person, Rachele did nothing to harm the family and the family business. He was likewise a kind-hearted and soft-spoken man, wise enough to know that the company needed him as he needed the company. Time passed, and although he seemed resigned to the new leadership scheme, he remained deeply disheartened. More than sixty years after this sad event, Aunt Cirilla summed up most of the family's feelings about this abrupt power grab: "Yes, they had the power, but Rachele had the key!"

After the passing of almost seven decades, I can now recognize that this new arrangement possibly allowed the company to concentrate its efforts on immediate growth and greater short-term profitability. But surely this matter should have been handled differently. What the three brothers overlooked was the spiritual principle that teaches "whatever is sown will be reaped." In this case, unfairness and greed eventually produced great loss for the brothers, the extended family, and the company.

After being ousted, Rachele continued to work on other experiments, some still having to do with pumping water. In August 1937, several weeks after visiting Gilia, he was tinkering with another pump idea that would convert solar energy into electricity to power a Jet Pump. Much of his work was done on a new well at our ranch, with my brother Dante, who was working summers for the company, assisting him. Sadly, before these—and perhaps many, many more future experiments—could be completed, Rachele, my family's beloved uncle, brother, and son, and my own godfather, died of a heart attack on August 24, 1937, as he bent over to tie his shoelaces. He was only fifty at the time, a mere two months after being stripped of his title and authority.

Fondly remembered by all in the family, he was especially cherished by his nieces and nephews. My sister Teresa recalled how patient Uncle Rachele always was with all of the Jacuzzi children. He used to love to pile all the kids in his car and take them for a ride. Along the way, he would sing happy songs in English like "Bye, Bye, Blackbird" and "Springtime in the Rockies." He talked with each child in the family as if he were speaking with a peer. During these conversations, he often shared his knowledge of the mysteries of nature and the universe. Like his mother, he especially enjoyed introducing the constellations of the night sky to the younger Jacuzzis.

My brother Virgil had a very vivid recollection of an incident involving Uncle Rachele that occurred when he was about fifteen years old. On one of our uncle's visits to our ranch, he found that his car would not start, so he asked Virgil to tow him to the garage in Oakley. All was going well until Virgil approached the end of our private road and was ready to cross the railroad track. He was so intent on the towing that he didn't notice the fast-approaching Southern Pacific train. In the nick of time, Uncle Rachele slammed on the brakes to stop the cars from being hit.

Uncle Rachele was buried in St. Joseph's Cemetery in San Pablo. Years later, Jacuzzi Brothers, under Uncle Candido's direction, commissioned a large bronze plaque for the grave. It proclaims an immigrant of genius, a man responsible for many successful inventions, and it seems to have been written, for the most part, by Uncle Candido.

Growth

My father, Valeriano, had not yet gone back to work for the company. Uncle Gelindo left farming full-time and returned to work there in 1938, making Pa the only one of the brothers not employed by Jacuzzi Brothers, Inc.

Uncle Gelindo initially started on the road selling pumps and later was in charge of the wiring and final assembly of water systems. He always tested the injectors and foot valve combinations. To test the foot valves, he would use his mouth to blow into each, making absolutely sure there was no leaks. As a result of his diligence, he often had a black ring around his lips!

My brothers, Virgil and Dante, worked for the company in the summers of 1936 and 1937, and they boarded with Uncle Joseph and Aunt Rena. Lola and Lola's sister, Olga, also worked for the company during those summers. Virgil recalled that most of his summer work was in the assembly department for Uncle Joseph, and later, for Uncle Gelindo. Toward the end of the second summer, he started going on installation and service jobs with Louis Beggio.

My brother Dante told me of a time he was greatly hurt and offended by Uncle Joseph, during the time he was boarding with him and Aunt Rena. Joseph spoke disparagingly against our father because he would not let our sisters, who went to Aunt Felicita's to learn how to sew, also stay with them. He was going to leave their home but Aunt Rena apologized for her husband and persuaded him to stay.

Pa continued to earn his living from our ranch and from the small dividends of his Jacuzzi Brothers' stock. However, in 1940, the other brothers convinced him to return to the company. Pa went directly to the machine shop and was responsible for the drilling operations. He was always adept at creating specialty tools and fixtures that increased productivity and efficiency.

Beginning almost immediately after the first unit was installed in 1926, numerous improvements were made to the Jacuzzi Jet Pump. These improvements included the Jacuzzi Jet Charger to maintain proper air quantity in pressure tanks; a broad line of single and multiple stage Jet Pumps for a wide variety of applications, featuring horsepower from one-quarter horsepower to fifteen horsepower; inner pipe injectors for one-and-one-half-inch-, two-inch-, three-inch-, four-inch-, and five-inch-diameter wells; and a number of pump construction refinements to improve operating efficiency and reduce cost.

These technical enhancements, aided by an increased sales force, expanded factory space, and a growing demand, steadily brought Jacuzzi Brothers, Inc., to the top of the water pump industry.

It is a sad postscript that neither Grandfather nor Uncle Rachele were alive to see their family company's most successful days. But their diligence, leadership, and sacrifice have never been forgotten.

Valeriano and Giuseppina Jacuzzi home with vineyard in foreground –1941

Valeriano Jacuzzi with dogs Pronto and Milecca, west view of home – 1941

Valeriano and Giuseppina Jacuzzi family photo – c.1941
Back row: Mary, Dante, Virgil, Jaconda, and Teresa
Front row: Flora, Rachel, Valeriano, Giuseppina, and Remo

Chapter 11

Our Ranch

"Le mandorle cominciano a sorridere."
"The almonds are starting to smile."
—Valeriano Jacuzzi, my father

For several years after his return to Jacuzzi Brothers in 1940, Pa lived in a small room above the offices at the factory in Berkeley, commuting home to our ranch on Wednesday nights and then on Friday nights to stay for the weekends. He did not want to move our family to the city. Rather, he preferred that we know what it was to be self-sufficient and to earn our keep, and he felt that farming was the best way to learn this.

Pa's rejoining his brothers at work caused several changes at the ranch. One of the most immediate of these was Pa's decision to hire a ranch hand to help Ma and us younger children with our daily farm chores and responsibilities. Another result of Pa's working full-time for Jacuzzi Brothers was that part of his salary could be used to invest in the ranch. Therefore, during the 1940s, the ranch's productivity was greatly enhanced because of the capital improvements that Pa's salary brought and as a result of the hard work of our new employee.

An Employee Becomes a Friend

Soon after Pa started working again at the Jacuzzi Brothers' factory, Ma and Pa hired Enrique Banuelos—or as we called him, Rico, to help at the ranch. Rico was a widower, whose wife had died in Mexico, and then met his new love, Giovanna, in California. Rico and Giovanna had a son, Manuel, born in 1939. Through the years, our family and Rico's family became very good friends. Rico and Giovanna decided to marry prior to Manuel's receiving the Sacrament of Confirmation. They asked my parents to stand up for them in their Catholic church ceremony. Ma and Pa were delighted to take part in this joyous event.

When we were children, Manuel, my sister Rachel, who was also born in 1939, and I used to play together at the ranch. Rachel also spent time with Giovanna, who was an excellent cook. Her specialty was enchiladas, which she enthusiastically taught Rachel how to make.

When Manuel wanted to marry a young woman named Wanda, we learned that according to the customs of their Mexican homeland, the groom's family was supposed to ask a respected person to approach the young lady's father regarding the marriage request. Manuel and his father, Rico, asked my father to do this. Pa was honored and agreed. His formal request that Wanda be allowed to marry Manuel was accepted graciously by Wanda's father.

Manuel and Wanda had four children before her death from cancer after twenty-one years of marriage. Manuel married again, but his second wife also died of cancer after they had been married thirteen years.

Pa helped Rico and Giovanna buy one acre of land in Oakley. Manuel bought them an older home and moved it to the site. Today, Manuel owns this property.

Rico worked for us for about ten years, when he left to work in a lumberyard. He returned several years later and asked for his old job back, but Pa already was sponsoring another man, Juan Ramos, to work for us. Although Rico sometimes worked for us on a part-time basis, and since he couldn't hire two people full-time, Pa directed his trusted friend, Rico, to Aunt Rosie, who hired him.

The Grape Harvest

The harvesting of our crops was always a family effort, and it became even more so when Pa went back to work for the company. So as soon as I was able, I joined my mother and siblings in the many chores and duties involving the running of the farm. Our ranch hand—first, Rico, and later, Juan—was also essential to this work effort. My family worked together much like Grandmother Teresa and her children had done in Casarsa. Pa managed to sandwich in ranch projects during the weekends.

As I grew older, I was given more work to do. My main chores included feeding and milking our cows and feeding our other animals, except for the chickens, which were usually tended by my mother or sisters. For many years, we continued to use our wood-burning stove for cooking, heat, and for heating the water-plumbed firebox. I kept the two large wooden boxes in the kitchen full of firewood for the stove.

The grape harvest, however, was a full-fledged Jacuzzi family effort. Of our ranch's 161 acres, 33 were planted with grapes. How well I remember the grape harvest and how we used our two horses, Nellie and Mollie, to pull the farm wagon as we distributed empty boxes throughout the vineyard for the pickers to fill! We returned later to pick up the full boxes. Like my older siblings in the first years of the vineyard, I helped prune the vines, burned the brush in the winter, and hoed and sulfured the vines in the springtime.

We sold most of the grapes we grew, but part of the Zinfandel crop was harvested late for greater sugar content. This late crop we used for our own family wine. Every year we obtained a permit to make wine for home consumption from the Bureau of Alcohol, Tobacco and Firearms. I helped my father produce about two hundred gallons of wine per year.

The winemaking involved passing the grapes through a grape crusher into a large redwood tank and periodically using a pitchfork to push the floating grape skins, stems, and seeds into the fermenting juices. When the wine was sufficiently fermented, we used a hose to siphon the wine from the tank into wine barrels. Then Pa and I used our wine press to squeeze out the last juices that remained in the grape skins, stems, and seeds.

For storage, we used fifty-gallon whiskey barrels that, with proper care, could be reused for a number of years. The barrels, which we bought in San Francisco from a company near the Embarcadero, always had a very strong whiskey odor until we washed them carefully with fresh water and left them to drip dry.

Sometimes when we washed barrels that had been used for wine, we added some sand to the water to help scour the barrels. After a thorough rinsing, we then used sulfur to eliminate any remaining bacteria. We wired a sulfur stick to the bottom of each barrel's bung or stopper. We lit this stick and left it to burn out in the sealed barrel.

We also produced excellent cooking and salad vinegar from our wine, which was similar to the balsamic vinegar that has now become so popular. Our vinegar also was kept in one of our fifty-gallon barrels, which was equipped with a spigot, so we could easily draw the vinegar into bottles.

Scrambled Eggs on Highway 4

In the early 1940s, when my sisters Teresa and Mary were in high school, Teresa drove herself and Mary to school with the added duty of delivering eggs to Mrs. Marian Beedi, one of their high school teachers.

One morning they had quite an adventure. They were in the ranch's 1939 Ford pickup truck, and Mary remembered that they carefully placed the fresh eggs on the seat ledge behind their heads. While on their way, Teresa stopped at the intersection of Highway 4 and Live Oak Avenue. Unfortunately, she misjudged the speed of an approaching car. She pulled out to turn left on the highway and discovered too late that the car was already dangerously close, forcing her to swerve off the road to avoid an accident. They hit an almond tree, and although they were uninjured, the eggs broke all over them, splattering their heads, faces, and clothing!

Teresa and Mary both became frightened by having hit the tree and broken all the eggs. Rather than returning home they drove on to the home of our friends Wayne and Jessie Hawkins, later my sister Jaconda's in-laws, and their daughter Rosemary to ask for help. Jessie and Rosemary helped the girls clean up and Mr. Hawkins checked the truck and found it to have suffered little damage. He calmed them down, reassuring them it wasn't anything to worry about. Rosemary Hawkins later married my cousin John Lanza, my aunt Felicita and uncle Luigi's son.

None of them ever forgot which tree they hit. Whenever passing it on Highway 4, Ma would inevitably point it out: *"Vedi li la pianta!"* ("Look there, the tree!") The incident also was covered on the front page of the *Antioch Ledger* with a headline, "Scrambled Eggs on Highway 4."

A Craft Passed Down

Mary's son, my nephew Fred Cline, is now a successful vintner with his own wine labels. He spent his last two years of high school and post-high-school summers, when not in school, living on our ranch with his grandparents. In the fall, when not doing his daily ranch work, Fred was taught winemaking by my father, just as Grandfather Giovanni taught Pa all about producing quality wine on the Casarsa farm. After my father's death in 1973, Fred's younger brother, Matt, also worked several summers at the ranch with Fred.

In 1977, Matt was given the farm's 1950 Ford pickup for his summer of ranch work, the same truck I used in high school. Matt spent many hours restoring it and used the Ford as his primary vehicle until 1981. He still owns it.

Both of the Cline brothers continued their interests in agriculture and the skills they acquired at our ranch. During their college years, Fred obtained an agricultural science and management degree from the University of California at Davis and Matt received a degree in entomology with a minor in pest management from the University of California at Berkeley. Matt also studied enology (winemaking) at UC Davis. They worked together for a number of years at Cline Cellars, begun by Fred in 1982 and located in Sonoma, California. One of Cline Cellars' finest wines is its Late Harvest Zinfandel, which my father taught Fred to make. Matt left Cline Cellars in 1999, and later started his own winery, Trinitas, which produces a number of excellent premium wines.

Grapes to Almonds

All went well with our vineyard until the late 1940s, when an infestation of phylloxera, a near microscopic root louse that attacks and destroys the vine's roots, started to attack and kill our vines. As the grapevines started to die, we interplanted our vineyard with almond trees, using a 30 x 30-foot spacing. We expanded the almond orchard to about forty-five acres. When the trees were about five years old, we pulled out most of our vineyard to give the almond trees more room. Fortunately for the California wine industry, but too late for our own vineyard, phylloxera-resistant grape roots were developed.

We grew the IXL, Neplus, Jordanolo, and Baker almond varieties, which matured for harvest at roughly two-week intervals starting about mid-July. The IXL was the first variety to be harvested, then the Neplus, followed by the Jordanolo. These varieties normally were harvested before school started in mid-September. The Baker almonds and our English walnut trees usually were harvested in October. As the English walnut required irrigation, the few trees we had were grown mostly near our home, where it was easy to water them.

From the 1940s through the 1970s, we sold all of the walnuts, almonds, and barley crops we grew, except what we needed for our family's use. The hay from some of our open fields was cut and raked in windrows with our horse-drawn rake. When it was sufficiently dry, we hauled the unbaled hay on a hay wagon, either to our redwood barn that also included stables for our horses and cows, or we stacked it outside.

Most of our open fields were used to grow barley, and occasionally wheat, but to conserve the soil, every other year we didn't plant crops and grew only hay in the fields. We sold this hay crop, on a "share crop" basis to a farmer who would cut, rake, and bale the hay. We usually sold our share of the crop to the farmer who baled it.

Smiling Almonds

When my father would say *"Le mandorle cominciano a sorridere,"* or "The almonds are starting to smile," we knew he meant that the outer hull of the almond was starting to split. This exposed the shell containing the almond nut, indicating that harvest time was near.

When the almond trees first started to produce, we hulled the almonds by hand and dried them in the sun. In 1950, we built a cinder-block building to house the Miller Almond Huller we bought in Stockton. About that same time, we also installed a ten-horsepower submersible pump and bought aluminum irrigation pipes and sprinklers so we could irrigate all our almond trees for greater production.

For the harvest, we used a long, slender homemade almond sled, approximately three feet wide, twenty feet long, and twelve inches high. We attached a thirty-foot square canvas to its right side, which was split halfway through the side opposite the sled. When the sled was drawn along the side of a tree with a tractor, the canvas could be pulled out and extended around the tree.

We used rubber mallets to strike the tree limbs to shake the almonds to the canvas, and we took long poles and knocked down any almonds that remained on the tree. Two people gathered the canvas and pulled it over the sled so that the almonds on the canvas would drop into the sled. The sled was then drawn to the next tree and the process repeated. When the sled was full, we shoveled the almonds into large, used burlap coffee sacks that were usually from Brazil. We then took the sacks from the field to the almond huller at the end of the long, nine-hour harvest days.

The almonds harvested had to be hulled about every three days or they would mildew. It took three to five people, and many times Pa, after his retirement from Jacuzzi, my sister Rachel, visiting grandchildren, and/or others would work the huller's conveyer belt to assure that only hulled clean almonds went into the Almond Growers Association sacks. Someone also had to check to make sure that good almonds were not discharged with the hulls on the machine's discharge belt. My mother always took this last job, which was the worst because of all the noise and dust in the air.

My job was to maintain the equipment, place the almonds to be hulled into the machine, and tag and sew up the sacks of hulled almonds. I also made sure the machine was adjusted for maximum efficiency for the different sizes of the almond varieties.

The hulled, sacked almonds from the machine still had to be dried to remove excess moisture. Because we didn't have our own dryer, we took them to Ivan Winger, who operated a commercial almond hulling and drying operation. His dryer consisted of a long chamber with openings on the top, over which the sacks of almonds to be dried were placed. Heated air was blown into the chamber and through the almonds until they were dry.

We brought the dry almonds to the California Almond Growers Association in Knightsen, a small farming town about ten miles away. From there, they were shipped to the association's processing plant in Sacramento.

One of my most memorable almond-harvesting experiences was when

I was about eleven or twelve. By then, I was driving our Holt two-ton, track-type tractor to pull our almond sled from one tree to another during harvest. One morning, I was driving it up a steep hill to the harvest area, and my sister Rachel, who was about eight, was sitting on the hood. About halfway up the hill, I stopped to down shift, but the tractor's brakes were worn out, so I was unable to stop and shift the tractor fast enough into a lower gear. It started to roll backwards in neutral, completely out of my control.

The heavy machine picked up considerable speed, but fortunately, instead of crashing into a tree, which could have seriously hurt us, it backed up in a large arc through the orchard, completely missing all the trees. Finally, I was able to stop. Our friend and farm helper, Rico Banuelos, was as scared as Rachel and I were. Thankfully, our guardian angels were doing their job.

By the 1970s, new diseases, such as root knot, golden death, and crazy top started to take a toll on ours and the other almond orchards in our area. Since then, most of our trees have died. In addition, a disease called "black line" that affects the graft of the English walnut to its wild walnut root stock, started to kill off many of the walnut trees in our area. Today, no one in the vicinity of our ranch grows almonds commercially, because of these diseases and increasing residential development.

Today, Californians who do grow almonds are involved in an entirely different process than the one our family used when I was growing up. California's San Joaquin Valley is now planted with many thousands of acres of almonds on flat land. Highly developed mechanical tree shakers and harvesting equipment are now used. These innovations mean that the harvest requires only a fraction of the labor we needed.

Flood irrigation also is used, a much easier process than the use of daily-moved water lines and sprinklers that were required for hilly terrain. In addition, today both grape vines and orchard trees are planted much closer together. Finally, improved root stocks with innate resistance to disease are readily available.

Refuge

My friend Romano Marchetti's mother, Inez Marchetti, and my mother first met during World War II. After Italy declared war on America in

1942, residential and travel restrictions were enforced against Italian-Americans who were not American citizens. For example, these immigrants had to live away from major towns and cities, displacing many families whom kindhearted women like my mother and Mrs. Marchetti wanted to help.

Antioch residents Anna Biancalana and her daughter, Betty, moved in with us and lived in our home for about one year. My mother and Anna, very close friends, often cooked and did other chores together. Mrs. Marchetti also invited an Antioch Italian-American friend to live with her. Anna knew Inez Marchetti's live-in friend, and it was through the friendship of the two displaced women that Ma came to know Inez Marchetti.

Anna Biancalana and Inez Marchetti are just two examples of the many vibrant, interesting friends of my mother's who were in and out of our home while I was growing up.

Inez, at this writing, is ninety-seven. She graduated from the University of Florence before immigrating to America. During a visit with her while I was writing this book, this Italian language scholar helped me with the translations of the quotes that introduce each chapter. We talked of the war years when both she and Ma gave refuge to friends. She had countless fond memories of my mother, including Ma's ability to do multiple tasks at once, such as knitting while walking and talking with Inez and other friends! We also discussed how much Inez's husband Vittorio and my father loved to play dominoes during their visits.

Family Times at the Ranch

I remember many social gatherings shared with Uncle Gelindo, Aunt Rosie, and their children. Like many kids, I was interested in trick devices. One evening, I was especially proud of myself, for I had an opportunity to use a "trick spoon" that our family friend John Continenti had given me. It appeared to be a real spoon, but it had only the outer rim, with a hole in the center of the scoop.

I placed it in the sugar bowl before passing it to Uncle Gelindo, who usually liked three or four teaspoons in his coffee, but he didn't notice that it was a fake spoon. He laughed as he saw the sugar spilling out before he could get it into his cup, but Pa did not! I discovered that Pa thought my trying out a new trick on an uncle was very disrespectful. A quick learner, I never did that again.

During World War II, our two ranch families often gathered in the evenings to listen to news on the radio. Many Jacuzzi uncles, sons, and brothers were involved in this conflict, and, like all Americans, we were eager for daily news.

As they had from the beginning days on the ranch, my grandfather and grandmother continued to visit our ranch many times through the years. Grandfather Giovanni died before I was born, but I fondly remember my grandmother Teresa. We called her *Nonna*, Italian for Grandmother. A splendid storyteller, she recounted all of her tales in Italian, of course. She liked to sit on a bench under our spreading fig tree and gather the children around her so she could entertain all of us with her lively stories.

Nonna used to enjoy the figs I picked for her. As the figs were high in the tree, I made a "fig picker" fashioned out of an open top tin can which I nailed through its bottom to a long pole. The top of the can was left with a jagged edge to more easily cut the fig, which would drop into the can. Simple, but effective!

Like Ma and Pa, Grandmother Teresa also enjoyed singing at mealtimes. Some of her favorite tunes were: *"Quel Mazzolin di Fiori"* ("The Bouquet of Flowers"), *"La Bella Violetta"* ("Beautiful Violet"), *"Volevo Baciare Ninetta"* ("I Wanted to Kiss Ninetta"), *"Le Campane di San Giusto"* ("The Bells of San Giusto"), and *"La Mariana"* ("Marianne").

My older brothers and sisters were always especially kind to my younger sister, Rachel, and me. Virgil, and his wife, Beulah, gave me a guitar one Christmas. I learned to play a little, although I also learned that I didn't have much talent for music. My son, Matthew, who, on the other hand, loves music and plays several instruments well, had my guitar restored for me as a remembrance.

When I was about seven, Dante gave me a Benjamin pump BB air rifle. As I used the gun practically every day for years, it's a wonder that any sparrows or other birds ever came around our barns and yard. The only time I remember abandoning it for a period of time was shortly after I received it, when my grandmother died. Out of reverence for her, my father asked that we be solemn and that I not fire my air rifle.

Dante also gave me my first and only bicycle in 1946, shortly after he got out of the Navy. I used it for years and then after I finished high school, I gave it to my nephew, Bobby Hawkins. After his discharge, Dante spent several weeks at the ranch with us. He and I worked very hard together to build a large, beautiful outdoor aviary, complete with a double entry to keep the birds from flying out. The structure included a big screened-in outdoor area in which we hung a carefully crafted nesting house. Over the years, I raised many Roller canaries, Strawberry and Zebra finches, and parakeets, some of which I sold to the local pet store.

Many of our young nieces and nephews regularly visited the ranch. So, I suppose, it should have occurred to Dante and me that little children and an aviary don't always mix well. One day, when my niece, Josephine DeShields Avery was about five or six years old, she went into the aviary and left both doors open. To my dismay, I found dozens of canaries, finches, and parakeets flying all around the yard, and I lost most of them when they flew to parts unknown.

As I am a number of years younger than my older brothers and sisters I don't have a lot of memories of them before they left high school. But I know that like my sister Rachel, they were all popular in school and well liked. My brother Dante also played high school football, as did Virgil and I, but unfortunately he broke his nose in the process as the helmets in those days did not include face guards. According to my sister Mary, Dante also taught her and his other sisters how to jitterbug.

My parents' grandchildren were, in fact, a regular part of ranch life. When they were young, many of my nieces and nephews liked to ride the tractor with me when I worked the fields. This was a red International Harvester Model T6 tractor that Pa had bought as a new model in 1950.

The new machine was a dramatic improvement over the Holt tractor that had given Rachel and me such a scare when I was driving it at almond harvest time. Much safer and easier to drive, it was equipped with lights, which I sometimes used when I wanted to disk our fields in the cool of the night. It also had excellent brakes!

One or two of my nieces or nephews liked to sit on the tractor for hours as I worked. They rode on either the hard battery cover on the left or on the hard toolbox installed on the right side of the driver's seat. They loved it! Before my father passed away, my parents had forty-six grand-children, and I was fortunate enough to give all of them tractor rides at one time or another. More recently, I have also given tractor rides to most of my own grandchildren—on this same tractor.

We retained some of the farm machines and implements from earlier days, but mostly, we—my brothers and sisters and our ranch cousins—have our memories. Almost all of these memories involve our parents.

My Father

It is impossible to separate my life on the ranch from my life with my father, for buying the ranch was very much his idea and, in many ways, our years there fulfilled his vision for the type of life he wanted for his family in America. As the son who led the Jacuzzi family's immigration, Pa firmly believed in the promise of the new land, and, although he eventually served as chairman of an international corporation, he was always most comfortable on the ranch.

Pa was a gentle, unassuming man with a quiet wit and demeanor who was very much a philosopher. He used few words, which meant that when he spoke, he had something important to say. He did not approve of arguing among our family members and his favorite answer to a loud and heated dinner discussion was to slap his hand on the table and say, "*Abbastanza!*"

This meant "I've heard enough." After he stopped our bickering, he would usually leave the room for a short time. During these minutes, Ma would gravely counsel us that we had really done it this time. But later Pa would be his usual calm self, as if nothing had happened.

He believed that a job worth doing was worth doing well. His tools were always neatly kept in place and the trees, vineyard, buildings, and fences around our home were always well maintained. The large fig tree that was planted outside our kitchen was an evidence of his meticulous care. The branches of this very large tree, planted in 1936, the year I was born, were supported and pruned to give this tree a large umbrella shape that provided excellent shade. The grandchildren all had wonderful times climbing the branches of this tree and playing in the sandbox area on swings that were maintained underneath it.

At Christmas time we always bought a spruce Christmas tree that was

ORIGINAL JACUZZI FAMILY

Giovanni and Teresa Jacuzzi – c.1929

Jacuzzi ancestral home, from side view – recent photo

Aerial view of ancestral home – c.1970

*Family gathering
at Jacuzzi
Byron Street home
in Berkeley –
c.1930*

*Stella and
Gilia
Jacuzzi –
c.1922*

Cirilla Benassini – c.1922

Jacuzzi brothers with mother, from left: Candido, Frank, Gelindo, Teresa, Joseph, Valeriano, and Rachele – c.1935

Jacuzzi family, from left: Ancilla Bianchi with son Leo, Felicita Lanza with son John and Rachele Jacuzzi – c.1928

Cousins, from left: Virgil, Dante, Aldo, Giocondo, and Ugo – c.1934

Jacuzzi brothers and sisters – c.1950

Jacuzzi cousins, March Creek,
CA – 1936

Valeriano Jacuzzi, Felicita Lanza, and
Frank Jacuzzi – 1973

Bay Area Jacuzzi family reunion at Valeriano Jacuzzi Ranch, Antioch,
CA – 1992

JACUZZI BROTHERS, INC.

Jacuzzi Brothers Airplane Works – 1921

Rachele Jacuzzi "Aeroplane" Helicopter Design Patent – 1930

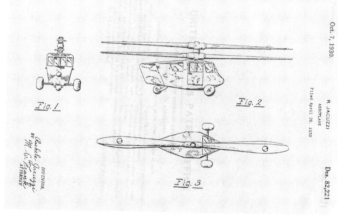

Jacuzzi J-7 Monoplane – 1921 (Courtesy of the Oakland Museum of California, Herrington-Olson Collection)

Aldo Jacuzzi with valves assigned to be manufactured by Jacuzzi Bros by the WWII War Administration – 1942

Dante and Tullio Jacuzzi with swimming pool filter system, St. Louis – 1958

Jacuzzi Family Spa – 1965

Jacuzzi J-500/J-600 built in whirlpool bath – 1962

Vietnam PBR Patrol Boat with
Jacuzzi Marine Jet propulsion units

Jacuzzi Brothers inauguration of
Jacuzzi Little Rock plant – 1964

Remo Jacuzzi at Jacuzzi do Brasil
new plant dedication in Itu,
São Paulo, Brazil – 1979

Jacuzzi do Brasil LTDA plant – 1979

Valeriano Jacuzzi family members planting his memorial tree at Jacuzzi do
Brasil's new plant in Itu, São Paulo – 1977

Valeriano Jacuzzi Family

Jaconda (Jacuzzi) Hawkins 1923-		Dante Jacuzzi 1921-1997		Teresa (Jacuzzi) DeShields 1924-
Rachel (Jacuzzi) Bruce 1939-	Giuseppina (Piucco) Jacuzzi 1898-1984		Valeriano Jacuzzi 1887-1973	Mary (Jacuzzi) Cline 1926-
Remo Jacuzzi 1936-		Flora (Jacuzzi) Nicoletti 1939-1990		Virgilio (Virgil) Jacuzzi 1919-2003

Giuseppina Jacuzzi
passport photo – 1920

Valeriano Jacuzzi
passport photo – 1920

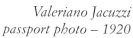

Giovanni Battista Piucco,
Giuseppina Jacuzzi's father – c.1920

Valeriano, Virgil, Dante, and
Giuseppina Jacuzzi – 1922

Flora with Mary Margaret, Mary,
Jaconda, and Bobby Hawkins

Valeriano and Giuseppina Jacuzzi family, Jacuzzi family reunion – 1958

Grandchildren at ranch under fig tree – 1959

Grandchildren at ranch – 1958

Grandchildren at ranch – 1960 Jim, Charlie, and Fred Cline and Remo V. Jacuzzi

Remo Jacuzzi giving children a ride on tractor, Antioch family ranch – 2001

Grandchildren at ranch: Maria, Jennifer, Loretta, and Teresa

Remo Jacuzzi hunting jackrabbits with Virgil T. Jacuzzi – 1958

Giuseppina and daughters,
under the fig tree – c.1960
From left: Rachel, Giuseppina,
Jaconda, and Flora

Enrique Banuelos (left) and
Juan Ramos – ranch workers
and friends – 1967

Harvesting almonds – 1963

Rena Jacuzzi, Valeriano Jacuzzi, and
grandchildren tending almond
huller belt – 1963

Grandchildren in fig tree at
ranch – 1962

Daniel Peregrin, Remo Jacuzzi's
grandson, with the ranch
home in background – 1999

Valeriano and Giuseppina Jacuzzi in front of home rose garden – 1965

Valeriano and Giuseppina family reunion at ranch. Siblings from left: Virgil, Rachel, Teresa, Jaconda, Mary, and Remo – 2001

Valeriano and Giuseppina Jacuzzi at their fiftieth wedding anniversary celebration with children and their spouses – 1969

Remo and Rachel Jacuzzi riding
Mollie – c.1950

Brothers Virgil and Remo
Jacuzzi – 1939

Remo Jacuzzi (66), U.C.
Berkeley Football, blocking for
quarterback Joe Kapp – 1956

Remo Jacuzzi, University
of California Berkeley
Football – 1955

Remo and Paula Jacuzzi wedding day – 1957

Remo and Paula Jacuzzi, Remo's graduation from Cal Berkeley School of Engineering – 1962

Valeriano and Giuseppina and children, Remo's wedding day – 1957

Remo V. Jacuzzi, helping his grandfather make wine – 1966

Remo and Paula Jacuzzi home in Oakley, Calif., before leaving for Brazil – 1967

Remo and Paula Jacuzzi family in São Paulo, Brazil – 1970. From left, back: Loretta, Remo V., and Jennifer, middle: Matthew, front: Paula with baby Paulo, Gretchen, and Remo

Remo and Paula Jacuzzi children, Jacuzzi ancestral home, Italy – 1977 From left: Gretchen, Paulo, Loretta, Jennifer, Matthew, and Remo V.

Remo and Paula's home in Brazil, with friends – 1975

Remo and Paula's home in Brazil, with friends – 1977

Remo and Paula Jacuzzi family at Brazil home – 1975
From left: Gretchen, Loretta, Jennifer, Paula, Remo, Remo V., Matthew, and Paulo

Beulah and Virgil Jacuzzi and Paula and Remo Jacuzzi in Israel with Sea of Galilee in background – 1981

Remo and Paula Jacuzzi family at home in Little Rock – 1984

Remo and Paula Jacuzzi with grandchildren – 1991

Remo Jacuzzi on Great Wall of China – 2004

Remo and Paula Jacuzzi fiftieth wedding anniversary celebration and family reunion – December 30, 2006

JASON INTERNATIONAL, INC.

Behind Every Jason Product Stands a Jacuzzi. From left: Remo V. Jacuzzi, Matthew Jacuzzi, Remo Jacuzzi, Paulo Jacuzzi, and Jennifer Jacuzzi Peregrin – 1996

Remo Jacuzzi in the tool shop – 1982

Jason Portable Spa – 1992

National Spa and Pool Institute
(NSPI) Show – 1983
Victor Jacuzzi (left),
Phil Adamo

National Kitchen and Bath
Industry Show (KBIS) – 1991

KBIS Show – 2001

KBIS Show – 2005
Jason personnel behind new Jason
Forma™ pedestal bath

KBIS Show – 2006

Jason MA635 Air-Whirlpool Bath – 2006

Jason IC635P Translucent Acrylic Bath – 2006

Jason HSC650 Home Spa – 2006

*Rachele and Olympia Jacuzzi
wedding – 1916*

*Olympia, Rachele, and Giordano
Jacuzzi – 1929*

Rachele Jacuzzi – c.1935

*Rachele and Olympia Jacuzzi family
Jacuzzi family reunion – 1958
Gordon and Eda Jacuzzi and sons*

FRANK AND RENA JACUZZI FAMILY

Giocondo and Ugo Jacuzzi First Communion – c.1928

Frank and Rena Villata Jacuzzi wedding – 1919

Frank and Rena Jacuzzi panning for gold with sons Giocondo and Ugo – 1932

Frank and Rena Jacuzzi family, Jacuzzi family reunion – 1958

JOSEPH AND RENA JACUZZI FAMILY

*Joseph and Rena Jacuzzi's family
From left: Joseph, Aldo, Roy,
Granuccia, Victor, and Rena*

*Joseph and Rena Beggio Jacuzzi
wedding – 1920*

*Joseph and Rena
Jacuzzi – c.1960*

*Joseph and
Rena Jacuzzi
family,
Jacuzzi family
reunion – 1958*

GELINDO AND ROSIE JACUZZI FAMILY

Gelindo and Rosie Meinero Jacuzzi wedding – 1918

Gelindo and Rosie Jacuzzi family with mother Teresa – 1939 From left: Rosie, Daniel, Olga, Tullio, Teresa, Lola, Rudolfo, and Gelindo

Gelindo and Rosie Jacuzzi – c.1920

Gelindo and Rosie Jacuzzi family, Jacuzzi family reunion – 1958

GIOCONDO AND MARY JACUZZI FAMILY

*Giocondo Jacuzzi's paint-
ing of his brother
Valeriano – 1921*

*Giocondo and Mary Guarneri
Jacuzzi wedding picture – 1919*

*Anna Jacuzzi and Olympia Jacuzzi
– c.1933*

*Giocondo and Mary Jacuzzi family,
Jacuzzi family reunion – 1958*

LUIGI AND FELICITA LANZA FAMILY

*Luigi and Felicita Jacuzzi
Lanza wedding – 1921*

John Lanza – 1935

*Luigi, Felicita, and John
Lanza – c.1945*

*Luigi and Felicita Lanza family, Jacuzzi
family reunion – 1958*

PETER AND ANGELINA TUNESI FAMILY

Pete and Angelina Jacuzzi Tunesi
wedding – 1921

Angelina Jacuzzi Tunesi – c.1925

Pete Tunesi and
Valeriano Jacuzzi

Pete and Angelina
Tunesi family, Jacuzzi
family reunion – 1958

PETE AND ANCILLA BIANCHI FAMILY

Pete and Ancilla Jacuzzi Bianchi
wedding – 1922

Leo and John Bianchi – c.1935

Leo, Pete, and John Bianchi
– c.1965

Pete and Ancilla Bianchi family with
Pete's second wife, Paulina, Jacuzzi
family reunion – 1958

CANDIDO AND INEZ JACUZZI FAMILY

*Candido and Inez Raneiri Jacuzzi
wedding – 1925*

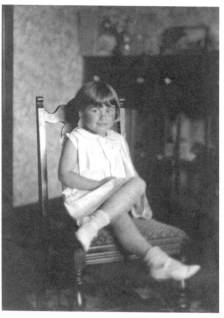

Alba Jacuzzi – 1930

*Candido and Inez
under mulberry tree,
Jacuzzi ancestral
home – c.1973*

*Candido and Inez Jacuzzi family, Jacuzzi family
reunion – 1958*

JOSEPH AND CIRILLA BENASSINI FAMILY

*Joseph and Cirilla Jacuzzi
Benassini – c.1935*

*From left: Harold and Lydia
Benassini, and Remo, Flora, and
Mary Jacuzzi – c. 1938*

*Cesar and Norma Benassini Nuti
in Little Rock – 1982*

Cirilla Benassini – 1996

*Joseph and Cirilla
Benassini family, Jacuzzi
family reunion – 1958*

RINO AND STELLA MARIN FAMILY

Rino and Stella Jacuzzi Marin –
c.1955

Silviano Marin – c.1933

Stella Marin with
son George – 1996

Rino and Stella
Marin family,
Jacuzzi family
reunion – 1958

JACK AND GILIA PERUZZO FAMILY

Jack and Gilia Jacuzzi Peruzzo wedding – 1925

Jack and Gilia Peruzzo – 1963

Gilia Peruzzo – 2001

Jack and Gilia Peruzzo family, Jacuzzi family reunion – 1958

supported with a wooden cross stand he made. If the tree happened to have uneven branches or bare spots he would make it look perfect from every side by transplanting some of its branches into holes he drilled in the tree trunk, fitting in branches as needed.

Pa was a skilled wood craftsman and he enjoyed working with different types of wood, using the techniques first handed down from his grandfather to his father. For relaxation at the ranch, he would often play a game of dominoes or the Italian card game, *briscola,* with family or friends, including Inez and Vittorio Marchetti, Monsignor Raymond Reali, and Silvio and Luigini Cesa.

Pa had many sayings, some of them a bit cryptic. Undoubtedly he had learned these in Casarsa and on his road through life. Once, my sister Rachel asked him if he thought a certain person would ever be able to change his basic character. He replied, "You can't change a dog's leg over night."

Pa was a tolerant man, a loyal friend, and a consistent parent and grandfather. He did not believe in giving excessive verbal advice but took time to talk to everyone, including his children and grandchildren. He showed his beliefs with his actions. One piece of advice that he did give to all of his children and grandchildren was to "study diligently, and get a good education because whatever you learn no one can take from you." He also admonished his children that if one of his siblings—our aunts and uncles—upset us, we didn't have to agree with them but we must respect them.

Pa's early life had been forged by hard times, and he never forgot a friend or a relative who had helped him during this period. I remember the woolen cap that he always wore at night, a reminder of his close escape from death in Italy during World War I.

When I was a young boy, I was rummaging through a storage shed on the ranch. To my delight, I found my father's old WWI Italian Bersaglieri uniform. Although tattered and barely holding together at its seams, this discovery was a tangible reminder of the roots of my father and of my family.

Pa held fast to the traditions and spiritual training of his youth. He often read his prayer book under the shade of the fig tree that stood outside our kitchen. Believing that any material success should be shared with the poor, when the ranch and his work with Jacuzzi Brothers became more productive, Pa regularly gave to many religious and secular charities.

One of my remembrances of my father was of him holding and bouncing a grandchild on his knee, singing *"Trotta, trotta, trotta una gamba rotta,"* an Italian verse, or seeing him with a child sitting on his knee listening to the ticking of his pocketwatch. When his young children and grandchildren were at the meal table with him, he would sometimes add a little bit of his sweet, late harvest Zinfandel wine to their water for a little color so they could share a little wine with the family.

My Mother

Like my memories of my father, most of my remembrances of my mother are linked irrevocably to our ranch days. Ma was always working hard on the ranch from early morning to late at night, to provide for her family and as a helpmate for my father. She was kind, considerate, and loved by all. She also was the disciplinarian of our family. While my father never spanked me, my mother wouldn't hesitate to set things straight! Once when Ma was particularly furious with me she chased me with a broom!

Her hands were very strong, undoubtedly from her years of hard work. She endured a tough childhood while she was growing up in the Italian Alps, later worked long days on the Jacuzzi farm in Casarsa, and then labored on our ranch in California. Life continued to be hard for her for many years in America. With no running water the first few years on the ranch, and no electricity there until after World War II, her life was busy and very demanding. My sister, Jaconda, recalled Ma getting up early in the morning to light all the fires before the rest of the family stirred. She was usually one of the last family members to go to bed.

She loved to knit and made all types of clothing, including sweaters, stockings (also argyle), baby blankets, etc., which she made for all of her family plus some for relatives as well. She used a system of knitting she learned in the Alps, in which the left knitting needle was held in place by sliding it into a wooden rod that was about one-half inch in diameter and twelve inches long. This rod was drilled in one of its ends with a hole that allowed the needle to be slid into it after the cap of the needle was removed. She called these wooden rods, which my father made for her, a *"cuchett."* She held the *cuchett* firmly at her side by wrapping it a couple of times in her apron string or cloth dress belt when she knitted.

Ma was a terrific cook. She managed a very welcoming home that had her kitchen as its heart. Friends would often visit her in the kitchen, where she would usually be working on a dish made from what we grew on the farm. Her food offerings were always delicious and quite varied.

My sister Teresa's husband, Don DeShields, said that coming directly from World War II into the warmth and graciousness of Ma's ranch home and kitchen created a dramatic contrast: "For me, it was just like stepping out of hell into heaven."

After all of the cooking and dining, Ma, along with the children, would be responsible for the cleaning up. Dante recalled our father washing dishes perhaps once or twice a year. For Pa, this task was very exacting, for he carefully went over each dish with scalding water. Ma managed the work in a fraction of the time!

My mother was also a great flower and vegetable gardener. She managed the ranch's large, one-acre vegetable and fruit garden. Ma was proud of her produce and sometimes entered a particularly spectacular representative in the Antioch Contra Costa Fair. My sister Mary remembered Ma's winning a blue ribbon one year for one of her gigantic red onions.

I was reminded of my mother's kind and generous nature during one of my recent trips to Italy. While there, I visited with members of her family. They told me that after World War II, Ma and Pa regularly sent them supplies like sugar, coffee, salt, clothes, and linens in packages she had fashioned from burlap. Additionally, they always sent them a generous check at Christmas. My relatives said that without these regular gifts from my father and mother, they couldn't have survived those years.

I still have a pair of *scarpetti* (slippers) my mother made for me using techniques she learned from her family before she left Soffranco to work for the Jacuzzi family. First, penciled outline's of one's feet were traced on a piece of paper for size. The soles of the slippers were made from remnant cloth layered to about one-inch thickness that was then lightly held together with stitches and trimmed with scissors to the needed sole size and shape. The sole material was then tightly sewn together with close hand stitches with thimble and strong linen thread to about a 3/8-inch thickness. The upper parts of the slippers were fashioned with strong canvas cloth and velvet outer coverings that were cut out from a pattern she made. The velvet outer covering was typically black, but she also used red, dark green, or dark blue velvet. She also sometimes embroidered white *Stelle Alpine* (Edelweiss) flowers, which grew in the Alps around Soffranco, on the front of some of the slippers she made for children or women. My mother then sewed the upper parts of the slippers together using her treadled Singer sewing machine; then these were tightly hand sewn and stitched to the soles using strong linen thread.

Her handmade slippers were extremely comfortable and long lasting. She must have made hundreds of them over the years for not only our own family but also for many other members of the Jacuzzi family.

In 1949, on her first trip to Italy after leaving the country in 1920, she brought along a pair of her slippers. Her relatives in Soffranco were both amazed and amused to see her pointed-toe-design slippers, which there were considered very old style. I was told that my mother's pointed, slightly upward-curved-toe design was a result of ancient Turkish influences. The new slippers they were then making in the Alps used a rounded-toe design. After my mother's passing, and while my older cousin Pierina DeCesero who lived in Soffranco was still alive, she would graciously provide me and my family with slippers she made. The most recent slippers she made were fashioned with purchased machine-produced rubberized soles but with uppers still made with canvas and velvet.

I remember when my sister Rachel and I were children, on cold winter evenings we would pull the kitchen table benches close to both sides of our mother who would sit near our wood-burning kitchen stove, which usually had some apples baking for dessert. As she told us stories of Italy and the Alps, we would help her thread her needles with linen thread so she could continue to sew the *scarpetti* soles without stopping to rethread.

The pair of *scarpetti* I now use are very much worn but comfortable. They were given to me by my cousin Federico DeCesero about six years ago when I visited him at his home in Longarone. He had them made for himself by someone in the town of Forno di Zoldo near Soffranco—they were too big for him but fit me perfectly.

We were raised on the ranch by Ma and Pa in a wondrous blend of the old world and the new. All of my parents' children have been grateful and blessed to have had Valeriano and Pina Jacuzzi as our father and mother.

A BRAND NAME

Jacuzzi windmill

Jacuzzi employees with Jet Pumps – c.1940 Front row from left: Candido, Gelindo, Joseph, Frank, and Valeriano Back row: Virgil Jacuzzi, first on left, engineer John Armstrong in center

Board meeting – 1950s

Chapter 12

Growth

"Piano, piano si va lontano."
"Slowly, slowly we go a long way."
—Giuseppina Jacuzzi, my mother

I've heard it said that it takes about thirty years to become an overnight success. When Jacuzzi Brothers, Inc., hit its stride in the early 1930s, my uncles and father had been working to build the company for more than fifteen years. I guess they hit the mark a little early. Obviously, the success Jacuzzi Brothers began to enjoy with the popularity of the Jet Pump was anything but overnight. But now the company had momentum in its favor, and that would propel it through the challenges of the Great Depression and then through three decades of growth and expansion.

The significant growth the company enjoyed during the 1940s, '50s, and '60s was centered on research and development of a comprehensive and very competitive product line. In turn, our production, distribution, and marketing needs became more global. Pa and my uncles led the company during this time, joined eventually by other family members, including my brothers and me. Here are some of the highlights of this expansion.

Product Line

In the mid-thirties, there were still a few places where wind-driven pumps were preferable, if not the only option, so the company devoted some effort toward improving that type of pumping mechanism. This had been Uncle Rachele's motivation in 1932, when he installed a wind-driven turbine pump on Uncle Gelindo's ranch in Antioch. Later versions of this prototype would be able to produce up to 200 horsepower and pump 1,200 gallons of water per minute.

The water-driven injector pumps, however, continued to be the company's backbone. During the first few years of the Jet Pump's existence, the only real changes were to make them more powerful for greater pumping depths and capacities. Then, in 1934, Jacuzzi Brothers joined with a motor manufacturer to redesign the pump's mounting plate. The goal was to transform the horizontal pump driven by a coupled motor into a totally integral, vertical pump and motor unit.

This alteration corrected a shaft alignment problem and increased the load that could be carried by all of the different sizes of Jet Pumps. In 1937, the pumps underwent another major design change. This time, the modification allowed the well pipes to be directly connected to the pump, which was installed vertically over the well rather than the pump being offset and "plumbed into" the well pipes.

Soon, other companies began to perceive Jacuzzi Brothers as the leader in the pump industry. In 1938, a contract was signed with Red Jacket Manufacturing Company that allowed that manufacturer to use the Jacuzzi patent on a royalty basis.

The Passport Product

After some scouting in the eastern states, the company learned that many wells in that part of the country were "driven" rather than "drilled," meaning they were typically made by driving a one-and-one-half- or two-inch steel pipe into the ground. If the water level was below about fifteen to twenty feet, depending on the altitude above sea level, it would be impossible to draw the water out. By modifying the deep well injector to use the driven pipe as the pressure pipe, and a smaller diameter suction pipe installed within it, water could be pumped from depths of as much as 120 feet. The company also developed and sold some inner-pipe injector pumps that used well casings of up to 5 inches in diameter.

While the inner-pipe injector pump filled a need, the company's original Jet Pump design, utilizing parallel well pipe plumbing, was the company's volume product, which was produced for a wide spectrum of pumping applications. The Jet Pump was effective for small diameter wells, as it was for larger ones, and for water pumping depths of over three hundred feet and in pump sizes from one-third to fifteen horsepower. In retrospect, the real significance of Jacuzzi's product modifications was that they set a course for serving the entire country, and perhaps the entire world, with its product. It is, therefore, no surprise that in that same year, 1938, the company signed several contracts with national mail-order houses that wanted to list Jacuzzi pumps in their catalogues and sell them on an international basis. Jacuzzi Brothers, the family company that started in a small Berkeley shop, had grown indeed.

By the close of the 1930s, in addition to Jet Pumps, Jacuzzi Brothers also manufactured a variety of other types of pumps: single and multi-stage centrifugals and line shaft turbines for residential, municipal, agricultural, and industrial applications.

Design improvements continued, as did the development of pump components. The company already had designed an air control to maintain the proper cushion of air in pressure tanks for automatic water systems. Later, it manufactured foot valves to replace the unreliable ones produced by other suppliers. Jacuzzi Brothers was moving closer to becoming a provider of a full line of water systems and related accessories.

After the War

After my brothers and cousins completed their World War II military service and returned home to work for the company, our product line grew significantly. By 1955, the majority of all residential water pumps sold in the world were jet pumps made either by Jacuzzi Brothers or patterned after its design. The company's success in the pump industry paved the way for our development of other related products. For example, many California winemakers were so impressed with the quality and performance of Jacuzzi pumps and related products that they asked us to begin making more efficient filters for wine and water.

This venture with filters evolved even further and in 1956, Jacuzzi Brothers opened a swimming pool equipment division that produced items such as filter systems, fittings, valves, underwater lights, ladders, diving boards, and skimmers. Silviano Marin, my aunt Stella's oldest son, was named division manager. For several years during the 1950s, '60s, and '70s, Jacuzzi was one of the largest makers and suppliers of swimming pool equipment in the world.

We launched two lines of air compressors, air cooled and water cooled, in 1960. In 1962, at a National Home Builders Show in Chicago, we introduced the model J-500 and J-600 whirlpool bathtubs, which were the first built-in baths produced by Jacuzzi for homes. Hydrotherapy products, which would impact my entire family in many different ways, deserve their own chapter in my family's story. I have given it this distinction in the following chapter, "Household Word."

A Military Partner

In 1962, the company entered the recreational boating industry when it introduced the Jacuzzi Marine Jet Drive, a revolutionary boat propulsion system. This was essentially built around a modified, mixed-flow, single-stage turbine impeller. The system operated by drawing water through a suction device on the bottom of the boat, passing the water through the impeller, and shooting it under high pressure through a nozzle toward the stern. This thrust the boat forward. The beauty of this propulsion system was that it operated smoothly, and it had fewer moving parts than a conventional propeller-driven system. With no exterior moving parts, the boat could navigate easily through shallow water. Additionally, the risk of a swimmer being struck by a propeller was eliminated.

In 1964, the U.S. Coast Guard began using the Jacuzzi Marine Jet Drive to power many of their survey boats, and in 1966, the U.S. Navy used the jet drive in Vietnam for "Operation Game Warden." The April 1966 issue of *Injector* magazine announced:

> The Jacuzzi Marine Jet has gone to war!
>
> A 120-boat fleet of river patrol craft are being used by the U.S. Navy in Vietnam for combat operations. Each boat is propelled by two Jacuzzi Marine Jets and powered by twin 220-hp diesel engines.
>
> This is the navy's first use of jet propelled craft under combat conditions. The decision to use jets was dictated by the necessity

for shallow-draft boats which can navigate the channels and mud-flats of areas such as those surrounding the Mekong Delta. Propeller-driven craft have had problems maintaining steerage in the shallow, weed-choked waterways.

Submersible Pumps

While the Jacuzzi Jet Pump revolutionized the water pumping industries starting in the 1920s and '30s and continue to be produced today, an even more efficient water pump—the submersible—was introduced in the 1950s by Jacuzzi and a number of other companies. A submersible pump is a pump-motor combination that is installed below water level at the bottom of a single well pipe. An electric power cable, typically banded to the well pipe, provides power to the submerged motor. Starting in the '50s, Jacuzzi developed a full line of one-third to five horsepower submersible pumps for four-inch diameter wells, as well as very large horsepower submersibles for larger diameter wells that were capable of pumping thousands of gallons per minute.

Today the introduction of the more efficient, easier-to-install submersible pumps has rendered Jet Pumps mostly obsolete, even though some are still sold because of their lower cost.

Frostifugo Revisited

Through these decades, we had many products that were proven winners. The business was thriving, and just as in its early years in Uncle Rachele's shop, Jacuzzi Brothers, Inc., continued to experiment, test, and introduce new products. Some of them seemed to be based on sound concepts, but for several reasons, they were not successful, and they never made it in the market place.

In 1965, we ushered in a new product called the Hydrocel, hoping this device would replace pneumatic pressure tanks in a water pumping system. Small enough to be held in two hands, the Hydrocel basically consisted of a rubber sleeve within an aluminum tube. The expansion of the sleeve, created when water was pumped into it under pressure, released that same water still under pressure when needed. It was believed that this invention would reliably do away with the nagging problem of water-logging, which often occurred with pneumatic tanks that were not properly maintained. Water-logging occurs when the tank's air, which acts as a cushion or spring, is absorbed by the water, resulting in a loss of effectiveness.

Any number of Hydrocel units could be installed in parallel; the more Hydrocels, the greater the volume of water readily available under pressure. While thousands of these units were sold, the concept was never greatly embraced by consumers, mainly due to field problems and the introduction of steel tanks, equipped with rubber bladders that mechanically separated the water from the air. The Hydrocel was dropped a few years after its introduction.

Nineteen sixty-five was also the year of the Auto-Infusor, another idea that worked on the principle of the Hydrocel. It, too, never really caught on. Following up on our success with the whirlpool bath, this device was intended as another product for the health-care industry. Its purpose was to automatically inject medicines into a patient at a preset, regulated pressure, while allowing the patient to move about. Although a licensee worked for several years in the testing and development of this principle, there were difficulties in obtaining approval from the Food and Drug Administration. This roadblock resulted in little enthusiasm for the product's development and the Auto-Infusor was eventually abandoned.

One year later, we introduced Spanline swimming pools. Because these pools were constructed using numerous gelcoat, fiberglass-reinforced panels, they could be used to build a pool of any size or shape. Eventually, however, problems emerged when the panels started to blister, which compounded the installation difficulties that were also encountered. Jacuzzi Brothers withdrew the product from the market. Some of the financial losses were recovered from the company that provided the panels.

Another very troublesome period for the company occurred in the early 1960s. Jacuzzi Brothers tried replacing metal pump components such as impellers, diffusers, and injectors with plastic replacements to lower costs. While the plastic parts were more efficient because of their smooth surfaces, they simply were not reliable and would lead to costly failure and field repair. A lot of Jacuzzi's prestige as a high quality product was lost during this time with a corresponding loss of sales.

Eventually better designs and plastics that were better suited for pump application were introduced, and these problems were resolved.

Fortunately, our successful products and services definitely outnumbered the less successful ones. As our product line expanded, so did our marketing territory.

Going Global

As the 1940s began, Jacuzzi Brothers had the best and most comprehensive pump line available. Like any dynamic business, Jacuzzi Brothers' physical growth and reach developed over time in direct response to the needs and demands of our customers. By 1940, Pa, Virgil, and Uncle Gelindo were working full-time at the company, and they, along with the other brothers, could see that the company had outgrown its manufacturing facility in Berkeley. So, Jacuzzi Brothers purchased ten acres in nearby Richmond, California, just a few miles to the north, and across the bay from San Francisco. There, the company initially built a 90 x 100-foot building.

Our ability to expand more dramatically began during World War II, when the federal government imposed restrictions on many manufacturers in an effort to conserve natural resources. Jacuzzi Brothers, however, was allowed to expand during these years, because the War Administration assigned the company the task of manufacturing a large line of valves. Additionally, the design of our products and the processes we used to make them demanded less material and workmanship than comparable products made by others.

In 1943, we built an addition to the factory in Berkeley. In that same year, because several pumps had been sold there, the company began to investigate the possibility of expanding into Mexico with a factory and distribution center. In 1944, the War Administration gave Jacuzzi Brothers permission to expand its Richmond and Berkeley facilities.

We purchased a large building in St. Louis in 1945. Due to its location in the center of the nation, this proved to be a strategic spot for the shipment of pumps from the factory in Richmond, California, and the distribution of these pumps to the growing marketplace east of the Rockies. During this same year, the company established a subsidiary company that eventually was named Universal Pumps. The purpose of this company was to allow more distributors to carry Universal-brand, Jacuzzi-manufactured products.

A branch factory was established in St. Louis in 1945, and my brother Dante was named factory manager and my cousin Tullio Jacuzzi, plant superintendent. The company also decided, in 1947, to retain the Berkeley plant, where the up-and-coming whirlpool bath would later be developed and manufactured.

Uncle Joseph and Aunt Rena became one of the first Jacuzzi couples to take a long airplane flight when they visited South America on business in 1949. After the tragedy of Uncle Giocondo's death, his brothers and sisters understandably had been hesitant to fly unless it was absolutely necessary. However, expedient travel was becoming more and more important as the company continued to enjoy dramatic growth.

In 1950, Jacuzzi-Universal, S.A., officially went into operation in Monterrey, Mexico. Uncle Candido's son John, at the age of twenty-one, had been named manager of this subsidiary, which Uncle Frank was instrumental in tooling up for production. Jacuzzi Brothers was now on its way to becoming an international corporation.

It is open to conjecture as to whether or not John, who was only twenty-one, was prepared to take on the responsibility of founding and managing a new start-up subsidiary in a foreign country. It was felt that Candido made the decision to start this Mexican subsidiary for John to manage to allow him to avoid being drafted into the military.

Lamentably, when John was subsequently drafted, he did not return to the United States and fulfill his obligation. Later, an arrangement was presumably made to allow John to reenter the United States and to volunteer for the army, but instead he was arrested (ironically, on Veteran's Day) for draft evasion. He served a six-month sentence.

Uncle Candido tried to persuade my father to try to keep me out of the draft. Pa would not hear of it. Apparently, Candido did not consider the fact that both my father and his two sons Virgil and Dante served their country.

One of the by-products of the revelations that surfaced in the *Jacuzzi* vs. *Jacuzzi* lawsuit covered in Chapter 15 resulted in the sale of all the assets of Jacuzzi Universal S.A.-Mexico, except for the Jacuzzi name.

Jacuzzi Brothers found it extremely difficult to deal with the management of this subsidiary in trying to trace the questionable financial transactions that were revealed during the trial. As Jacuzzi Brothers was being postured to go public in the early to mid 1970s, it was decided it would be best to abandon litigation and sell the assets of Jacuzzi Universal S.A.-Mexico to a group of Mexican investors.

Between 1943 and 1952, the Richmond plant and its attached corporate offices were enlarged several times, resulting in the facility's 1952 value being placed at $2.5 million. In the same year, Jacuzzi Brothers, Inc., surpassed $10 million in sales.

As product sales continued to climb, it became necessary to define the distribution regions even more strictly, and in 1953, Jacuzzi Brothers opened a distribution center in Binghamton, New York. In 1954, warehouses also were placed in Milwaukie, Oregon; Louisville, Kentucky; Orlando, Florida; Atlanta, Georgia; and Houston, Texas. We opened new warehouses in Minneapolis, Minnesota, and Dallas, Texas, in 1955.

In 1956, there was another expansion. A new subsidiary factory, Jacuzzi Canada, Ltd., opened in Toronto. My brother Virgil was named manager, and my brother-in-law Joe Nicoletti, my sister Flora's husband, the plant manager. They and their families both moved to Toronto from California in 1955 to build and equip the factory and offices and then to start production. This plant was expanded in 1959, again in 1963, and once more in 1967.

Eventually branch offices were opened in Montreal, Winnipeg, Calgary, and Vancouver. Under Virgil's leadership, Jacuzzi Canada became the most profitable entity within the Jacuzzi Brothers' structure. When I later became a plant manager, I often sought advice from him.

In 1959, Jacuzzi Brothers opened a plant in São Bernardo do Campo, a city on the outskirts of São Paulo, Brazil. An older cousin of mine, Aunt Cirilla's son, Harold Benassini, managed this operation for eight years.

Then, in 1963, we opened a factory branch in Honolulu, and the following year, in the largest expansion we had ever undertaken, a 175,000-square-foot manufacturing and office facility was opened on a forty-seven-acre site in Little Rock, Arkansas. The following year, this officially became Jacuzzi Brothers, Inc.'s new corporate headquarters.

With its location in the center of the country, combined with favorable supportive economic conditions, a business-friendly environment, and a willing workforce, the Little Rock market site was a good choice. However, transferring our manufacturing know-how to the Arkansas workforce proved to be much more of a challenge than we originally anticipated.

On the day of the Little Rock dedication in April 1964, the announcement was made that sales had surpassed $20 million, and that company assets had reached $10 million. In 1965, a 70,000-square-foot factory was opened in nearby Lonoke, Arkansas. Only one year later, it was enlarged to 92,000 square feet.

In 1965, Jacuzzi Brothers' golden anniversary year, the *Injector* magazine reported that more than fifty U.S. patents had been granted for Jacuzzi inventions. That same issue stated we had more than seventy-five factory-trained sales representatives, and operated twenty-two distribution centers throughout the world. I believe that Jacuzzi Brothers was fortunate enough to draw from a number of capable family members to fill the management positions required to expand the company worldwide. In my own family of eight children, three sons and three sons-in-law, in addition to my father, participated in this growth.

My Early Years with Jacuzzi Brothers

Because I was raised on the farm, from the late 1930s through the early 1950s, I thought I wanted to be a farmer. I continued to think this until my early high school years, when I decided that I really wanted to work for Jacuzzi Brothers, Inc., like my father, my two brothers, and most of the Jacuzzi clan.

So, with this plan, I attended the University of California at Berkeley to study business. While at Berkeley, I played fullback and linebacker for the freshman team and right guard and linebacker for the varsity football team and lived in my Sigma Phi fraternity house. During my last couple of years at Berkeley, instead of returning in the summers to work on the ranch, I worked at the main Jacuzzi factory in Richmond. I also worked at the Richmond facility on a part-time basis during the school year. After working in various production departments, I was assigned to the order desk, and then eventually to customer service.

I married Paula Putnam on January 20, 1957, at St. Anthony's Church in Oakley, California. We had a wonderful wedding feast at the Veterans Hall in Antioch, catered by Ottino's of Oakland. Our wedding was attended by many friends and most of the Jacuzzi family in the area. After a honeymoon visiting places of interest along the California coast, I returned to school at the University of California. Our first son, Remo Valerian Jacuzzi, was born on December 15, 1957.

In January of 1958, I completed my prerequisite courses for my B.S. degree in Business Administration from Berkeley, and I immediately began working full-time in sales engineering at the Richmond plant. I received my diploma in June 1958 when I participated in Berkeley's graduation commencement exercises.

Paula and I were soon blessed with two daughters. The first, Jennifer, was born on June 29, 1959, and our third child, Loretta, came on February 21, 1961. Both of them, and our son, Remo V., were born at Oakland's Kaiser Permanente Hospital, where Paula graduated as a nurse.

By this time, I realized that I had a keen interest in learning more about product research, design, and development, as I was now learning the technical side of how our products worked. I was also taught how to match pumps to specific customer needs by Floyd Nash, a brilliant company engineer. As I discovered more about how our products were made, designed, and selected for specific applications, I decided I could contribute more to the company by formally studying engineering. Therefore, after completing some required lower division math and science courses at Oakland City College, and after passing my entrance exam for the School of Engineering with a 96th percentile score, I returned to the University of California at Berkeley in 1960 to study for a degree in Mechanical Engineering.

I found it fascinating how much Berkeley had changed. While the School of Engineering area of campus was much like it was when I completed my earlier degree, the hippie and "freedom" movement permeated the liberal arts areas of the campus, creating a dramatically different environment from my earlier years there.

As I continued part-time at Jacuzzi Brothers, I was grateful for being able to work my way through college in pursuit of this second degree.

Paula and I also were thankful for the added help of my parents and for the Jacuzzi Brothers' dividends from shares which my parents had early on given their children.

I graduated with my second University of California degree, a B.S. in Mechanical Engineering, in June of 1962 and am proud to be a member of the Tau Beta Phi Engineering Honor Society for being in the top 20 percent of my class. President John F. Kennedy was our commencement speaker. However, another speaker, one of our engineering professors, made a remark that proved prognostic for me. He said that although the majority of our class was looking forward to working as engineers, in the end, most of us would find ourselves in management positions.

Two months after I officially became an engineer, on August 25, 1962, our fourth child, Gretchen Lynn, was also born at Oakland's Kaiser hospital. Then, Paula and I, along with our four children, moved to Fresno, California, where I began a job in field sales, allowing me to experience this area of the business. I was named the company's territory salesman for the San Joaquin Valley area, where much of my work involved the agricultural industry, mostly furnishing large turbine pumps used for irrigation.

By 1964, I had been transferred back to the Richmond plant and was the sales engineer for the western United States. In this position, I was responsible for all the technical sales aspects of our pumps, swimming pools, and compressor lines. I specialized in configuring and quoting large centrifugal, submersible, and deep well turbine pumps for customers throughout the entire country. I was also charged with planning and troubleshooting, and would often go into the field to determine what corrections, changes, or modifications should be made. During this time, I designed my first product, a high-capacity, deep-well turbine pump for an 8-inch water well application.

After I was transferred back to the Richmond plant, Paula and I bought a two-story country home with seven acres of land in Oakley, California. We had returned to our roots, for Oakley is very near Antioch, where Paula and I had met and graduated from high school. Our last child to be born in the United States, Matthew Paul, arrived on March 15, 1965, at the Kaiser hospital in Walnut Creek, California.

Brazil and Italy

In December of 1967, Uncle Candido, the company's general manager and chief executive officer, sent me an intriguing letter. In it, he asked me to take over the management of Jacuzzi do Brasil, headquartered in São Bernardo do Campo, a city near São Paulo. I will have more to say about Jacuzzi Brazil's operation and my response to Candido's letter in Chapter 16.

During that same year, it seemed as if the Jacuzzi family had circled the globe, for the company opened Jacuzzi Europe S.p.A. in Valvazone, Italy, just a few miles from Casarsa, where the Jacuzzi legacy began. The local priest blessed the Valvazone plant when it opened.

A few years after the Valvazone plant's opening, Uncle Candido completely modernized the old family home in Casarsa, now fallen into disrepair after being vacant for many years. His plan was to make the ancestral residence into a Jacuzzi historical museum as well as the European home base for family members and other Jacuzzi Brothers' management. We truly had come full circle.

The Family in Sorrow and War

While I have summarized the growth and expansion of the company during the decades of the 1940s, '50s, and '60s, and the role I played in this productive period, I am also aware that my family knew its share of sadness and wartime stress during that time. In fact, while much of the Jacuzzi family's history intertwines with that of the company's, we had a life apart from it as well.

On August 7, 1943, Grandmother Teresa was supposed to come to our ranch for a chicken and *polenta* dinner. That same day, my parents learned the severity of her heart disease, called off the ranch dinner, and surprised Grandmother Teresa with a visit. The following day, the family was devastated when the matriarch, Teresa Arman Jacuzzi, died suddenly and unexpectedly of congestive heart failure at the age of seventy-seven. Her death was quick and unexpected.

War also crossed our threshold several times. Nearly twenty family members were called for service during either World War II, the Korean War, or the Vietnam War. Like other American families, we have stories of many of these family members' amazing adventures during war time.

For example, Aunt Ancilla's son, Leo Bianchi, was a pilot during World War II. He often flew cargo planes over the Himalayas. Once, flying solo, he was forced to land in a remote mountain area. Though shaken up, he reported that the locals who found him helped him clear the area and unload the plane, so Leo eventually was able to take off again and make it back to his base.

Eventually, thank God, all of our family in the military returned home safely.

Family Reunions

During the early years of the company, since so many family members worked for Jacuzzi Brothers, company social gatherings and picnics became the occasion for family reunions. But by the end of the 1940s, given the growth of our family, we were ready for a mass reunion, one that would be thoroughly planned.

Thus, the Jacuzzis hosted its first big reunion, a dinner dance at Bellini's Restaurant in Oakland on December 28, 1949. Everyone was dressed in their Sunday best, with the men and boys sporting suits and ties, the women in silk and satin dresses, and the little girls wore new dresses, with festive ribbons in their hair.

Aunt Ancilla had passed away tragically on December 8, 1949, so several weeks later, at the time of the reunion, eleven of Grandfather and Grandmother's children were alive, and about a hundred people attended. Unfortunately, Uncle Gelindo, who, attended this gathering along with his family, died of cancer a few months later, on February 4, 1950, at age fifty-six.

Eight years later, on August 16, 1958, we held another reunion of the descendants of Giovanni and Teresa Jacuzzi at the Columbo Club in Oakland. This all-day affair began with a morning Mass and ended with a dinner and dance. In between, there were nurses and baby-sitters, cribs, and playpens, all to accommodate the many younger Jacuzzis. As at all of our reunions, there were many photographs taken.

In 1958, my father was seventy-one, and the oldest of the living brothers—a group that also included Frank, Joseph and Candido. The youngest member of the family in attendance was his grandson Michael Cline, my sister Mary's son, who was born on May 19, 1958. They were joined at this gathering by the families of Giocondo, Gelindo, and Rachele, as well as by the sisters Stella, Gilia, Felicita, Angelina, and Cirilla, and the sisters' families—including that of Ancilla. Ultimately, the Columbo Club was brimming with Jacuzzis, for more than two hundred of us united for the celebration.

It would be many years before the Jacuzzi family attempted to come together again, for by the end of the 1960s, we had scattered throughout the world. Almost anywhere there was a Jacuzzi factory or distribution center, there was a branch of the Jacuzzi family tree. Perhaps it was because we had so many family members that we were able to expand the company into so many locations.

Jacuzzi Portable Hydromassage

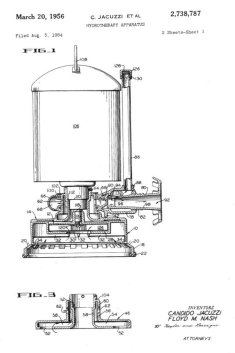

March 20, 1956   C. JACUZZI ET AL   2,738,787

HYDROTHERAPY APPARATUS

Filed Aug. 5, 1954   2 Sheets—Sheet 1

FIG.1

FIG.3

INVENTORS
CANDIDO JACUZZI
FLOYD M. NASH
BY *Taylor and Hassage*

ATTORNEYS

Candido Jacuzzi – Hydromassage Patent – 1956

Chapter 13

A Household Word

"Per ogni male è un bene."
"For every bad there is a good."
—Giuseppina Jacuzzi, my mother

The tale behind the product that made Jacuzzi a household word is so remarkable that it deserves a chapter unto itself. It begins with my cousin, Kenneth Jacuzzi, Uncle Candido's youngest son.

In 1943, when he was almost two, Ken came down with a severe case of strep throat. For a child his age, in an era that predated antibiotic prescription drugs, this was a serious illness. For nearly two weeks, he ran an extremely high fever, which occasionally would break, only to return within hours. It sometimes cycled as high as 105 degrees. Eventually, he developed rheumatic fever, which left him with juvenile rheumatoid arthritis affecting every joint in his body.

The crippling effects of arthritis set in on Ken almost immediately. Within a year, his body drew into an almost semi-fetal position. Seeing the severity of his condition and how rapidly Ken was declining, his doctors advised that he should be sent to the Children's Hospital in Oakland, California, for treatment and therapy. This was the only viable option for helping their son, and so, Ken's parents, Candido and Inez, consented. They placed Ken in the hospital a few days later.

One of the doctors' first priorities was to try to coax Ken's body to grow straight. To attempt this, Ken was suited in a full-length body cast, where he remained for nearly a year. The hope was that this treatment would not only combat any further drawing up of his joints, but that it also might reverse some of the damage already done to his body. Unfortunately, the confinement in the body cast did little more than increase Ken's pain and restrict his body's ability to grow. As a result of this confinement, Ken never exceeded four feet, two inches in height.

Over the next several years, various other treatments and therapies were tried. One regimen included "gold treatment," during which gold is injected into the patient. As a mineral, gold was believed to possess qualities counteractive to arthritis, and gold injection therapy is still practiced by some medical professionals today. While none of the treatments Ken received could reverse the effects of arthritis, one was particularly helpful in relieving him of some pain and in increasing his mobility—hydrotherapy. During 1948, when Ken was seven years old, his mother took him to the Herrick Hospital in Berkeley twice each week. Ken was placed on a bench inside a stainless steel whirlpool tank, also known as a Hubbard tank.

This oval-shaped vessel was about four feet high, four feet long, and two feet wide and was also known as a "hip tank." This moving water massaged Ken's stiff, aching joints. Hydrotherapy relieved Ken's pain much more than any other treatment. Ken recalled that physical therapy always immediately followed these hydrotherapy treatments and that the warm, soothing time in the water made the subsequent work with the therapist much easier.

Ken's mother, Inez, certainly noticed how much Ken was helped by his biweekly hydrotherapy sessions, and she felt that perhaps his condition would improve if he could receive these treatments more often. In fact, Inez even dared to hope that if Ken could somehow receive hydrotherapy every day, he might actually regain some of his lost mobility. Reflecting on his mother's optimism, Ken once remarked, "What they say about Italian mothers must be true—they believe if a little is good, more must be better."

Aunt Inez reasoned that since Jacuzzi Brothers was such a success in the water pump industry, the company could make a whirlpool unit for use in their bathtub at home. Since the whirlpool is essentially made of a centrifugal pump and air aspirator, both of which Jacuzzi Brothers excelled in manufacturing, Aunt Inez was correct in her assumptions.

Though Candido was skeptical, his wife persuaded him to accompany her and Ken to the next hydrotherapy treatment at Herrick Hospital, thereby allowing Candido to see firsthand the benefit his son was receiving from hydrotherapy and to let him observe more closely how the whirlpool operated.

This single visit was all it took to convince Uncle Candido: the relief of his son's pain—even if only temporary—was motivation enough. That same day, the excited Candido eagerly consulted a couple of Jacuzzi Brothers' engineers, Floyd Nash and John Armstrong, and together they conceived and built a portable whirlpool pump unit that Ken could use right in his home bathtub, undoubtedly similar in construction to Herrick Hospital's hip tank.

The unit resembled a vertical type sump pump, with the motor mounted on a column above the water level, and an air snorkel tube protruding down to an air aspirating venturi. The entire unit was supported by a frame placed across the drain end of the bathtub. Though somewhat crude in appearance, it proved very effective. Both Ken and Inez were delighted.

In addition to his being able to get in the tub every day, Ken was particularly happy about two things: he didn't have to be in a hurry to get out of the water, and he could actually stretch himself out in the tub and allow the water to massage his entire body. In the hospital whirlpool, his sitting on a bench inside the tank had prevented the massaging water from reaching any higher than his chest.

Uncle Candido and his family were so pleased with their prototype whirlpool that they invited Ken's doctor, Dr. Cecil Saunders, an arthritis specialist in San Francisco, to come to their house and see the unit in operation. Dr. Saunders was equally pleased and immediately envisioned all of his patients having one of these units available in their own homes. He strongly encouraged Candido to mass-produce a portable whirlpool unit and to market it to the elderly and arthritic. This doctor, a rheumatologist, was keenly aware of the suffering his patients experienced each and every day, and he longed to offer them some relief. He was convinced that if these people had a whirlpool bath in their homes, rather than having to travel to the hospital every few days for treatments, they could have pain relief readily available, all the time.

What the doctor said made sense to Candido, but he also had another motivating thought. He knew that Ken's working years would likely be shortened by his disease. This was the late 1940s and early '50s, and the workplace was generally inaccessible to people with physical disabilities. Candido was concerned how his son would live in the years to come. He considered that if whirlpool products really were marketable, they might generate an income which Ken could rely on for the years ahead.

Once again, one must remember the context of the times. It was not until 1966 that the federal health insurance program known as Medicare went into effect for those sixty-five and older, and it was not until 1973 that Medicare was expanded to cover those under sixty-five who were disabled and could not work. Prior to that, as in the early years of Ken's arthritis, people with disabilities had to fend for themselves. So, Ken's father began thinking ahead for his son's future.

Development

Given the experience of his own family, and realizing that hydrotherapy could provide similar benefits to many people, Uncle Candido quickly saw the sales potential of portable hydrotherapy bath units for the home. For the next few years, after the development of the first prototype whirlpool bath pump, a team of engineers at Jacuzzi Brothers, Inc., in Richmond, California, redesigned, tested, and improved on the first concept unit and in the process made the entire apparatus fully submersible and portable. After filing with the U.S. Patent Office on August 5, 1954, Candido Jacuzzi was issued patent #2,738,787, for the first whirlpool system designed for home use, on March 20, 1956. With this development of the portable hydromassage, Candido finalized his thinking on a way for Ken to be taken care of financially, if he were unable to work.

Royalty Agreement

Thus Candido argued on behalf of Ken's future income and persuaded the board of directors of Jacuzzi Brothers, Inc., to pay him one percent of the gross sales of the whirlpool product sold by the company. Candido then endorsed these payments over to Ken.

While I'm sure that all the directors and shareholders had compassion for Ken's situation, this royalty agreement was another example of Candido's abuse of his fiduciary responsibility as manager of the company and the coercive power he held over the board of directors. This was reinforced when I studied patent #2,738,787 and found it was granted in the name of both Candido and Jacuzzi's engineer Floyd M. Nash. In addition, as typical with most company/employee agreements, I noted that the rights to this patent were assigned by both Candido and Floyd Nash to Jacuzzi Brothers, Inc. Undoubtedly, Mr. Nash did not share in this royalty agreement.

The cost of this royalty agreement was borne by all the shareholders and was such an irritant that the plaintiff shareholders in their *Jacuzzi* vs. *Jacuzzi* lawsuit against the company, covered in Chapter 15, stated that one of the intents of the lawsuit was to ask the court to declare this royalty contract void.

The Jacuzzi Hydromassage

The portable whirlpool was ready to go on the market. The original unit weighed twenty-five pounds and was marketed under the name Jacuzzi Hydromassage. This product was a self-contained pumping device. To use it, one merely placed the unit at the drain end of a bathtub filled with water and turned on the pump's power. Since it had only an electrical cord attached, the portable Jacuzzi Hydromassage was fairly easy to move and store.

A 1955 edition of the company's *Injector* magazine contains one of the earliest printed advertisements for the Jacuzzi Hydromassage:

> . . . for the first time, a lightweight, portable, hydromassage unit is available for home use—for the tired business man or harried housewife, for the golfer with sore muscles, for the aches and pains of senior citizens, for frolicking youngsters and for those who just want to relax and pamper themselves with a hydromassage bath. The action of heat plus millions of tiny bubbles which are introduced into the water, backed by the force of the turbulent, moving water produces a massaging effect that benefits persons in every age group.

In the mid to late 1950s, the product was sold primarily through pharmacies and bath supply shops. The product still was largely unknown, and in order to generate national publicity, the Jacuzzi Hydromassage was included in gifts received by the winner on the very popular television program *Queen for a Day*. Ken was present at the television station for one of these presentations to a lucky housewife, who was showered with many premium gifts, like the Jacuzzi Hydromassage, and named that day's "queen." The publicity bonanza continued and soon the Jacuzzi Hydromassage began to receive testimonials from celebrities like Randolph Scott and Jayne Mansfield.

The portable whirlpool was accepted eagerly by the general public. Although its original marketing concept focused on the elderly and disabled, it didn't take long for American consumers to see the benefits of relaxing in their bathtubs after a long day of work or play. In 1956, the State of California issued a Certificate of Merit for the Jacuzzi Hydromassage. This was the highest award given by California to manufacturers of consumer products.

Although the product enjoyed success, there were design issues to be resolved. Though fully submersible and easily portable, the unit's electrical connection raised safety concerns. It was becoming increasingly difficult for the product to receive safety listings from agencies like Underwriters Laboratories (UL) and the Canadian Standards Association (CSA). The company needed to conduct research efforts in an attempt to find solutions, such as mounting an external pump.

Based on the need for further research and a realization the public was becoming increasingly interested in the product, the directors of Jacuzzi Brothers formed a subsidiary company, Jacuzzi Research, Inc., in 1959. Uncle Candido appointed his son-in-law, Pete Kosta, who was living in Stockton and working in an electrical supply store, as the general manager of this subsidiary. From that point forward, the special royalty payment to Candido and Ken came from that company.

The Whirlpool Bath

The portable Jacuzzi Hydromassage sold successfully for several years. Then, in December of 1962, the company launched the first built-in whirlpool bath units at the annual National Association of

Home Builders Exposition in Chicago. These self-contained whirlpool baths made use of a standard-size bathtub with a slightly modified drain opening that served both as a drain for the tub, and as an opening through which the whirlpool pump could circulate water to and from the bath.

Each of these units, marketed as the J-500 and J-600, included an electric pump located outside the bathtub. The pump was installed either in the floor joists beneath the tub or in the wall framing at the end of the bath. Floyd Nash, the remarkable Jacuzzi Brothers' engineer from whom I learned so much, was issued U.S. patent #3,287,741 for these units.

In 1964, Jacuzzi Brothers, Inc., made another forward leap when it introduced whirlpool pump-and-tub combination units known as the Family Spa. This unit was large enough to hold several individuals and featured a heater, a recirculation pump filter, and multiple wall-mounted jet fittings, as well as an optional safety rail and skid-proof steps. With these developments, whirlpool bathing became a mainstream recreational and leisure activity.

Two years later, the Luxury Line Hydro-Therapy Pool was introduced. The therapy equipment of the Luxury Line was similar to the Family Spa. Its versatility, however, made it unique: the bathing vessel could be configured in various sizes and shapes by adding any number of fiberglass panels. This same year also marked the Jacuzzi whirlpool bath's debut in a major motion picture, *The Fortune Cookie*, directed by Billy Wilder and starring Jack Lemon and Walter Matthau.

Many patents were issued during the mid to late 1960s, both to Jacuzzi Brothers' personnel and to others, for improvements to whirlpool bath products. Most of these patents reflect modifications to the water recirculating system, hydrotherapy fittings, plumbing to and from the pump, and air controls.

The patent for the whirlpool system closest to our present-day design is Candido Jacuzzi's patent #3,297,025, filed on June 16, 1964, and issued January 10, 1967. This design included hydrotherapy jets plumbed to the bath sidewalls and a separate suction opening to the pump, as did Jacuzzi's modular Luxury Line Hydro-Therapy Pool and Family Spa products sold in the infancy of the whirlpool bath industry.

In 1969, Jacuzzi introduced its Roman Bath line of whirlpool baths, covered by Roy Jacuzzi's patent #3,571,820, which included sidewall-mounted jets, but maintained the suction opening to the pump in the drain assembly, as did J. H. Everston's earlier patent #3, 263, 678, filed on June 19, 1965, and issued on August 2, 1966. The whirlpool bath industry soon moved to the basic plumbing design included in Candido's patent, filed on June 16, 1964, and Jacuzzi Brothers earlier Family Spa and Luxury Line baths sold in the infancy of the whirlpool bath industry.

A Household Word

The twenty-first-century market offers such a vast array of whirlpool bath models that some clarification may be helpful. For example, the terms *spa* and *whirlpool bath* are often confused with each other or used interchangeably. To add to this confusion, the term *spa* is frequently used to describe a health club or resort. However, in the field of hydrotherapy, there is a distinction. A spa is rarely drained of its water—this is usually only done for cleaning and maintenance purposes. Also, the water is kept filtered, chemically treated, and either at a constant hot temperature, or the water's temperature is controlled with a timer, according to the user's preference. A spa typically is installed outdoors. In contrast, a whirlpool bath is usually filled with warm water and drained after each use. And still, more recently, modern home spas are designed for indoor installation and are drained after every use. But when people speak of having a "Jacuzzi," they may be referring to either one of these products, confusing matters still further.

By the early to mid 1980s, Jacuzzi had become a household word, synonymous with whirlpool baths and spas, while prior to this, Jacuzzi Brothers, Inc., was still known primarily as a manufacturer of water pumps and swimming pool equipment.

This phenomenon came about in two ways. First, the company began to market its line of whirlpool products to the international market and the whirlpool bath virtually became a standard fixture in upscale homes.

Second, the whirlpool's use continued to be encouraged by trend-setters, like entertainers and popular movie stars, who advocated using it for a group or social bathing experience. It seems odd that this was once a hip social activity, since the whirlpool bath and spa have become such an integral part of twenty-first-century life. In the 1960s and '70s, whirlpool baths and spas were considered very avant-garde, counter-cultural, and "in."

By the end of the '80s, having a Jacuzzi had become a symbol of enjoying a luxurious and enviable lifestyle, and the word "Jacuzzi" began appearing in most English dictionaries, usually defined as "whirlpool bath."

I do not believe it has necessarily been a good thing for the name Jacuzzi to evolve into generic term, used to identify any, or all, whirlpool and spa products. I especially felt this way when the family still owned the company, and I always believed that the company should have done more to protect its name. Many hotels and home builders advertise a Jacuzzi when that is not necessarily the brand of whirlpool product they offer.

Ken

No discussion of the evolution of our family name into a generic term and the development of the whirlpool bath and modern-day spas would be complete without my telling you more about my cousin Kenneth.

Ken faced his circumstances not only realistically, but coura-geously. Before he reached the age of eight, his arthritis had advanced to where he needed a wheelchair, which, to the always-upbeat Ken, meant "mobility with limitations" rather than confinement. By the time he reached his mid-twenties, he had endured fourteen different surgeries.

Ken worked for Jacuzzi Brothers for several years. For a while, the company gave serious consideration to developing a line of health-care products specifically designed for the physically disabled. Ken served as the manager of that project. Eventually, however, the idea was dropped, but then another opportunity opened up for Ken.

In 1971, the Jacuzzi Europe S.p.A. manager resigned and Candido, who was then living in the Jacuzzi ancestral home, recommended that his son Ken be named to this position. This was the subsidiary plant in Valvazone, Italy, built on one of the parcels of land orginally owned by my grandparents, Giovanni and Teresa Jacuzzi. Ken was a student in Spain when he was eventually offered and accepted this management position. He served in this capacity until 1976, when he was replaced by George Regula, who is my cousin Esther Peruzzo Regula's husband.

Jacuzzi Europe S.p.A. was a company in trouble during the years prior to Ken's tenure and during. While Ken attempted to improve the company's performance, this subsidiary operation continued to lose money and was a negative factor in the eyes of the investment bankers who were trying to posture Jacuzzi Brothers to go public. It was even suggested that this subsidiary be sold to improve the company's financial position.

While in Italy, Ken met and married Daniela, a native Italian from Udine, one of the major cities of the Friuli region. Ken and his wife, Daniela, now live in Paradise Valley, Arizona.

Birthing an Industry

It's interesting that while the name Jacuzzi is now synonymous with whirlpool bathing throughout the world, the Jacuzzi Brothers company was really the first to make it available for home use. Whirlpool jet therapy was in existence a number of years prior, not only in hospitals, such as benefitted Ken, but also in a number of health spa resorts. The Arlington Hotel in Hot Springs, Arkansas, for example, has been in existence since the 1920s and still uses some of their one-person whirlpool baths from this era. These baths are filled with naturally hot mineral water. A column-type whirlpool pump with a jet fitting and air snorkel tube installed over the drain end of the bath provides hydromassage therapy much like the first prototype Candido developed for home use. The big advantage for the Jacuzzi Company is that they were the first to introduce this technology for residential use.

Today, however, we expect to find whirlpool baths or a spa in virtually every hotel, and certainly there will be at least one, if not several, in every resort and fitness club. Nearly every newly constructed, middle-to-high-end home includes a whirlpool bath, and the product is standard in sports training facilities, ranging from high school to the professional level.

A product that didn't exist fifty years ago has now become almost commonplace throughout the world. Hundreds of thousands, if not millions, of people have benefitted from the soothing, relaxing massage and therapeutic benefits of a whirlpool bath. But it all began for Jacuzzi when a mother and father simply wanted to relieve their son's arthritic pain.

Teresa Jacuzzi with her daughters – c.1940
Back row from left: Cirilla, Angelina, Teresa, and Felicita
Middle row: Ancilla in front of Felicita
Front row from left: Gilia and Stella

Chapter 14

Jacuzzi Ladies:
Sisters and Sisters-in-law

"Una buona moglie è un regalo di Dio."

"A good wife is a gift from God."
—Virgil Jacuzzi, my oldest brother

Of Giovanni and Teresa Jacuzzi's seven sons, six lived to build a global company, and the other died in that pursuit. I have shared the story of these brothers' successes and setbacks, their dreams and disasters, in building Jacuzzi Brothers. All tenacious men, they married equally strong women.

Giovanni and Teresa Jacuzzi's six daughters, though not directly involved as their brothers in company operations, were crucial to its ongoing success. Like most of the Jacuzzi wives, they formed the backbone of the family. So now, I will spotlight Felicita, Angelina, Ancilla, Cirilla, Stella, and Gilia—the Jacuzzi sisters—as well as the unique and stalwart women who married the Jacuzzi brothers—Olympia, Giuseppina, Rena Villata, Rena Beggio, Rosie, Mary, and Inez.

Hardships and Blessings

Most of the Jacuzzi sisters were very young, and some were not yet born when their brothers began to immigrate. The sisters' lives began in blessing and hardship. They entered the world in a family that showed love and support for one another, but they recognized that life was physically demanding, especially in the absence of brothers to share the load.

The sisters were small of stature, most of them never attaining a height of more than five feet, five inches, and yet they performed most of the long and taxing duties associated with running the family farm. Then came World War I, which made a hard life also a dangerous one. Although that same war halted their formal education in Italy, the girls kept up with their studies as much as possible, thanks to their keen and inquisitive minds.

In fact, I can personally attest to the fact that the Jacuzzi sisters were very intelligent and well read; one would never imagine that their formal education—except for that of Stella and Gilia—stopped before junior high school. Then again, life provides many lessons of the nonacademic sort.

The sisters also had a huge part in preparing the family to immigrate to the United States. The house and other buildings were prepared for the new tenants. Furniture and other household belongings were stored away, and the crops and livestock were harvested and sold. With Felicita and Angelina arriving one year earlier with Candido, by the time the last of the family departed Italy in December 1920, the other girls were nineteen, fifteen, thirteen, and twelve years of age.

Once the exciting voyage to a new world was behind them and the entire family was reunited, the girls quickly settled into a new life where their help was needed as much as ever. With only Stella and Gilia still young enough to attend school, the other sisters went immediately to work.

During the early 1920s, when the company was struggling to survive in the aftermath of the tragic plane crash and the end of its aviation industry work, the sisters often contributed financially to keep the company afloat. They also devoted their time and, certainly, their loyalty.

Then came the boom years for Jacuzzi Brothers, where the role of the sisters was perhaps not as obvious, but no less vital. Theirs became more of a nurturing role that kept the family united through success and, later, through dissension. Like their sisters-in-law, the sisters also reared sons and daughters, some of whom became managers and leaders within the company, while others enjoyed many other vocations and careers.

The Jacuzzi sisters always considered themselves exceptionally close since, with the exception of Candido, they were the last of Giovanni and Teresa's children. They were lucky to have shared this bond, and I am fortunate to have known each of them. I want to honor them now, by introducing, in the order of their birth, each of these unforgettable ladies.

Felicita Jacuzzi Lanza

Born May 15, 1897, Aunt Felicita was the seventh child and first daughter of my grandparents, and was named after grandmother's mother. She immigrated to the United States in 1919, along with her sister Angelina and brother Candido. Of all the sisters, Felicita was recognized as being the most expert and knowledgeable seamstress. Soon after arriving in California, she put her skills to work in a garment shop in San Francisco.

By the time the rest of the family arrived in California in January 1921, Felicita was engaged to Luigi Lanza. They wed on January 30, 1921. Luigi and Felicita had one child, a son named John. For the entirety of their married life, they made their home on Grove Street in Oakland.

Luigi was a gifted musician who loved to play his violin, which he thought to be a Stradivarius. In the early 1960s, hoping to raise some money, he and his wife, Felicita, had it appraised and were very disappointed to learn that, while of good quality, it was not a Stradivarius.

Luigi worked for Jacuzzi Brothers as a foreman in the machine shop and liked to tinker with various projects on the side. He received a patent on a sandblaster he developed, and he told me once that he hoped his son, John, or a grandson would develop a business around the device, but the boys were not interested and this never happened.

Luigi had a rough appearance, although he was an extremely kind man. My sisters, Jaconda and Teresa recalled Uncle Luigi liked to cut hair, but that his haircuts were some of the worst they ever received!

Felicita was renowned within the family for her ability to merely see a garment in a shop and then re-create it, stitch for stitch, without the benefit of a sketch or a pattern. She was very methodical, liked to experiment with sewing methods, and invented her own approach to the craft. In much the same generous way in which she assisted my mother with her wedding dress, Aunt Felicita created many of her sisters' and nieces' wedding gowns. She created especially beautiful wedding dresses for my sisters Jaconda and Mary.

In addition to the dressmaking she did for the family, Aunt Felicita also regularly sewed for local professional women. She worked with silks and velvets, designing and sewing her customers' ball gowns and bridal dresses.

Most family members believe that she is the author of the "Jacuzzi Family Creed," a lovely written affirmation of faith that stresses family unity, a preordained purpose for each family member, the belief that spiritual things are more important than material things, and an overarching testimony to honesty and truth. The creed also pays homage to Grandfather Giovanni and Grandmother Teresa:

Family Creed

We believe in *family unity*. We must always believe in *family unity*. We believe the past has taught each and every one of us that strength is achieved through *family unity*.

We believe that the world and each one of us has a *purpose* and that our lives are part of that *purpose*.

We believe that *spiritual things* are greater than *material things* because Man cannot live by bread alone. He must have faith in his Creator.

We believe that *honesty and truth* must guide our every action and that we must always be fair with our fellow men.

We believe in that which is *good, true,* and *honest*. Our parents taught us the fundamentals of clean, wholesome living, and we will remember them always.

Aunt Felicita also tried to instill sound values and behavior in younger family members. For example, my sister Mary remembers that her aunt patiently attempted to teach her the proper way for boys and girls to interact.

My sister Jaconda recalled that she and our sister Teresa used the money they earned during their high school summers to buy fabric for school dresses. When they were old enough, my two sisters went to Aunt Felicita's for a week or so and she taught them how to sew. My niece Beverly Jacuzzi Edgell also told me of the time spent with my sister Rachel at Aunt Felicita's home. They, too, were eager sewing students of Aunt Felicita.

During this visit, Beverly and Rachel learned more than the art of sewing. Aunt Felicita was very practical and believed that every teenager should be able to negotiate a city bus system. Therefore, in addition to sewing lessons, she sent the girls forth on various errands to secure sewing supplies. Each of these trips required that they work out the best Oakland bus route in advance and then successfully execute their mission.

Shortly after her eightieth birthday, Aunt Felicita suffered a massive stroke. She lost her speech and was fully paralyzed on the right side of her body. She lingered in an Oakland nursing home for more than a year, and passed away on November 17, 1978.

Luigi, her husband of fifty-seven years, survived her, and after Felicita's death, Aunts Stella and Cirilla faithfully visited him, helping him however they could with his domestic needs, and stayed in close touch with him for the rest of his life.

Uncle Luigi died two days after he attended Uncle Rino Marin's eightieth birthday party. Aunt Stella told me a neighbor found Luigi in his backyard, where he had suffered a heart attack. He was ninety-two.

Angelina Jacuzzi Tunesi

Aunt Angelina was born November 23, 1899. She was named after my paternal great-grandmother, Angela, in keeping with the promise Grandfather and Grandmother made to Teresa's father. I visited the city offices of San Vito al Tagliamento, Italy, and obtained Aunt Angelina's birth certificate, which shows that her given name was Angela. However, everyone always called her Angelina or "little angel."

Angelina had many things in common with her older sister, Felicita: they immigrated to the United States together; initially, they both worked in the same San Francisco garment shop; and both were engaged to be married within one year of their arrival in California. They waited to marry until the rest of the family arrived from Italy. In fact, Angelina married her husband, Peter Tunesi, in a double-ring wedding ceremony on January 30, 1921, with Felicita and Luigi.

Soon after marrying, Peter and Angelina moved to Monte Vista, near Cupertino, California, where Peter worked as a gardener. For many years, he maintained the twenty-six-acre palatial estate of a Dr. Karne. Peter also boxed professionally for a few years, and, as a hobby, raised homing pigeons. He sold the squabs as a part-time business. They had two daughters, Doris and Edith.

When their children were still young and could accompany them on the job, Aunt Angelina and Aunt Ancilla worked in a fruit-processing plant at harvest time. Aunt Angelina later worked with Aunt Stella in a San Francisco sewing factory.

I recall Aunt Angelina as being very well read and a great reciter of poetry.

Aunt Angelina was widowed in 1971. She lived alone for several years until it finally became necessary to hire a live-in caregiver. Although there had been no previous indications of violent behavior from the helper, this woman attacked Aunt Angelina late one night, breaking her hip and leaving her helpless on the floor. When Angelina's oldest daughter, Doris Adamo, phoned the next morning, and there was no answer, Doris knew something was wrong. The family was devastated.

Angelina recovered only partially; her latter years were spent in a wheelchair as a result of the beating. She alternated living with Doris and Edith. On the morning of February 17, 1990, she turned to Doris and said, "I am going now," and quietly passed away.

Ancilla Jacuzzi Bianchi

Aunt Ancilla was born November 8, 1901. She immigrated to the United States in December of 1920, along with her parents and the balance of the family who endured World War I in Italy.

While they were working on a sewer line in Bakersfield, Uncle Gelindo met Ancilla's future husband, Peter Bianchi, who had worked as a shoemaker in Italy. One day while he and Gelindo were at work, Pete was walking on top of the twelve-foot deep trench and accidentally kicked dirt down in the trench. A fellow at the bottom was hit by the dirt, became angry, and crawled up to see who had kicked it in. Uncle Pete admitted that, unfortunately, he had. The man started fighting with Pete, who, sadly, got the worse end of the fight.

Upset, Pete sought out his *friulano* friend (a fellow Italian from northeast Italy), Gelindo. Gelindo said, "Don't worry about it, I'll take care of it." After dinner, Uncle Gelindo found the man, fought him, and won the battle. After that, Pete and Gelindo were great friends. Later, Gelindo introduced Pete to his sister, Ancilla.

Aunt Ancilla married Peter Bianchi on December 23, 1922. Peter was a muscular, fairly short man of about five feet, five inches. His hobbies included amateur boxing and motorcycle racing. Peter was also in the construction business, a plasterer by trade. Aunt Ancilla worked with Aunt Angelina during harvest time, then in later years she worked with Uncle Pete in the building or repairing of homes. They had two sons, Leo, born in 1923, and John, born in 1933.

Aunt Ancilla and Uncle Pete bought a lot with Aunt Angelina and her husband, Uncle Peter Tunesi, in Monte Vista, California. The two couples divided the lot and each husband built a house. They lived side by side for many years.

Aunt Ancilla and Pa were always very close, and, in turn, Pa was especially fond of Uncle Pete. Aunt Ancilla, the tallest of the Jacuzzi sisters, with clear blue eyes and a fondness for cooking and family gatherings, was also beloved by my mother. I know my parents dearly enjoyed their visits to the ranch, and Pa was appreciative of the careful and highly skilled craftsmanship of Uncle Pete whenever he worked on our family's ranch. When they visited, Aunt Ancilla always brought wonderful baked goods from her kitchen, like rolls, cookies, and candy.

Aunt Ancilla had a beautiful singing voice and her sisters enjoyed singing with her. She would inevitably win any family singing "competitions." Aunt Ancilla and Uncle Pete also enjoyed dancing. In fact, after Ancilla's death, Uncle Pete attended dances until he was in his eighties.

Virgil recalled that, in the summer of 1933, he spent his first summer away from home and lived with Aunt Ancilla and Uncle Pete. Virgil worked with our cousin, Leo Bianchi, to help Pete with plastering and stucco jobs. He said the work was hard, but they were always happy to come home to Aunt Ancilla's fine meals.

Cousin Lola recalled that the highlight of a breakfast shared in Aunt Ancilla's home was her waffles with strawberries and cream.

My cousin Leo recalled an incident that occurred when he was a boy on one of his trips to our ranch with his father. He remembered driving along a country road near Brentwood and seeing an orchard full of ripe figs. His father, Pete, could not resist the temptation and stopped and picked a fig for each of them which they started to eat. As they were doing so, a policeman stepped out of the orchard and arrested them for stealing. Somehow, they got word to my father, who came and bailed them out of the Brentwood Jail for $25.00. Aunt Ancilla was so upset with the $25.00 fine, which was a lot of money at the time, that she tried to appeal and have the fine nullified and returned, without success.

Sadly, Ancilla died tragically in 1949, at the young early age of forty-eight, due to a series of difficulties resulting from a car accident that occurred while returning home from our ranch.

Because of her early death, I don't remember Aunt Ancilla as well as I do most of my other aunts. However, like Virgil and Lola, I recall her excellent cooking. One day stands out in my memory as very special, for it was a day our family visited her and she prepared delectable apple pancakes.

Uncle Pete passed away on June 25, 1988, at the age of ninety-three.

Cirilla Jacuzzi Benassini

Aunt Cirilla was born March 13, 1905. She, too, immigrated to America in 1920, with the last wave of our family to leave Italy. In Berkeley, on November 25, 1922, Cirilla married a homebuilder named Joseph Benassini. She was seventeen and Joseph was twenty-four. She had met Joseph at a dance party.

Uncle Joseph and his father had a successful home construction business in Oakland. When his father decided to return to Italy after several years of living in the United States, Joseph continued operating the business. Through the years, Uncle Joseph became a close friend and confidant of Uncle Rachele.

Aunt Cirilla was a very kindhearted and generous lady, and fairly formal in her bearing. I remember her as being always very well dressed and she seemed quite sophisticated in her outlook on the family, the family business, and world events in general.

Lola recalled Aunt Cirilla as being an expert cook, which I can confirm. Lola said that when her family visited Aunt Cirilla and Uncle Joseph, they always hoped Cirilla would prepare her veal pocket dish and apple pie.

Joseph worked as a home builder until, eventually, in 1943, my uncle Frank coaxed Joseph into coming to work for Jacuzzi Brothers. This was achieved by Uncle Frank offering Joseph 2,000 of Frank's shares in Jacuzzi Brothers in exchange for a Berkeley house Joseph and Cirilla owned. Cirilla told me that, at the time, the house was valued at about $5,000.

His ownership in the company helped convince Joseph to give up his construction business and join Jacuzzi Brothers as carpentry foreman. He served in this capacity for many years.

Under his skillful direction, Jacuzzi Brothers built several lovely tables with benches for family members who had eight or more children. Many of our most memorable family meals at the ranch were shared around our own family's table that Uncle Joseph designed and built. Because they each had nine children, my sister Mary and my cousin Tullio were also given similar tables.

Joseph and Cirilla's ownership in the company was disapproved of by one of the brothers, who did not want the sisters to own stock.

Cirilla and Joseph had three children: Harold, Lydia, and Norma. Uncle Joseph died in 1963 at the age of sixty-five. Aunt Cirilla, whose remembrances assisted me greatly in my writing of this book, passed away on May 15, 2000. She was ninety-five.

Stella Jacuzzi Marin

Aunt Stella was born April 3, 1907, and was also among the 1920 family immigration. Like her younger sister, Gilia, Stella's acclimation to her new country was enhanced by her years spent at Burbank Junior High in Berkeley, California. Later, Aunt Stella worked for several years as a seamstress in Berkeley and in San Francisco.

In 1925, she married Rino Marin, whom she met at a New Year's Eve party two years earlier. Her mother, Teresa, allowed Stella to go to the dance because Candido agreed to accompany her as a chaperone. Stella remembered it as a large, festive party, with immigrants attending from all over the Bay Area. Rino's heart had been so captured by Stella at that dance that he moved from Mendocino County to San Francisco the following summer, just so he could court her regularly.

Aunt Stella said that when she and Uncle Rino were leaving their wedding ceremony and headed for their small apartment in San Francisco, her father, Giovanni, said he wanted to give them some money. Grandfather told her he would like to give them more, but that he could only give them $20. Stella refused, thinking this was too much for her father to part with. She and Rino counted their money when they got home and discovered they had $7.65 between them for a week's worth of expenses. She felt foolish that she had turned down her father's offer!

Uncle Rino worked many years in the lumber industry, both before and after marrying Stella. Eventually he came to work for Jacuzzi Brothers as a salesman. Stella and Rino had two children: Silviano and George.

Grandmother Teresa sold the Byron Street house in Berkeley to Stella and Rino, who divided it into two flats. My cousin Lola and her husband, Lawrence—or "Bud," as we always called him—rented the upstairs flat. After Lola and Bud moved out they rented this flat to another couple. One evening during a dispute, the tenant pulled out a knife and stabbed Uncle Rino in the arm, requiring Rino to be hospitalized. Aunt Stella and Uncle Rino later sold the Byron Street House and bought a home in Albany, California.

In 1936, Aunt Stella and Uncle Rino purchased 11,000 shares of Jacuzzi Brothers stock from Giocondo's widow, Mary Jacuzzi. Mary needed cash in order to help her father with a business venture and send her daughter, Anna, to dress design school.

Aunt Stella said they paid $500 as a down payment to Mary, and then followed with monthly installments of $20. At the time, purchasing shares was more an act of charity than an investment, for during these Depression days, the stock was virtually worthless. In fact, a bank president advised Uncle Rino that he would not give two cents for the shares. But Aunt Mary was in a crunch, and Stella and Rino wanted to help her.

Again, this ownership in the company by a sister was not enthusiastically supported by one of the brothers, the same one who later expressed disapproval when Aunt Cirilla obtained company stock. Later, Aunt Stella and Uncle Rino sold Uncle Candido 1,000 of their shares because Candido told them he also wanted to have a total of 10,000 shares.

I recall Aunt Stella as being a strong and very opinionated person and, like all of the sisters, very intelligent. Like Felicita, she also willingly shared her sewing skills with her many nieces. Aunt Stella was deeply interested in the arts and was a skilled writer in both Italian and English. She wrote many informal remembrances, some dealing with her early life in Italy, and others focusing on her life in her new country. These writings proved invaluable to me as I reconstructed the family's early life in Casarsa.

Italy's entry into World War II as an opponent of the United States had a rather interesting effect on Aunt Stella and her family. At that time she was not yet naturalized, but was officially a citizen of Italy. Therefore, she was considered an enemy alien, and as such was required to live away from specified geographical areas of the country.

The San Francisco Bay Area was one of those restricted zones, so Aunt Stella and her family were forced to move temporarily further inland. They relocated to Grass Valley, a small town in the Sierra Nevada Mountains. They lived there for nearly a year until Stella could finalize her American citizenship. Soon after she accomplished this, Stella and her family returned to their Albany home.

Uncle Rino died in 1995 at the age of ninety-five. Aunt Stella passed away at the age of ninety-five, eight years later, on December 2, 2003.

Gilia Jacuzzi Peruzzo

Aunt Gilia, born September 15, 1908, was my grandparents' thirteenth and last child. She came to the United States with the last of the immigrating family in 1921, when she was twelve. Although still very young, Aunt Gilia already had seen much suffering and hardship during World War I.

Like Stella, Gilia benefited from being able to attend Berkeley's Burbank Junior High very soon after she immigrated. When she was fifteen, she began what would be a series of different jobs, always working as a seamstress in clothing factories. She made a variety of items, including silk blouses and ornamental pillows. At one point, she worked for the Levi Strauss Company.

Soon after her arrival in California, Gilia met a friend of the family, Jack Peruzzo. On November 7, 1925, Gilia and Jack married in Berkeley. Aunt Gilia had just celebrated her seventeenth birthday; Uncle Jack was twenty-five.

Uncle Jack worked in construction and helped build the San Franciso-Oakland Bay Bridge. He then began working for Jacuzzi Brothers part-time, selling and installing pumps. Later he joined the company full-time and was transferred to Portland, Oregon, where he managed the warehouse and shipping departments of the distribution center located there. He was with Jacuzzi Brothers for more than forty years.

Aunt Gilia, a great storyteller, assisted me every step of the way as I attempted to reconstruct our family's early years. As a young girl, she had beautiful blonde hair and bright blue eyes. She recalled that her grandfather, Teresa's father, Giuseppe Arman, once told her that she was the only child of Teresa's who resembled the Arman family.

Like her other sisters, Aunt Gilia drew on her many years of experience as a seamstress and was always more than willing to teach the art of sewing to her nieces and other family members. Lola remembered that, not only did Gilia teach her to sew, but our aunt also inspired her, when, as a young girl, she would visit Aunt Gilia's home, which was always lovingly decorated with table arrangements of fresh, beautiful flowers from her garden.

Sister Jaconda lived near Aunt Gilia on Ada Street in Berkeley. She said that Aunt Gilia regularly shared vegetables from her garden with Jaconda and her family.

Jack was a jovial man with a great smile. Like Gilia, he loved a very well-maintained garden. He was also helpful at our ranch and usually assisted with the butchering of our pigs and in the making of the *salsiccia, salami* and *prosciutto.*

Aunt Gilia and Uncle Jack had three children: Nilda, Esther, and Peter, born in 1927, 1937, and 1945, respectively. Uncle Jack died in 1979 at the age of seventy-eight. As of this writing, Aunt Gilia is ninety-eight and the only living child of Giovanni and Teresa Jacuzzi.

Regrets and Regards

In light of the sisters' shoulder-to-the-wheel support in the building of Jacuzzi Brothers, Inc., I have long been troubled over the negligible consideration the company showed my aunts pertaining to any ownership and profits. Though steps were finally taken to help correct this, it was too little, too late.

When the company was started, none of the sisters owned a financial stake in Jacuzzi Brothers. Of course, like Uncle Candido and my father, they were all still in Italy when the company was founded. When they did immigrate to the United States, six of the brothers wanted to offer shares of the company to them.

However, one brother opposed the gesture and, for whatever reason, he was not overruled. Regrettably, this created a subtle rift within the family. As the company grew and prospered, and as the family members with ownership finally started realizing profits from their stock, the inequity became an even more sensitive issue. As time passed, some of the sisters did acquire shares in the company, like the shares obtained by trade or purchase by Aunt Cirilla and Aunt Stella. Nevertheless, a later attempt to finally extend ownership in their family's company to all the sisters was again thwarted by Uncle Joseph—the same brother, who, in the 1920s, had opposed the gift of shares to the sisters. This sad episode also involved Grandmother Teresa.

Apparently, Grandmother had always regretted that she and Grandfather had not been able to give their daughters a larger dowry when each one had married. Therefore, after Grandfather passed away and before her death, she asked some family members, including my father, to purchase her shares so she could give each of her daughters a more significant, although belated, dowry.

But Pa suggested to Grandmother that it would be better if she simply divided the 6,000 shares equally between her six daughters. I can imagine Grandmother Teresa's liking this idea when she realized that it presented the perfect gift for her daughters and their growing families—ownership in the family company.

Somehow, Uncle Joseph learned of Grandmother's intentions and quickly acted to prevent her from following through. Showing up on her doorstep driving the company pickup truck, he told Grandmother Teresa

he had come to take her for a drive. However, he instead took her directly
to the American Trust Bank in West Berkeley, where he insisted that she
sell her shares to him. Grandmother, confused and intimidated, did what
Joseph demanded but was brokenhearted over such treatment by a son.

Through Joseph's acquisition of these additional shares, he and his
family became the largest shareholders of all the brothers.

When the sisters and other brothers learned what Joseph had done,
they were shocked. However, there was nothing they could do.
Grandmother Teresa died in 1943, several months after this incident,
and it was seldom mentioned. Without question Joseph's deep-seated
problem centered on greed, but a number of other instances of his inter-
actions with family members reflected a flawed moral character.

A few years later, Uncle Joseph, who continued to oppose granting
shares to the sisters, was collectively overruled. The company voted to
give each of the sisters, except Stella and Cirilla, 1,000 shares of company stock. Stella and Cirilla were left out of this agreement because of
their earlier acquisition of stock. This arrangement always seemed pecu-
liar to me, and I am saddened that Aunt Stella and Aunt Cirilla were
never actually given any shares as a gift.

However, the sisters all gained a financial stake in the company, and,
hopefully, enjoyed some profit. But I regret that they either had to pay
for it or wait so long. Their lives required much patience—and even
more forgiveness.

The Sisters-in-Law

Seven women, all of whom were of Italian heritage, married into the
Jacuzzi family. Upon doing so, each lady found herself forever linked to
a large, energetic clan. Most of these marriages were successful; all of
them were eventful.

My mother I held in the highest esteem, and I am happy that I
enjoyed good relationships with most of the sisters-in-law.

Olympia Calugi Jacuzzi

Olympia Calugi was born in Florence, Italy, on June 22, 1881. She
arrived in New York City in December 1907. Uncle Rachele and Olympia
married on June 15, 1916. Uncle Rachele was twenty-nine; Olympia,

thirty-four. They first met when Rachele was working in Los Angeles and he stayed in a boardinghouse Olympia managed. She also worked at the French laundry in Berkeley for a period of time, ironing clothes. As a result, Uncle Rachele's shirts were always meticulously pressed.

In 1920, when Jacuzzi Brothers was incorporated, Olympia became the first female to receive shares in the new corporation. She, along with each of the brothers present at the time of the incorporation, received 6,000 shares.

For most of their years together, Uncle Rachele and Aunt Olympia were not happy, and Olympia was not particularly liked by some in the family. While my mother liked her and treated her with kindness, I usually found Olympia to be very difficult and somewhat brash.

Uncle Rachele considered children the ultimate blessing of a marriage and he was often despondent over their lack of offspring. In his booklet *Creation*, Rachele offered several "social rules" for consideration. One of them seems particularly telling: "Matrimonial contracts shall be valid for only five years at a time until nature approve them with the birth of children, thus eliminating the unable, unfit, or malicious companions."

The couple separated at one point, with plans for a divorce, but reunited afterwards and stayed together until Rachele's death in 1937.

They adopted a three-year-old boy, Gordon, and Rachele and Olympia also were extremely close to Giocondo's daughter, Anna. Olympia was living with Anna at the time of her death on May 22, 1952. In her will, Olympia left Anna her Jacuzzi Brothers stock as her father Giocondo's shares were sold by her mother. Gordon inherited Uncle Rachele's shares.

After Rachele died, Aunt Olympia lived by herself for several years at the home she and Rachele owned at the corner of Addison and California Streets in Berkeley. When Olympia could no longer live by herself, she accepted Anna's invitation to live with her and her family. As Anna was helping Olympia move and ready her home for sale, she came across a number of boxes that were full of Uncle Rachele's writings, drawings, projects, experiment results, photographs, etc., and proceeded to start to burn them in the backyard.

Aunt Gilia happened to be visiting her sister Cirilla and her husband

Joseph, who lived next door to Rachele and Olympia, when she noticed Anna and asked her what she was burning. Anna proceeded to tell our aunt that it was all of Rachele's personal papers which she didn't have room for as they would take up space and she didn't think anybody would want the material. Who knows what could have been included in work papers and correspondence of this genius?

Giuseppina Piucco Jacuzzi

I often wondered who could possibly fulfill the qualification of the virtuous, hardworking woman described in the Bible's thirty-first chapter of Proverbs, but I believe my mother, Giuseppina, came close. Her Italian name, Giuseppina, is Josephine in English, but most people called her Pina.

Born on December 16, 1898, my mother was raised by her older sister, Giovanna, in the small mountain town of Soffranco, Italy. Her mother died of a stroke, when Ma was three, after working in the hot sun. Ma had the same birthday as my father, who was born eleven years earlier on December 16, 1887.

Ma was a hard worker. Her days always began very early and ended when the rest of us had gone to bed. She had a beautiful voice and loved to sing Italian songs, by herself or in concert with Pa or other relatives. She and Pa also liked to dance to Italian music, which I remember them doing many times around our large kitchen table.

Italian cooking is enjoying a rebirth of popularity in America. If only new Italian food aficionados could taste one of my mother's dishes! A fabulous, very confident cook, Ma made dishes she learned as a young girl growing up with her family in the Italian Alps.

She also prepared foods learned from Grandmother Teresa when Ma and her friend, Pasquetta, lived with the Jacuzzi family during World War I. In her later years, my grandmother often would sit in our ranch kitchen and knit or make quilts, while Ma prepared one of Grandmother Teresa's recipes. Ma also liked to prepare new recipes that she acquired through the years from her many friends in America.

Her dishes usually were made from what we grew on the farm, and they were always delicious and quite varied. I could devote an entire book to Pina Jacuzzi's cooking, but some of its highlights would include her *antipasto*, cracked Dungeness crab, fried *calamari*, *minestrone*, *cotochino*, and bean soup, her *polenta* and chicken, duck or rabbit stew, roasted duck, *gallina fritta* (fried chicken), roasted lamb with artichokes and new potatoes, escargot, and many different types of salads from our garden produce, including radicchio, *rucola* (arugula), endive, and more, as well as wonderful pastas and desserts.

My brother-in-law Don DeShields began dating my sister Teresa after his discharge from the Navy in February 1946. He recalled that he joined us for one or two meals a day for the next two months, until they were married, and his weight jumped from 130 to 150 pounds!

In the early lean years on the ranch, through the years of the Great Depression and beyond, through many decades, my mother was always very hospitable and quickly put together a meal for family and friends, even if they arrived unannounced. Extended family and friends often tell how, within an hour after their arriving for a visit, Ma would have caught a chicken from the coop, killed it, cleaned it, and have it cooking in a pot. Many of our relatives were frequent visitors to our ranch, especially for Sunday visits. After their son Aldo and his family moved to Little Rock, Uncle Joseph and Little Aunt Rena many times would join the family for Easter, Thanksgiving, and Christmas.

Ma loved her flower garden and we always had a large variety of beautiful flowers in our yard that included roses, geraniums, carnations, camellias, gardenias, stock, poppies, lilies, tulips, and marigolds. A statue of the Virgin Mary overlooked Ma's rose garden.

In her one-acre vegetable garden that was surrounded by fruit trees and grapevines, Ma grew blackberries and raspberries and planted artichokes, corn, beans, tomatoes, radishes, endive, radicchio, lettuce, peas, cauliflower, cabbage, broccoli, Brussel sprouts, onions, garlic, zucchini, squash, and other vegetables. We also grew kale to feed to our more than 150 chickens. She always sent ranch guests home with gifts of eggs, flowers, or produce.

Interestingly, the artichokes and different berries at the ranch are still producing. I doubt this longevity would have impressed us much when we were children, as the garden's laborious hoeing, watering, and weeding were our early morning summertime chores—all supervised by Ma.

At the age of seventy-six, Ma's amazing and productive life in Italy and on our Antioch ranch was featured in a 1975 newspaper story. The title of the feature story was: "Giuseppina Jacuzzi's Serene Life: The Old Customs Suit Her."

Pa passed away at the age of eighty-five, on March 10, 1973. Ma was also eighty-five when she died of Alzheimer's disease on February 2, 1984.

Giuseppina and Valeriano were blessed with eight children: my brother Virgil, born in Italy in 1919; my brother, Dante, their first child born in America, 1921; my oldest sister, Jaconda Jacuzzi Hawkins, 1923; sister Teresa Jacuzzi DeShields, 1924; sister Mary Jacuzzi Cline, 1926; sister Flora Jacuzzi Nicoletti, 1929; me, born in 1936, and our youngest sister, Rachel Jacuzzi Bruce, 1939.

Rena Villata Jacuzzi

Rena Villata was born in Italy on June 21, 1901. Uncle Frank and Aunt Rena married at the Saint Peter and Paul Cathedral in San Francisco on June 21, 1919. On their wedding day, Rena celebrated her wedding and her eighteenth birthday. Frank was thirty.

Since Uncle Joseph also married a lady named Rena, the family always used their difference in height to distinguish them. Rena Villata Jacuzzi was "Zia Rena Grande," or Big Aunt Rena" because she was about five feet, seven inches tall, while the other was "Zia Rena Piccola," or "Little Aunt Rena," since she was eight inches shorter.

Uncle Frank and Aunt Rena had two sons: Giocondo, born in 1921, and Ugo, born in 1922.

I recall several times when "Big Rena" brought a group of her girl-friends for a "girls only" visit to our ranch. They liked to party in our basement and enjoy Pa's wine. They did not want any of the kids around!

I also remember when she and Uncle Frank would come for ranch visits, usually on a Sunday afternoon. Aunt Rena typically drove. They always were very generous to us during these visits, bringing gifts of *salami*, cheese, sweets, and other foods.

After World War II, Frank and "Big Rena" bought a large Buick sedan. On several occasions, they shipped it over to Italy for their use during summer vacations. Aunt Rena told us that the sedan was very difficult to maneuver through the small Italian streets and roadways.

Big Aunt Rena's sister, Margaret Lepori, lived with Frank and Rena at their home in Berkeley a number of years before Uncle Frank's death at eighty-four, on September 24, 1973. Margaret continued to live with her sister, but died several years prior to Aunt Rena, who died on August 25, 1995, at the age of ninety-four.

Rena Beggio Jacuzzi

Rena Beggio was born on April 15, 1904, in Italy. She and Uncle Joseph married on June 12, 1920. Joseph was twenty-nine and Rena was sixteen. They lived for about five years in Berkeley with Rachele and Olympia, and Giocondo and Mary. In 1925, they built their own two-bedroom home.

Like most of the brothers' wives, Rena helped with the building of some propellers and, eventually, with the construction of the brothers' airplanes. She had several jobs, including "roughing" the propellers with a knife to shape them and placing the brass tips on the propellers.

While the brothers' airplanes were being built, Rena used Olympia's sewing machine to sew the unbleached muslin cloth for the wings. She also helped the wives, sisters, and brothers stretch the muslin over the wings.

After the tragic monoplane accident, there was a great need for extra money to keep the family going. Everyone pitched in: Ma took care of Rena's toddler, Aldo, so Rena could work at the California Bag Factory. Rena later worked for several seasons at a cannery.

Rena was four feet, eleven inches tall, and so she was always called "Little Rena." As the company grew, like most of the other spouses, Rena became a gracious hostess and support for her husband. In 1943, she and Joseph traveled to forty-two states on behalf of Jacuzzi Brothers. In 1949, the couple helped pave the way for global expansion with a trip through South America.

My brothers, Virgil and Dante, and my sister Jaconda lived with Aunt Rena and Uncle Joseph during some of their early work with Jacuzzi Brothers. Cousins Olga and Lola, also Jacuzzi Brothers employees, also were welcomed guests in the couple's Berkeley home.

Little Rena was a wonderful, giving person. She had a great memory; for example, she always remembered family birthdays, including those of all of her nieces and nephews—no small task in our family!

Joseph died in Berkeley on January 5, 1965, at the age of seventy-three, after which Rena moved to Little Rock and bought a home next door to my brother Dante and his family. Paula and I moved to Little Rock in 1980, and Paula became frustrated that our extended family didn't seem to see each other very much. So, Paula started a once-a-month card night, as a fun way to get the family together. Rena was an avid participant, until she passed away at the age of eighty-six, on December 2, 1990.

Rosie Meinero Jacuzzi

Rosie Meinero was born on December 12, 1903, in Cuneo, Italy. Throughout her long life, my godmother, Aunt Rosie, was always very resilient. After she and her parents first immigrated to America in 1904, they were caught in the 1906 San Francisco earthquake. Rosie's mother and younger brother were killed; Rosie and her father survived because he jumped out of a third-story window with the infant Rosie in his arms.

Rosie's father returned to Italy, remarried, and, in 1913, again brought his family to America. Her family life was difficult: Rosie worked long hours as a young child in a laundry and a cannery in the Bay Area.

Rosie's parents disapproved of Uncle Gelindo, and, at one point, they actually locked her up to keep her away from him. But she knew he was the right man for her, and she defied their orders to stay away from Uncle Gelindo. Rosie married Gelindo on December 14, 1918. Gelindo bought her wedding dress. He was twenty-four and Rosie was fifteen.

They shared more than thirty years together, almost all of them on the ranch. She had a tough time in the early ranch years. One of the first winters, Uncle Gelindo was bedridden for months with rheumatism. One evening, my cousins Lola, Olga, and Tullio needed milk, but Aunt Rosie had never milked a cow. However, as night approached, she grabbed a bucket and headed for the barn.

She succeeded by making several trips between the barn and Uncle Gelindo's bed, each time getting additional instructions. Finally, she was able to draw down enough milk to keep her children happy for the night. Uncle Gelindo told her that the cow would cooperate in the morning. Aunt Rosie persevered and eventually became the regular "milkmaid" until Tullio and later his brothers grew old enough to help with the milking.

When the apricot trees in the orchard that Uncle Gelindo had planted were still very small, he and Aunt Rosie planted garden peas, cabbage, onions, garlic, and black-eyed peas between them. These vegetables would generate money to keep the family going. Their daughter Lola said it was not uncommon to have a "garlic cleaning party" when Uncle Gelindo, Aunt Rosie, the children, and some of her fathers' brothers all sat around the kitchen table and broke down the heads for seed, which they planted the next day.

Aunt Rosie traveled into town to sell artichokes and other vegetables. However, this activity was often stopped because she did not have a proper license to sell food. This lack of paperwork never discouraged her and she had many regular customers. Rosie became known as the "Artichoke Lady." The *Antioch Ledger*, the local daily newspaper, ran a series of Rosie Jacuzzi's recipes on various ways to cook artichokes.

After Uncle Gelindo's death on February 4, 1950, Rosie lived for almost fifty more years. She passed away on August 4, 1999, at the age of ninety-five.

Their children were Lola, Olga, and Tullio, Rodolfo or Rudy, and Daniele. Cousin Lola, the first Jacuzzi grandchild born in America, has been one of the most enthusiastic supporters of this book. For that, and for her enduring friendship, I will always be grateful.

Mary Guarneri Jacuzzi

Mary Guarneri was born in New York on January 12, 1902. Uncle Giocondo and Aunt Mary were married on April 19, 1919. Giocondo was twenty-three; Mary was seventeen. They had a young daughter, Anna, born on February 20, 1920. Giocondo, Mary, and Anna lived in Berkeley with Olympia and Rachele, and with Joseph, Rena, and Aldo.

After Uncle Giocondo was killed in the crash of the *J-7* on July 14, 1921, Grandfather Giovanni felt strongly that Aunt Mary and Anna should continue to live with the Jacuzzi family. But Mary's father felt otherwise, and so Mary and Anna moved back in with her parents. She soon found herself, however, taking care of her bedridden mother, and since she was of small stature, she found it difficult to lift her mother while giving her care. As a result, she needed help in caring for her young daughter Anna, a pleasure which childless Aunt Olympia and Uncle Rachele were happy to help with.

The Jacuzzi family remained in close contact with Mary, particularly Uncle Rachele and Aunt Olympia. At the time of the accident, they had no children of their own, so they often took little Anna into their home for visits.

Always kind and generous to children, Uncle Rachele found a special place in his heart for Anna, thus forging a lifelong bond between him, the child, and Aunt Olympia. After Rachele and Olympia adopted Gordon, the two children were more like brother and sister than cousins.

Eventually Aunt Mary married a man who had two sons, though that union was not a happy one. She soon felt treated more like a servant and as a person who needed to be supervised—rather than as a wife—in her own home. One particularly disturbing habit of her second husband's was his tendency to count all the eggs and chickens before he left for work each morning, and to account for each of them again in the evening. Mary soon divorced him, took her Jacuzzi name back, and she and Anna returned to the home of Mary's parents.

After Rachele died, Anna remained a comforting companion to Olympia. Anna devoted almost all of her time to Olympia when her own husband, Vince Liotta, was off fighting in World War II. Anna continued to watch over Aunt Olympia during the years leading up to her death.

Gordon inherited Rachele's shares in the company, but when Olympia died in 1952, Anna inherited Olympia's shares, as an expression of gratitude for her loyalty. Anna received a special inheritance from her father, some of Giocondo's creative talent, for she worked several years as a successful dress designer in San Francisco.

Aunt Mary died on May 3, 1990, at the age of eighty-eight. When she passed away, her beloved husband, Giocondo, had been dead for almost sixty-nine years. She had truly lived another lifetime without him: At the time of Uncle Giocondo's accidental death, Warren G. Harding was president; when Mary died, our president was George H. W. Bush.

Inez Ranieri Jacuzzi

Inez Ranieri was born on November 21, 1908, in Italy. Candido and Inez married on December 26, 1925. At the time of the wedding, Candido was twenty-two and Inez was seventeen.

Although Candido received the patent for the first Jacuzzi whirlpool for the home, Aunt Inez should really receive some credit for this product. At least within the Jacuzzi family, she will be remembered as the person who conceived of the possibility of home-based water therapy. Her disabled son Kenneth's response to hydrotherapy in the hospital was the catalyst for her idea, which she then presented to Candido.

Inez always had an outgoing and happy disposition even though for much of her life she was busy and preoccupied with Ken's medical condition, which required numerous surgeries and treatments. In addition, her husband Candido's argumentative, haughty spirit and heavy travel schedule must have given her many times of stress.

Aunt Inez and Uncle Candido lived in many different places around the world. Throughout their later years together, when Uncle Candido's legal difficulties sometimes seemed insurmountable, she continued to live her life with dignity, and served as a caring and supportive helpmate during Candido's last years of ill health.

Candido and Inez had four children: Alba, John, Irene, and Kenneth. After Candido's death on October 7, 1986, at the age of eighty-three, Aunt Inez lived for almost nine more years. She died on February 21, 1995, at the age of eighty-six.

Jacuzzi Sisters and Sisters-in-Law

I am appreciative of the lives and examples of all the Jacuzzi ladies. In addition to my special thankfulness for the honor and love that my mother's life brought to me and our entire extended family, I am also especially grateful for the lives of the last three Jacuzzi sisters, Aunts Cirilla, Stella and Gilia, who freely shared their many remembrances with me as I gathered research for this book. Given the unifying strength and support provided by the Jacuzzi sisters and sisters-in-law, it is little wonder that our family accomplished so much. God has truly blessed us.

Candido Jacuzzi with the company's largest and smallest Jet Pumps

Candido and Inez Jacuzzi at the entrance of the restored ancestral home in Italy – c.1973

Chapter 15

Jacuzzi vs. *Jacuzzi*

"Io sono IL Jacuzzi!"
"I am THE Jacuzzi!
—Candido Jacuzzi, tenth child and seventh son
of my grandparents

"Alla fine, solo gli avvocati vinceranno."
"In the end, only the lawyers will win."
—Valeriano Jacuzzi, my father

Valeriano's Parable

My father used to tell a story. Two people were walking on a beach. They both saw a clam at the same time. Both of them reached for it, touching it simultaneously. They started to fight over the clam, and argued violently about which one of them owned it.

A lawyer passed by. He told them to calm down and that he could settle the argument. The lawyer took the clam, opened it, and scooped out its sweet, fresh meat. He then proceeded to eat all of it.

After he had finished eating, the lawyer held up the clam and broke it at its hinge. He gave one half of the shell to the first person and the other half to the second. So, as my father used to say, during an argument, *"Alla fine, solo gli avvocati vinceranno"*—"In the end, only the lawyers will win."

Biographies should be truthful. And since this book is a biography of my family, I want to be forthright about our blemishes and blunders. We didn't always do everything right.

People are flawed. Sometimes they turn right when they should turn left. Sometimes they buy when they should sell.

And sometimes, their own arrogance clouds good judgment.

There were some dark moments in the Jacuzzi family history when a few family members made most of the decisions and the rest felt the repercussions. This is the story of the most controversial of those decisions and the darkest of those moments.

The Trio

From the 1950s through the 1970s—the heyday of Jacuzzi Brothers, Inc.—everything was not always well in the front office. According to the flow chart, the company was run by a board of directors, all of whom were shareholders and family members. However, in reality, the company was run by Uncle Candido who held the position of general manager, with the unwavering support of Uncle Joseph and Uncle Frank.

Candido was the central power, wielding great influence. Joseph, on the other hand, though officially president, was not a strong leader and functioned principally as a figurehead in his position. Rounding out the alliance was Frank, who was on the board of directors, and almost always echoed the opinions and wishes of Candido.

At the risk of sounding disrespectful to deceased family members, I must admit that the dictatorial leadership of Candido, Joseph, and Frank was not always principled. Their style was lead-by-intimidation, with decisions often boiling down to "their way or no way." Nevertheless, they were neither ignorant nor incompetent men and the company prospered and expanded under them.

But at what cost?

Jacbros

In the late 1950s, Candido had an idea. Jacuzzi Brothers was profiting in nearly all of its international locations, but the corporate tax structure in the United States was taking a huge bite out of those profits. Why not establish another company in another country, a company that could own and control all foreign subsidiaries?

It was intended that the Jacuzzi Brothers shareholders could purchase their pro rata ownership of stock in this company, thereby soon enjoying a substantial increase in their income dividends. The foreign subsidiaries themselves would also benefit from this restructuring because more capital would be available to reinvest in their expansion and development. The preferred location for such a holding company, to be called Jacbros, was, of course, Switzerland.

Candido enthusiastically sold the concept to the Jacuzzi board of directors, who, on February 12, 1959, agreed that he should go to Switzerland to conduct further feasibility research. After some preliminary investigations, Candido visited Geneva. He secured a local attorney and a bank, and established a three-man board of directors for the new corporation, which included Candido, the attorney, and a bank representative.

On April 2, 1959, without authorization from the board and with no notification given to shareholders, Candido secretly transferred $115,500 of Jacuzzi Brothers' money to Switzerland into the Jacbros S.A., Geneva, account. The Jacuzzi board met on April 9, when Candido reported in very vague terms about his advance trip to Switzerland, without telling the board he had sent the money required for the incorporation of Jacbros.

The minutes of this meeting record that Rosie and Rudy Jacuzzi and others warned that "too much pressure was being used to push this through." But, it was clear that Candido was not going to put the brakes on his pet project. In this same meeting, he said, "This Swiss company would be the best thing we could possibly do for the best interests of the Jacuzzi stockholders."

Jacbros' incorporation was completed on May 20, 1959.

On May 28, Candido, representing Jacbros, announced the new Swiss company's decision to buy the foreign holdings and contract rights of Jacuzzi Brothers. The agreement for sale is dated May 30, 1959. Candido took the advice of his Swiss attorney and did not sign this document on behalf of Jacbros. On June 10, now acting as a director and general manager of Jacuzzi Brothers, Candido recommended that Jacuzzi Brothers sell these assets to Jacbros for the prices stated in the Jacbros' minutes. Most of the board went along with Candido's opinion as to what was a fair market value of these assets, and the recommendation was approved. In reality, although never officially disclosed to the board, the sale of the assets had been consummated thirteen days earlier.

I must mention that Candido did continue to pitch the new company to the shareholders and board of directors of Jacuzzi Brothers. He sent a November 10, 1960, letter to all shareholders that outlined the plan. This first formal communication on the subject of Jacbros ever given to shareholders stated the pro rata cost for Jacbros participation. But by the time he did this, and had persuaded most of the shareholders to join the venture, Jacbros S.A., Geneva, had already been in existence for about sixteen months.

The November 10 shareholder letter also disclosed for the first time that Jacuzzi Brothers' foreign assets were sold at less than book value to Jacbros. Candido's explanation for this was that the risk of operating a business in a foreign country more than made up for any cost discrepancies.

Still, based on what had been presented and disclosed, it sounded like a good idea and most of the Jacuzzi Brothers shareholders, including me, invested. I received Candido's November letter while I was back at Berkeley, working on my second undergraduate degree, and working part-time for Jacuzzi Brothers.

Like me, more than half of the Jacuzzi Brothers' shareholders were company employees. Although Candido's flamboyant style often was questioned, most shareholders respected his power. Aware of his dominant position, he had assumed everyone would accept the benefits of his plan. He never counted on strong resistance.

Jacbros, a Swiss corporation with limited tax liability and the capacity to provide more capital for all Jacuzzi foreign subsidiaries, made perfect sense to Candido. He had thought the structure through and could see only good coming from it.

Others weren't so sure. They had questions, mostly about the proposed tax advantages, and they wanted those questions answered before the books were closed and investment options were withdrawn. They didn't want to miss out on a good opportunity . . . if it really was a good one. But neither were they happy about losing earnings from the foreign subsidiaries of Jacuzzi Brothers, a side effect of Jacbros. Furthermore, the purchase of assets from Jacuzzi Brothers for less than their book value bothered them. Candido's statement about linking the price to the "risk of operating in foreign countries" didn't reassure everyone.

It was a classic catch-22 for the hesitant shareholders: They would either miss a good opportunity or lose part of their own profit base.

Confrontation

On the morning of November 14, 1960, Aunt Stella's son, George Marin, visited Candido's office to examine documents, including the Jacbros by-laws. On this same morning, George's father, Rino, met with Uncle Joseph and Uncle Frank to discuss Jacbros. Then, later that same morning, Rudy Jacuzzi, Aunt Rosie's son, called Uncle Candido. Rudy requested an appointment for the purpose of discussing Jacbros. The meeting was arranged for that afternoon.

When Rudy arrived, he explained to Candido that he and a few other family shareholders had some misgivings about Jacbros and wanted some issues clarified, or perhaps reconsidered. Others, including my father and I, also were present at this meeting.

The conversation was amicable until Rudy began jotting down notes. Candido adamantly objected to this and informed Rudy that if he wished for notes to be taken, he would call in his secretary, Janet Gregor. Janet, and Janet, alone, Candido insisted, would take notes in *his* office. Rudy must have considered this ridiculous, for he soon got up and left. I, too, was quite surprised at Candido's reaction. Mistrust was quickly gaining momentum.

Looking back, I think it may have been at this point, on November 14, when the frustrated shareholders decided that this matter could not be resolved on a personal level. Just a few days later, they hired attorney Richard F. Swisher to represent them.

On November 17, 1960, a petition was delivered to Joseph, president; Candido, vice-president; and Giocondo (Frank's oldest son who was named after our uncle who died in the crash), secretary—the officers of Jacuzzi Brothers, Inc.

The document was signed by ten shareholders: Rudolfo Jacuzzi, Rino Marin, Silviano Marin, Giordano Jacuzzi, Anna Liotta, Frank Negherbon, Lydia Negherbon, George Marin, Stella Marin, and Rosie Jacuzzi.

The petition requested that a meeting of all shareholders be called to discuss "the transfer, assignment, conveyance, or delivery of domestic and foreign assets of this corporation, and all other acts directly or indirectly relating thereto. . . . "

The fact that the family members felt it necessary to communicate through an attorney indicates where this confrontation was headed.

The meeting request was never granted.

Instead, Candido immediately sent a letter, dated November 18, 1960, to his sister Stella, imploring her to reconsider her actions. He bluntly requested that she withdraw her name from the petition, which a few other petitioners had done by this date. He advised Stella that by doing so, she would remain neutral in this matter, which was what he said he desired.

He quoted in Italian some proverbs of their mother and my grandmother, Teresa, including: *"Con buona volonta non esiste problemi che assieme no si puo risolvere."* "With goodwill, there is no problem that exists, that together, we cannot resolve."

However, on November 17, Rino Marin, George Marin (Aunt Stella's husband and son, respectively), and Rosie Jacuzzi (Uncle Gelindo's widow) had also signed a paper appointing Mr. Swisher to investigate certain corporate documents on their behalf—a legal request in keeping with the company by-laws and corporation laws in the state of California.

Mr. Swisher then sent a letter to Joseph, Candido, and Giocondo, via certified mail, saying that he would call at the Jacuzzi Brothers offices on November 21, at 1:30 p.m., to make this inspection.

This group of shareholders was disgruntled for several reasons. First, they had suspicions that Candido had been receiving income from the Mexico operation managed by his son John, and that Candido had not been reporting this income to the board of directors or to the Internal Revenue Service. Many months later, these suspicions were proved correct.

Furthermore, some were displeased with the royalty arrangement that Candido had established wherein he received one percent of the gross sales of the Hydromassage product, money he personally designated for the support of his son Kenneth.

His style also worked against him. It was no family secret that Candido had closely managed things within the company, including appointments and salaries, to favor those within his immediate family.

All together, these actions cost him the respect and trust of the family-at-large.

Candido also made an unpopular decision when he dismissed Mr. Nathan Gray in May 1956. Mr. Gray, who had been Jacuzzi Brothers' corporate attorney for about twenty-five years, was hired by Uncle Rachele in the early 1930s and served for a while as the company's board chairman. Candido retained Mr. Joseph Alioto of San Francisco as Gray's replacement. Mr. Alioto, who would later serve as the mayor of San Francisco, from 1968–76, had not had the time to earn the respect of many shareholders and of the family. In retrospect, some began to view this appointment as another of Candido's crafty maneuvers.

Upon receiving Mr. Swisher's letter, Candido attempted to reach Alioto, only to learn that he was out of town and would not return for a few days. Candido talked by telephone to Alioto, who recommended that Candido request that this investigative visit to the Jacuzzi Brothers offices be delayed long enough so that Alioto could be present. Perhaps this was just lawyering, or perhaps it was a legitimate request. Either way, it appeared that the sides in this disagreement were growing more distant. The makings of a bitter battle seemed to be brewing.

Even though tension was building, there was still some effort being made by certain family members to talk directly with one another, rather than through their respective attorneys. I believe that at this point, both parties sincerely wanted a solution without litigation.

As he had reached out earlier to Stella, Candido continued to telephone unhappy shareholders in attempts to answer their questions regarding Jacbros. He was not willing, however, to consider abandoning the idea. He only wanted to gain their support for a decision that was already made. So even though there was communication, the tone was tense rather than conciliatory.

Mr. Swisher arrived at the Jacuzzi Brothers offices on the day and time he had designated, and he was denied access. Candido asked Swisher if he had received his letter requesting a postponement. The ethics of Uncle Candido and Alioto seem questionable to me, since surely another attorney from Alioto's office could have been assigned for the document review, if one was indeed necessary. A case can also be made that Candido was illegally denying board members access to company records.

Swisher replied that, yes, he had received the letter, which was not an outright refusal. As legal representative of certain shareholders and directors, he had a right to inspect the books, but still Candido refused him access. Swisher then went immediately to the county courthouse in Martinez, where he obtained a court order demanding access to the books and documents in question.

When presented with this court order on November 22, 1960, Candido again denied the request, using the excuse that the court order gave the company until December 2 to comply. In addition to Swisher, this court document lists Nathan Gray as the petitioners' second attorney—the same Nathan Gray who was the well-respected, former counsel for Jacuzzi Brothers.

A legal showdown was now inevitable.

On November 23, Candido, Joseph, and Giocondo met with Alioto. During that meeting, Alioto called Swisher and informed him that the way was now clear for him to come to the Jacuzzi Brothers' offices and make his inspection. The plaintiffs learned that no permit for the sale of Jacbros stock had been obtained from the State of California.

That same afternoon, two gentlemen from the Division of Corporations of the State of California presented Candido, Joseph, and Giocondo with a "Desist and Refrain Order." In part, this document, instructed:

> You are hereby directed not to offer, solicit, negotiate for the sale of, issue, deliver, or collect any consideration for the sale of issuance of any shares of capital stock, promissory notes, or any other securities in connection therewith of JACBROS S.A. GENEVA. . . .

Jacbros was, for the time being, dead in the water, even though Candido was fully engaged in attempting to revive his project. On December 13, 1960, he sent an eight-page letter to Jacuzzi family shareholders, employing his best rhetoric in calmly reviewing the chronology of events that led up to the "Desist and Refrain Order." Each time Candido discussed a dissenting family member and shareholder in this letter, he used patient and reasonable language, but also dismissed most of their objections by stating: ". . . I felt we were dealing with family and it would not be necessary to become so formal when dealing among ourselves."

In this same letter, Candido claimed that he revealed pertinent Jacbros information in a board meeting six months earlier, but because this data was not in its "finished form," it was omitted from the official minutes.

Perhaps the most interesting passage dealt with Uncle Rachele. Uncle Candido discussed how the management of the company was thrust upon him with Uncle Rachele's death. This revised the company's history, because, in 1937, Uncle Rachele had been abruptly removed from his position as head of the company by Uncles Candido, Frank, and Joseph. This overnight power grab occurred months before Uncle Rachele's death.

Strangely, Candido closed by discussing a psychiatrist's viewpoint of paranoia, and then shared his hopes that this dissent will end, because "we would like to celebrate the coming Christmas holidays in harmony; bringing peace again to all concerned and working toward good will together."

But there would be no peace in sight for the Jacuzzi family.

Jacuzzi vs. *Jacuzzi*

The disagreement between the shareholders worsened in 1961. Rudy continued to ask Candido for more information, both by phone and by letter. In the Jacuzzi Brothers' shareholders meeting of April 20, 1961, Rudy and Rino questioned the basic issues swirling around Jacbros: its formation, the sales agreement regarding the Jacuzzi Brothers' foreign assets, and the tax implications.

The likelihood of reconciliation grew more remote.

During this same period, in an effort to have their side represented in the ongoing struggle, the minority shareholders had elected Mr. Swisher to the company's board of directors. But upon his election, the board's membership was suddenly reduced from seventeen to six, and the frequency of board meetings was simultaneously reduced from monthly to quarterly.

On September 18, 1961, Mr. Gray and Mr. Swisher met with Mr. Alioto and his associate, Mr. Grant Calhoun, to discuss a possible compromise. The lawyers on both sides seemed to make headway, as Alioto asked for specific proposals from Gray so that Alioto could, in turn, communicate these requests to Candido. These were given to Alioto the morning of September 20 and Alioto assured Gray that he would get back to him very soon.

Twelve days passed. Gray telephoned Alioto, but was unable to reach him. The next day, on October 3, Gray received a letter from Alioto, stating that Candido "will be out of the country for two weeks. Upon his return, we will be able to conclude the matter of arriving at a decision with respect to your proposal."

This continued pattern of evasion ignited a furious response, and that same day, Swisher resigned from the Jacuzzi Brothers board of directors. His primary reason for quitting was stated in his letter dated October 3, in which he said that since Jacuzzi Brothers board members are unwilling or unable to be autonomous "due to their being completely dominated by Candido Jacuzzi, I feel any efforts by myself to serve the company by continuing as a director are utterly futile and a waste of time."

Also on October 3, 1961, Gray sent a letter stating that an official complaint had been drafted, and that if steps were not taken by October 13 to resolve the stipulated issues through a compromise, a complaint would be filed in court.

Such steps were not taken, a compromise was not reached, and the lawsuit, *Jacuzzi* vs. *Jacuzzi*, went forth. The plaintiffs were Rudy (Rodolfo) Jacuzzi, Rosie Jacuzzi, Rino Marin, Stella Marin, Silviano Marin, and George Marin. This group—Aunt Rosie and her son, Rudy, together with Aunt Stella and her family—owned a substantial, although minority, interest in the company, approximately 19 percent of the voting shares and 15 percent of the nonvoting shares.

Aunt Stella recalled the day that she, her husband, Rino, and her sons signed the complaint as being a very sad day for all concerned. Rino and her sons, Silviano and George—all Jacuzzi Brothers' employees—were fired and told never to attempt to enter the company's property. Other plaintiffs immediately received equally rough treatment:

Aunt Rosie's pension was cut off and her son Tullio, a Jacuzzi employee, was followed by a private detective. Aunt Rosie's pension, which was earned by Uncle Gelindo, was never restored. In fact, the last check she received and had already deposited, was not honored by the bank as a stop-payment order was placed on it by the company.

The complaint's defendants were: Jacuzzi Brothers, Inc., Candido Jacuzzi, Joseph Jacuzzi, Giocondo Jacuzzi, my brother Dante, Carmelo Guarneri, and Jacbros, S.A., Geneva.

Specifically, the intent of the suit was twofold, as explained in Nathan Gray's October 3, 1961, letter:

> . . . to set aside the purported transfer of a substantial part of the assets of Jacuzzi Bros., to Jacbros, S.A., Geneva . . . [and] to ask the court to declare void the contract that Candido Jacuzzi obtained from the corporation for the payment to him of sums of money equal to one percent of the gross sales of Hydromassage over a period of approximately seventeen years. . . .

The plaintiffs also requested Candido's removal as a director, based on the allegations in the complaint. Jacbros was now on full hold and there was nothing to do but to carry on or attempt to carry on with "business as usual" at Jacuzzi Brothers—a difficult task when coworkers, who are also family, have a lawsuit pending between them. During this same time, our new plant and corporate offices in Little Rock and a plant in nearby Lonoke, Arkansas, were opened and established.

Attempts for a compromise continued. Dante and Virgil consulted with Mr. John Gilmore, a St. Louis attorney who had represented Jacuzzi Brothers for many years. Mr. Gray made what seemed to be a reasonable proposal to Gilmore. The proposal was basically for a mediation and a judgment by unbiased parties. Gilmore agreed that the idea made sense. Candido fired Gilmore when he heard of his approval of the mediation plan.

My father also tried many, many times to seek a compromise between the two parties. He recalled how frustrating this became, for it seemed that most of the time, key decisions had already been made between the attorneys or between Candido and an attorney, before a critical meeting started. He found it particularly heartbreaking when he reached out to Aunt Stella, who refused to see him.

On February 26, 1965, the plaintiffs sent a letter to all shareholders. This mailing also contained a letter from Gray that outlined the plaintiffs' efforts to date to reach a peaceful solution.

Finally, courtroom proceedings began on January 13, 1967, some five years and three months after the complaint was filed.

In the meantime, much work had been done through collecting evidence and conducting depositions. One huge accomplishment had been the valuation of certain Jacuzzi Brothers holdings, including the company's operations in Canada and Mexico, as well as determining the amount of royalty income that had been paid to Jacbros by way of licensing agreements from factories in Mexico, Canada, the Philippine Islands, Chile, Argentina, Columbia, Pakistan, Australia, Brazil, Sweden, and New Zealand. This information was needed in order to determine precisely how much Jacuzzi Brothers' money had already been placed in the Jacbros coffers.

The case was tried in Superior Court, Alameda County, California, and was heard by the Honorable Lyle E. Cook. There was no jury.

After many weeks of listening to testimony, examining evidence, and reviewing corporate documents, Judge Cook issued an interlocutory opinion on April 14, 1967. The court ruled in favor of the plaintiffs, stating that they had "met their burden of proof." The judge further instructed that when his final judgment was issued, all transactions involving Jacbros would be made null and void. He then urged the Jacuzzi Brothers' family members and company shareholders to make every effort to work out agreeable terms to settle the matter financially, although he said in Candido's case "there is evidence . . . of hardheadedness."

The judge also addressed the fact that many of Candido's statements, both in court and in his depositions, were inaccurate, especially regarding the company's Mexican subsidiary. He noted in particular the detrimental effect of not producing John Jacuzzi, Candido's son and manager of the Mexican operation, as a witness. The court further cited certain tax exposure problems inherent in Jacbros, one of which was the possibility that Jacbros could be considered a personal holding company.

Judge Cook added that he had "admiration for this great family. . . . The fact that the actions that led to this lawsuit cannot be condoned . . . is no denial of the genius which has manifested itself throughout the history of this organization."

Negotiations between parties took place through their attorneys during the summer and fall. Virgil, taking a lead in many of the Jacuzzi Brothers, Inc.'s strategic discussions, noted that Candido often seemed understandably distracted and agitated. Sometimes, however, Candido's mood would turn hostile, with his animosity often aimed at Virgil.

One of these incidents occurred when Candido learned that Virgil, under the direction of our Little Rock attorney, Bill Bowen, called two of the plaintiffs to see if they might be amenable to something short of a total "buyout" of their shares. Virgil did all the computations and was afraid that a complete buyout could prove disastrous to the fiscal health of the company. Candido reacted by calling Virgil a "Judas" and a "second-class citizen." Virgil was upset and angered by our uncle's callous behavior, especially since this scene played out in the presence of several other individuals.

In these internal company discussions, Candido always argued that the Swiss partners would be very agitated if Jacbros was dissolved and that there could be legal actions taken. Bowen countered that Judge Cook couldn't care less. As the summer waned, Candido strongly lobbied for an appeal, but his attorneys, and most of his fellow defendants, including Dante, discouraged him. They told Candido that any appeal would simply extend the entire sordid affair by about three years, and that the chances for the company's winning on appeal were slim to nonexistent.

Also, during the summer of 1967, Mr. Alioto began showing decidedly less interest in his client's case. For example, Alioto promised Candido he would attend an important planning meeting in Little Rock on August 4, but at the last minute, he sent a substitute. When the other attorney showed up, Candido tried to reach Alioto on the telephone, but was told that "Mr. Alioto is too busy to take your call." This perceived slight greatly depressed and angered Candido.

However, by the time Judge Cook issued his final judgment on December 11, 1967, the matters had been negotiated and settled. It was agreed that:

- All transactions pertaining to Jacbros were null and void, and that all assets would be restored to Jacuzzi Brothers, Inc.
- Jacbros would pay Jacuzzi Brothers back all royalty income received through licensing agreements.
- Payment would be made to all Jacuzzi Brothers shareholders who had not invested in Jacbros, bringing them up to an equal financial standing with those who had invested (proportionate to the amount of stock they owned in Jacuzzi Brothers).
- All court costs and legal fees incurred by the plaintiffs would be paid by the defendants.
- All litigation between plaintiffs and defendants would be terminated and all rights of appeal waived.
- All plaintiffs had the option of selling their stock back to the company for an agreed upon price of $53 per share.

This nearly seven-million-dollar settlement was a solid victory for the plaintiffs. The judge cited several bases for his decision. Candido, the judge noted, had been "strangely reluctant" to fully disclose certain information about both the entire Jacbros plan and his dealings as general manager.

Also, the fact that certain Jacuzzi Brothers personnel were never called as witnesses by the defendants was a negative, as it was assumed that their testimony would have been damaging. Central to this ruling was that the defendants could not prove that the transactions involving the sale of assets from Jacuzzi Brothers to Jacbros had been carried out in good faith and fairness.

Life Inside the Executive Suite

Janet Gregor, later Janet Gregor Merker, Candido's secretary from 1955 until 1964, offered a true insider's perspective of Jacbros and Candido's managerial style. Having begun her career with Candido and Jacuzzi Brothers in Richmond, California, Janet followed Candido to Little Rock, where, among many other assignments, she was responsible for setting up the Jacuzzi Brothers' new management offices.

Candido, or C.J., as she always called him, was remarkably candid with Janet, who, in turn, was generous in sharing her memories with me.

In addition to her work for the company, Janet also did almost all of the Candido Jacuzzi family's personal banking. This included handling personal accounts for Candido, his wife, Inez, and his son, Kenneth.

She told me of meeting minutes that, at Candido's direction, were either filed with their contents incomplete, destroyed entirely, or not sent to a participant who might disagree with the accounting of what had happened in the meeting.

Janet described these actions as: "Old C.J. was a great one for keeping the facts hidden."

Janet said that in the early 1960s, all of the Jacbros materials and documents were "filed" in the locked trunk of Candido's Cadillac. Any time Janet needed to work with any of the documents in the Jacbros file, such as its check ledger, deposit slips, et cetera, she drove the Cadillac away from the Jacuzzi office property, usually to her own home, and worked from there.

Janet thought this was ridiculous, but as a dutiful employee, she cooperated with this cloak and dagger routine. As a professional, though, she did not agree with many of Candido's decisions. Admitting that she and Candido frequently argued, she felt he eventually understood her views. Others were not so lucky: Any other employee questioning Candido would invariably storm out of his office, sometimes, Janet noted, in tears.

According to Janet: "C.J. could be very cruel and if he felt an individual crossed him, he let him or her know."

Her written version of the Jacbros time line showed internal dissent forming early against the plan, from staff members such as a Jacuzzi Brothers accountant and a C.P.A. Janet also said Joe Alioto advised Candido that it might be possible for the Jacbros corporation to be judged as a "personal holding company," making its individual shareholders responsible for the taxes levied. But Candido dismissed this early advice and instead pushed on with his project.

After the "Desist and Refrain" order was delivered, Janet witnessed Candido instructing a few family shareholders to predate their checks, so Jacbros could continue.

Candido was a smart person who realized that Janet was an invaluable and very sharp secretary, so in June of 1962, he sent her as his emissary to Geneva, where she contacted the Jacbros attorneys on Candido's behalf. She was told that a "stamp tax" had not been paid, so after a telephone call was placed to Candido in Little Rock, another secretary drove the Cadillac off the Jacuzzi Brothers' premises to obtain the checkbook. After this, Candido realized that this "protection" of the Jacbros file caused too many logistical problems. From that point forward, most of the Jacbros information was kept in his own office.

Some Jacbros paperwork, however, was never part of the Cadillac filing system. These documents were always stored in Monterrey, Mexico, and, whenever Candido felt it necessary, Janet made trips there to work with the file. For example, all the Jacbros stock certificates were held there.

Certain monies from the Jacbros account were sent directly to Candido's Mexican bank account. As later investigations revealed, Candido also received about $17,000 each year from 1959 through 1966 from the Mexican subsidiary. This was his Mexican "salary." (In today's dollars, that's approximately $106,000 per year, since according to the U.S. Department of Labor, it now takes $6.25 to buy an item that cost one dollar in 1962.)

Candido told Janet that any money he made for his work in Mexico stayed in his Mexico bank. All the Mexican subsidiary reports, unlike those from our other foreign subsidiaries, were sent to Candido's home and never came across Janet's desk. She later discovered that Joseph Jacuzzi also was putting money in Mexican high-interest-yielding investments. She did not believe Uncle Joseph fully understood the implications of not properly reporting the interest income on these investments.

Janet also interpreted the company's headquarters move to Little Rock in an interesting light. She suspected that Candido embraced the idea because he was tired of dealing with California law and courts and, for whatever the reason, thought that life in Arkansas would be "loose and free."

By the conclusion of the lawsuit, Janet had decided to leave Jacuzzi Brothers. Just before her departure, Candido withdrew all his money from his United States banking accounts and put them in his Mexican ones, and also gave his Jacuzzi Brothers shares away to his family and put his home in his wife's name.

After this, Candido told Janet: "So if they come after me, I don't got no money."

In 1965, back in California, Janet became concerned about how much damaging information she knew, both about Candido's personal affairs and his operations of the company. On January 12, 1965, at the advice of attorney Dick Swisher, she began to meticulously record events that had happened, always noting if there were any witnesses present. This apprehensiveness was certainly a sad turn of events for an employee who had been so faithful and, who, in the beginning, had put so much trust and hope in Candido's abilities.

In her February 26, 1966, letter to attorney Nate Gray, Janet wrote about her time with Candido and Jacbros:

> Every time I talk to you and try to remember back about certain things, I get upset and often out of balance. I fought the old boy as long as I could. I put up with things that very few (if any) people would tolerate; I became involved in situations that were possibly fraudulent and certainly underhanded. . . . I watched the web being drawn tighter and tighter and knew I had to get out. . . . I am sorry for a few people who became involved and didn't know how to get out of it.

Having already served as a witness in the *Jacuzzi* vs. *Jacuzzi* lawsuit, on June 15, 1966, Janet began what would be a series of interviews and sworn depositions for the IRS, "in the matter of the income tax liability to the United States of Mr. Candido Jacuzzi."

Clearing the Air

I have my own thoughts about why the Jacbros issue became so volatile within our family, and it didn't happen overnight. It's about trust—and the lack thereof.

Candido did not enjoy the trust of many family members. Mistrust isn't usually formed in a vacuum; usually there are concrete reasons for its existence. In Candido's case there were several. His leadership had been dictatorial. His financial arrangements were sometimes questionable, and he favored his own household over others.

It seemed to some that Candido forgot that it was not he, but Uncle Rachele, who had founded Jacuzzi Brothers, an attitude which many family members viewed as the most severe form of disrespect and arrogance. I remember at our wedding, Paula had relatives present who had not yet met all of my family. One of them innocently asked Uncle Candido if he were a member of the Jacuzzi clan. He answered, "I am THE Jacuzzi!"

With all his misdeeds soiling his reputation, Candido had been courting disaster for a long time. His secretive dealings raised suspicions against him, and when he tried to establish Jacbros, the stakes were just too high for the family to acquiesce. I would like to think Candido intended to benefit all Jacuzzi Brothers shareholders, but he lost their trust by his hardheadedness and by stifling any and all opposition.

In the end, it is difficult to estimate the total damage of the Jacbros episode. Needless to say, during the more than five tumultuous years of the lawsuit, the family suffered greatly. Social functions and family gatherings remained civil, but something had been lost forever. There is no joy in knowing that your family had to go to court in order to settle a dispute. There is shame. There is tension. There is regret. And, for some, there is bitterness.

The company suffered also. Bank loans were necessary to fund the stock repurchasing program mandated by the trial verdict. Court costs and legal fees were astronomical. Several family members left the company's employment, and we all lost some of our heart.

Royalty Payment Revisited

While the lawsuit's final judgment resulted in Jacbros being declared null and void, it did not address the 1 percent royalty agreement that the dissident shareholders asked the court to void, undoubtedly because they sold all their interest in Jacuzzi Brothers back to the company.

After Kenneth Jacuzzi returned to the United States in 1976, after his tenure as manager of Jacuzzi Europe in Italy, he filed a suit against the company, claiming he should be receiving a 1 percent royalty on the gross sales of all Jacuzzi hydrotherapy products such as the jet fittings sold by the Jacuzzi Brothers company and therapy products manufactured by its foreign subsidiaries. However, in researching the original royalty contract that was made with his father, Candido, it was found that the royalty was only to have been paid on the Jacuzzi Portable Hydromassage covered by Candido Jacuzzi et al.'s patent #2,738,787. Somehow he was being paid 1 percent on the gross sales of all Jacuzzi Research hydrotherapy products, which were then predominantly complete whirlpool baths.

As the Jacuzzi Brothers were trying to go public at this time, rather than addressing this controversial royalty agreement and risking possible troublesome publicity, Jacuzzi's president, Ray Horan, proposed and obtained board of directors approval to replace the royalty contract with a yearly adjusted remuneration agreement for the balance of Ken's life.

A Downward Spiral

Soon after the Jacbros lawsuit was settled, Candido began to have serious trouble with the Internal Revenue Service, due to the revelations about his business affairs that came to light during the lawsuit. In 1969, he was indicted by a U.S. grand jury in San Francisco on five counts of income tax evasion.

He escaped to Italy, where he remained a fugitive in the renovated home of his youth, and also spent time in Canada and Mexico. As his problems with the IRS worsened, he moved to Puerto Vallarta, Mexico, where he and his wife, Inez, built a villa. He always proclaimed his innocence, as he did in an August 18, 1975, *Sports Illustrated* story about Candido and the whirlpool bath: "I had reasons for not facing trial, but I'm guilty of nothing. Nothing! The government was trying to persecute me."

He further rationalized by oddly blaming his situation on the spectacular growth of Jacuzzi Brothers: "When there were just us brothers, we'd put a bottle of wine on the table and solve our problems. Today, there are too many of us to do that."

Sadly, in 1975, just before the fiftieth wedding anniversary of Candido and Inez, Uncle Candido suffered an aneurysm in Puerto Vallarta. He needed sophisticated medical treatment and wanted to go to Houston, but before he could return to the United States, his condition worsened and he became paralyzed from his waist down.

Upon his arrival in Houston, Candido was put under "hospital arrest" by the IRS. He finally was able to settle with the government for about

$400,000, based on his reputed original liability of more than one million dollars. He sold his Mexican home, and lived for a few years in Lafayette, California, near his daughter, Alba. I visited Uncle Candido several times while he was living in Lafayette, where he had round-the-clock care.

At the end of his life, Uncle Candido must have undergone a significant amount of soul searching, for he had someone take him to many family members so that he could apologize face to face for the way he had conducted himself within the family and in his management of the company. During my visits with him in Lafayette, he was a repentant man. An indication of his change of heart was a discussion he had with my sister Teresa, when he asked her if she thought he would be allowed into heaven in light of his actions.

On October 7, 1986, Candido Jacuzzi, the youngest of the Jacuzzi brothers, died in Arizona. His daughter, Irene, passed away from cancer a few months later.

Candido's apology did not erase the wrong that was done, but it went a long way toward rebuilding lost respect. I remember some of the wrong things my uncle did, but I also remember that, at the end of his life, he tried to right his wrongs. On my part, I have forgiven him.

Happily, I have some good memories of him. One of these recollections is from 1973, the year in which my father died. After Pa's passing, my sister, Rachel, her husband, Neil, and I brought Ma to Italy so she could visit her family in the Italian Alps. We also spent some memorable days with Candido and Inez at the Jacuzzi ancestral home in San Vito al Tagliamento, where they were very gracious and hospitable hosts.

One day while there, I visited the Jacuzzi-Europe plant with Uncle Candido. After work, we stopped in at several cantinas to taste Candido's favorite fruit-flavored *grappa*. I'm glad I was able to share these light-hearted moments with him while he once again lived in his childhood home.

Jacuzzi Ancestral Home

It is with regret for many of the Jacuzzi family members that the Jacuzzi ancestral home in San Vito al Tagliamento is somehow no longer in the family. The home, which my grandparents so tediously strived to build and where all their thirteen children were raised, was leased to others when the family left for America in 1920. It eventually sold in 1975.

As mentioned in the narrative of this book, my grandparents retained ownership of the home and their separate remaining parcels of land when they immigrated to California in 1920. Later, before the decade was over, they sold these properties to Jacuzzi Brothers for $3,000, plus 6,000 shares of Jacuzzi stock that Giovanni had already received from his sons several years earlier.

When Jacuzzi–Europe S.p.A. was built in Valvazone, Italy, it was built on one of the parcels that was owned by Jacuzzi Brothers as a result of the purchase of the family properties. In 1969, when Candido fled to Italy, he immediately embarked upon an ambitious restoration project to turn the home of his youth into a well-appointed residence, complete with an elevator and an additional wing that was to serve as a Jacuzzi historical museum. This wing replaced the stables and the hayloft.

The cost of this restoration project was estimated to have been over four hundred thousand dollars, as a good part of the old stone works and structure of the house had to be taken apart and rebuilt.

These restoration costs—which were born by Jacuzzi–Europe S.p.A., —along with this subsidiaries' poor performance and cash position, compounded by a desire to clear up the financials for an anticipated public offer of Jacuzzi Brothers stock, led to the sale of the ancestral home for a reported $100,000.

When Candido restored the home he equipped it with a very elaborate and ornately crafted wrought-iron gate. Before the home was sold, he had the gates removed and buried on the property of Jacuzzi–Europe S.p.A. for a reason known only to him. They were later discovered after the sale of Jacuzzi Brothers in 1979, when Jacuzzi Europe constructed an addition to the plant.

CHANGES

Valeriano and Giuseppina Jacuzzi visit to Brazil. Shown from left:
Adults, back row: Paula, Giuseppina, Remo, and Valeriano
Children front row: Jennifer, Gretchen, Loretta, Remo V., and Matthew

Paula Jacuzzi introduction at São Paulo Women's Luncheon – 1968

Chapter 16

Brazil

"Chi non risica non rosica."
"Nothing ventured, nothing gained."
—Rachel Jacuzzi Bruce, my sister

Uncle Candido's letter of December 20, 1967, asking me to take over the Brazil subsidiary arrived soon after the Jacbros lawsuit was settled. I soon learned this was a last-ditch effort to make a go of a subsidiary that was losing money. If I were unable to turn the company around, Jacuzzi Brothers planned to close it. The Brazilian subsidiary faced difficult times in the years before my arrival. An unstable social and economic period culminated in the Brazilian military's taking over power. So, although I was startled by the offer, I also was inspired by the challenge.

I met with Uncle Candido on January 4, 1968, and told him I felt the job was a challenge, but that with all due respect the Brazilian job should report to the board of directors, rather than to him because of his misdeeds revealed during the Jacbros lawsuit. These included his unwillingness to try to compromise with the plaintiff shareholders prior to litigation, his unauthorized Mexican salary, and his unwillingness to testify during the lawsuit. We ended the meeting with Candido stating he was not going to be a figurehead president.

On January 12, I received a letter from Candido acknowledging my desire to work more closely with the board of directors, which he asked all the board members to sign as well. In response, I wrote that I appreciated the job offer and the promised relationship with the board, but that in fairness to both the company and to me, I wanted to take an exploratory trip to Brazil for several weeks, and if I found the prospects favorable, I would then return with my wife, Paula, to explore what life in Brazil would mean for our family. I also asked that if we decided not to accept the responsibility that it would not be held against me for future advancements with the company.

To be quite frank, Candido's response of January 23, 1968, took me aback. He said the company could not set a precedent with these conditions, and that my answer had to be yes or no. In response, I wrote to him and the board of directors, declining the offer. In the midst of this correspondence, my brother Virgil wrote to advise the board of directors that Jacuzzi should liquidate its investment in Brazil after eight years of losses, and no single person could be expected to take on such a responsibility. Not surprisingly, I started to look into other employment opportunities.

On February 8, Candido wrote me a three-page letter, which he indicated that he read to the entire board of directors, basically asking me again to please take the responsibility. He stated that Virgil was trying to discourage me with his letter to the board, and my decision declining the offer was made without my knowing anything about Brazil, and that the company had confidence in my ability. He closed his letter giving me the opportunity of going to Brazil, saying that no one could expect me to stay there. After I declined the offer again because it did not address the consequence of my being able to decline the offer after an exploratory trip, Candido wrote me again on March 6, 1968, stating that if his resignation from the board of directors would contribute to a better relationship between me and the board, he would do so immediately, and having removed all obstacles it was clear for me to leave for Brazil immediately.

Upon receipt of this letter from Uncle Candido I felt that he had acknowledged my request, and that I didn't have anything to worry about if I went to Brazil and found conditions adverse to staying.

Finally, after all the preliminary discussions regarding the Brazilian job opportunity were resolved, I left on a two-week exploratory trip— March 16 to March 31.

When I arrived on March 16, my cousin Harold Benassini met me at São Paulo's Viracopos International Airport. Harold, who was ready to return to the United States, was the manager of our Brazilian operation.

I stayed at the Jarugua Hotel, located near the center of the city. Since it was the middle of the summer in Brazil, it was very hot. The hotel room had no air conditioning, and, with all the automobile traffic, it also was very noisy, even in the middle of the night. Needless to say, I didn't sleep very well during that first visit, in part, due to the heat and noise, but also each night I was thinking about the opportunity in evidence at this Jacuzzi factory.

The plant was located in São Bernardo do Campo, a city located near São Paulo. I found this subsidiary had a narrow product line, out-of-date equipment, and antiquated manufacturing processes. But I also sensed potential and an exciting opportunity to turn the business around.

Upon my return I had a long discussion with Paula and my children about the potential I saw for the company, housing, schools for the children, the beauty of the country, et cetera. I was definitely excited and enthused about the opportunity the job offered me and what I felt would be a wonderful opportunity for my family. Based on all the positives I felt existed, we decided I should commit to the job. I then wrote the board of directors accepting the responsibility, and advised that I was prepared to move there for at least two to three years as soon as the children's schooling terminated for the summer. I also asked for home leave to the United States every year for me and my family, plus resolution of some other matters such as salary, health insurance, and tuition for the children in Brazil.

The Move

Satisfied with the arrangements for my new Brazilian position, Paula and I visited São Paulo in May. After looking into housing, schools for the children, living conditions, and opportunities for Jacuzzi in Brazil, we embraced the opportunity of living and working in a new country and agreed to stay in Brazil for at least three years.

During our visit, my cousin Harold and his wife, Marcella, were very helpful and supportive, introducing us to a number of their friends, who, in turn, became our friends, and providing local business and social contacts that eased our settling into the city. They also introduced us to the staff at Escola Maria Imaculada (School of Mary Immaculate), where their children attended school, so we decided to enroll our children there for the next school year, beginning in August. The home in São Paulo, which we rented for our family's return in July, was obtained with the kind help of this couple, who also recommended their well-trained and efficient cook and housekeeper, Benadita and Urides, who worked for us for a number of years.

Before moving to Brazil, we rented our country home in Oakley, California, and prepared for our transfer. We obtained the necessary medical examinations, inoculations for ourselves and our five children, police statements of clear records, plus the residency papers and work permits required by the Brazilian immigration authorities.

This was an exciting time for my family as we looked forward to our move to a country with a new culture and language. But at the same time, it was somewhat difficult to leave our family and the comfortable rural Oakley home we bought a few years earlier. It was located about five miles from my parents' ranch and my childhood home and close to Antioch where Paula and I met in high school. Her mother and other family members still lived there. Her father, Paul Putnam, had died in 1965.

After packing and shipping our furnishings in lift van containers, Paula, our five children, and I left California in early July, stopping to visit family in Toronto, Minneapolis, and Little Rock, Arkansas, before departing for Brazil. The stop in Little Rock also gave me an opportunity to meet with Jacuzzi management at the head office.

Though we shipped part of our furnishings by air freight so we could occupy our home upon our arrival, we were forced to stay several weeks at the Grande Hotel Ca' Doro near downtown São Paulo until the shipment arrived and cleared customs, a much lengthier process than anticipated. This was a pleasant family hotel, where we made friends with several other American families who also were transitioning into lives in São Paulo. We were pleased to learn they, too, planned to send their children to the School of Mary Immaculate.

We finally were able to move into our home in early August, but we waited nearly sixty more days before the ocean-shipped part of our furnishings arrived and cleared customs.

Our first home in São Paulo was located in the Cidade Jardim area of the city. It was a nice four-bedroom home with a rather small yard, surrounded by a tall security wall. It was located about 300 meters from the front entrance to the São Paulo Jockey Club. While our home was in a good neighborhood, we joined our neighbors in hiring a private security guard in accordance to local custom. He would walk around the neighborhood at night on the lookout for problems or anything out of the ordinary. What didn't make much sense, however, was how he would blow his whistle periodically to let us know he was patrolling, which at the same time also warned potential troublemakers he was in the vicinity. Actually, we never had problems with house or personal theft during the years we lived in Brazil, but we learned that this home was broken into several times within six months after we left it.

Our older children started school at the School of Mary Immaculate soon after we arrived in São Paulo, and they began classes in mid-August. Eventually, all of our children would attend this school, which was built and run by the Oblate Fathers of Mary Immaculate. Responsible for instruction, the Felician Sisters assigned one sister to each of the first through twelfth grades but other lay teachers were also on staff. A small private school bus picked up and returned our children home along with other children who lived in our area of town. As Mary Immaculate did not have a kindergarten class when our son Matthew started school, he was enrolled for kindergarten at the English-speaking American Graded School.

The original Mary Immaculate was located near downtown São Paulo, but the school had recently moved to its new facility in the Chacara Flora area of the city. While all classes were taught in English, Portuguese was mandatory, and our children quickly learned this new language. I always found it fascinating that the children usually spoke in Portuguese during their recesses and sporting events, slipping into their second language in much the same way the Jacuzzi children of my generation happily switched back and forth between English and Italian.

Since my brother Virgil was so successful in managing the Jacuzzi subsidiary in Canada, I asked him to visit and help me assess our operation. When he and his wife, Beulah—our first visitors in Brazil—arrived in September, we were delighted to have them stay at our home. Unfortunately, it was only furnished with our air-shipped belongings, so some of the younger children slept on couches and cots during their stay.

With them, we had fine times sightseeing in São Paulo and attending a soccer match between our company team and one sponsored by our customer from the city of Itu, who later prepared a big barbecue that everyone enjoyed.

Virgil was a tremendous help to us during this trip! One of his suggestions was that I should employ, as quickly as possible, someone adept at production and manufacturing. He recommended Tony Presot, an Italian immigrant and foreman for him at Jacuzzi Canada, and a master of machine shop operations. After an exploratory visit to São Paulo, Tony agreed to move to Brazil to head up our production. On July 23, 1969, three days after Neil Armstrong became the first person to land on the moon, Tony arrived in São Paulo with his wife, Sandra, and their four daughters. He proved to be a godsend. Virgil was right; Tony really knew manufacturing and was especially good at developing tooling and assuring that products were shipped promptly. He played a key role in our eventual success.

Shortly after Virgil and his wife returned to Canada, my sister Rachel and her friend Tiia arrived for a visit en route to a tour of more of South America. Afterwards, Rachel returned to São Paulo for a few days to join my parents, who had arrived for their first visit there. They really enjoyed seeing Brazil and spending time with our family. As a group, we visited the renowned Butanta Institute in São Paulo, where many species of venomous and non-venomous snakes were kept outdoors in concrete-lined pits. Anti-venoms still are developed there for distribution throughout Brazil. We also took them to the beautiful Jequiti Mar Resort and Beach near the port city of Santos, to São Paulo's large zoo, and to the Clube de Campo de São Paulo (Country Club of São Paulo).

Soon after Rachel's departure, we discovered our home was literally splitting in two and was in need of major repairs. Since it had been built on a concrete slab on a gentle slope, the plumbing beneath the bath had broken, causing the drain water to wash out the supporting earth beneath the slab. The repairs required excavation in the middle of the home to jack it up into proper position. We had to move out for several days, giving my family and parents a fine opportunity to spend a few days at Campos do Jordao (fields of Jordan). This beautiful vacation town in the mountains, where the homes and hotels are built in the style of Swiss

Tyrolean chalets, is just a few hours drive from São Paulo. All of us, except Ma and Pa, rented horses for an enjoyable ride around the area.

We concluded Ma and Pa's first stay in Brazil with a quick road trip to picturesque Rio de Janeiro. From where they left directly for home.

During this visit Pa was able to visit Jacuzzi's facility a number of times with me and met all of our employees. Always interested in the quality of Jacuzzi products, Pa was able to make some suggestions about how we could improve our production methods and efficiency.

Brazil's Portuguese, a Romance language like Italian, and its open air markets, food, customs, and traditions brought back many memories of Italy to my parents. They enjoyed trips in the country, visiting our favorite winery owned by Italians, and seeing the horse-drawn carts still being used in São Paulo. They loved the Brazilian people, who in turn loved them, but the *favelas*, the terrible slum areas, distressed them greatly.

While Brazil is a very beautiful country with rich natural resources, living side by side with the wealthy there exist millions of less fortunate people, many of them desperately poor. Large numbers of them migrate to large cities such as São Paulo looking for work, often ending up worse off than they were in the rural interior. One Sunday morning I took my children to the Praça de Republica (Republic Square) in downtown São Paulo to visit the many artists and vendors who sold arts and crafts, paintings, petrified stones, fossils, and much more. After shopping, while waiting in my car on a side street for all of them to arrive, I noticed a poor man whom I thought was drunk, stumbling along the sidewalk. He collapsed as he came alongside my car, so several of us went to see what was wrong. It turned out he had come to São Paulo from the countryside to look for work and hadn't eaten for several days. He gulped down a glass of milk and a bread roll a woman gave him. I learned he couldn't get a job because he didn't have money to buy a work permit and couldn't work to get money in the first place. This poor fellow was in a dilemma. I gave him money for a work permit and money for a few days of food and lodging. I often wonder what became of him.

Water Outages

Water is the most precious of our commodities of life. We got to know the truth of this when we lived in our first home in São Paulo, where we suffered through a number of water outages that lasted sometimes for several days. We found we could get along fairly well without electricity but life without water is nearly intolerable!

Because of low water pressure and service interruptions, most of the homes in São Paulo are provided with a 1,000-liter water reservoir in their attics, equipped with a float valve to keep them full. The water in the reservoir was then gravity-fed to the home. With a large family, however, we often used more water than what was available in times of water outages. Fortunately, our next door neighbor had a well with a pump and would let us fill our water vessels and bathtub during these outages. Unfortunately, our first outages occurred during the visit by my brother Virgil and his wife, Beulah.

After months of these periodic difficulties, after which service was restored very slowly, I learned one of the principal causes: the *lava carros,* or car washers, who peddled their services to customers at the local horse races. A valve in the parking lot would be left open, draining water from the neighborhood mains.

Our Brazilian Son

Less than a year after our arrival in Brazil, our third son, Paulo Andrew Jacuzzi, was born on May 24, 1969, at the Samaritano Hospital in São Paulo. Paula's mother, Freda Putnam, came in time for our blessed event and was able to spend a couple of months with us. We had a wonderful time with her and, even with our newborn son, we were able to take her to the beach and show her many points of interest in São Paulo. She returned to California with us in early July when we left for home leave.

Jacuzzi do Brasil Challenges

The military government, which overthrew civilian rule in 1964, provided the country with not only relative economic stability, but a period of phenomenal growth and expansion that continued until almost the end of the 1970s, when the nation again suffered from hyperinflation. During my years in Brazil, the country's government and its growing—although somewhat inflationary—economy were the good news.

Our Jacuzzi plant was a different story. It was located in São Bernardo do Campo, about twenty kilometers from São Paulo. When Jacuzzi do Brasil was founded in 1959, the company was a completely new, start-up operation. Jacuzzi Brothers, Inc., purchased a square block located in a new, fairly undeveloped area of the city. The company built the factory and administrative offices in the block's center and bought a few machines. The company also owned and operated a cast iron and bronze foundry that was located across the back street of our plant.

This combined plant and office building in the middle of a city block with few neighbors was operational in 1959, but by 1968, the Jacuzzi-owned block was surrounded on all sides by homes, our foundry operation, and some small businesses. I knew we eventually would need to expand our product line and upgrade the plant to improve profitability, but for now those projects would have to wait.

In addition to the many anticipated and unexpected challenges, I soon attacked a major legal issue. One of our largest competitors was a former employee. He had taken our jet pump designs and had begun manufacturing pumps under his own label. We hired and trained the man in the United States and then sent him to Brazil to oversee the manufacturing operations under the direction of my cousin Harold Benassini. When the company learned he had started a rival company while he was a Jacuzzi employee, he was terminated. The legal challenge that followed was costly, but we prevailed.

Another employee crisis came on November 25, 1970, when I received an anonymous letter, claiming our assembly foreman was stealing some of our products. This was proven true after a police search of his and other employees' homes. One of these employees, Antonio, was a young man of Italian descent who had been hired to help install what were now stolen pumps. I considered Antonio's plea to keep his job, since I knew his father had a strong influence on him, so I requested a meeting with the two of them. I told them that if he would share everything he knew about the theft, and if his father would vouch for him, I would allow Antonio to return. They both cooperated completely and I never had any more problems with the son. I learned that sometimes giving a person a second chance can pay off, especially in this case, where the father's involvement was so positive.

Plant and employee issues needed urgent attention, yet some of the most demanding challenges, often involving technological break-throughs, centered on one area: communications. During my first years in Brazil, we had to schedule long-distance telephone calls to the United States—and sometimes even within Brazil—in advance. By the time I left in 1980, direct-distance dialing to and from Brazil, and anywhere in the world was commonplace. But in 1968, the telegram was the pre-ferred "fast" mode of communication, but after dealing with this limited, cumbersome, and often painfully slow medium, the advent of the overnight courier delivery systems seemed a minor miracle. However, by 1980, we were sending and receiving faxes with the greatest of ease.

Company Payroll

When I first arrived, the payroll system at Jacuzzi do Brasil was a concern to me, as we paid our employees in cash. Due to high inflation and the low value of individual paper bills, our payroll officer went to the bank to pick up our payroll in a suitcase, opening a large exposure for theft both for us and our employees, who had to carry their full salary in cash. Accordingly, we convinced them that they would benefit greatly if we made direct transfers to their individual bank accounts.

Jacuzzi Executive Committee Meetings

Principally due to communication difficulties but also to keep Jacuzzi Management abreast of the company's various branch and sub-sidiary operations, the managers of Jacuzzi Brothers USA and foreign subsidiaries would meet twice a year either in Little Rock, Arkansas, or at one of the subsidiary operations.

During the time I was in Brazil, instead of meeting in Little Rock, we had several meetings of the executive committee at the Jacuzzi Canada facility in Toronto, one at Jacuzzi Europe's facility in Valvazone, Italy, and one in Brazil. It was never possible to meet at the Jacuzzi Mexico operation in Monterrey.

I recall the preparation for one of these meetings well. The day prior to embarking for Little Rock I worked rather late to get my report in final form and left the Jacuzzi plant in São Bernardo do Campo about 7:30 p.m. On my way home I was stopped in a police roadblock, in which the police were checking every car and driver for any possible infraction.

Any infraction meant your car would be impounded and driven or towed to the police yard until the infraction was resolved. Unfortunately, my car, which I just bought new the day before, had only a temporary license permit and not the actual plates. The police told me I was not permitted to drive the car without proper plates, then impounded my car and said they would have it towed to the police yard, or I could drive it there. There was no way I would let them have it towed, so I stayed with it until after 11:00 p.m., when their roadblock mission was completed. By then they had over a hundred automobiles lined up by the side of the road. By the time I drove my car to the police yard in a long procession, parked it, and received an official receipt, it was after 12:00 midnight. I flagged down a taxi to take me home. Without the convenience of roadside telephones or much less a cell phone, I was unable to call home and tell Paula what had happened, and by the time I got home, she was quite concerned. The next day I left for the United States, and our company controller and attorney were able to resolve the issue with the police. I always felt I would never have had a similar experience in the states.

Jacuzzi Comes to Brazil

In November 1977, Paula and I hosted the Jacuzzi Brothers' executive committee and their spouses, most of whom had never been to Brazil. I had suggested that the committee meet in Brazil both to see our operation on a firsthand basis and to better understand the unique challenges and the promise of this market.

Some of our group began their journey by visiting Belem, a city in northern Brazil located at the mouth of the Amazon River. Next, all of us met up river at the beautiful Hotel Tropical in Manaus, a town in the heart of the Amazon jungle. I was pleased to point out the hotel's swimming pool was completely outfitted with Jacuzzi do Brasil products.

While in the jungle, we particularly enjoyed a boat tour that took us to the "meeting of the waters," the place where the black or tannic waters of the Rio Negro River merge with the lighter waters of the Amazon River.

We flew to and visited Brazilia, Rio de Janeiro, and finally arrived in São Paulo, where we held our last formal executive committee meeting. While in São Paulo, we visited our plant under construction in Itu, where we planted thirteen flowering trees, in memory of the thirteen original Jacuzzi brothers and sisters. Paula and I later hosted a beautifully catered dinner party for the group and a number of our friends in our home, complete with entertainment by a Brazilian band.

Prior to their return to the States, most of the party traveled to the falls of Iguassu, the largest falls in the world, based on the volume of water flowing from them. It was a trip of many wonders, not the least of which was our demonstration of the vigorous nature of Jacuzzi's Brazilian subsidiary, which had made a quantitative comeback after its earlier troubled years.

Pumps to Pools

No finished Jacuzzi products were imported from the U.S. to open up Jacuzzi's South American market. The company built its own cast iron and brass foundry to make our pump castings. Other components were purchased locally, with one exception, a line of mechanical shaft seals imported from the U.S. Despite a slow beginning, the company's products did well for several years, but failed to stay current. We had some serious catching up to do if we were to survive, let alone compete.

As we came of age in our production department, we were able to update and expand our growing product line. First, we concentrated on updating and expanding the injector pump and the centrifugal pump lines. Later, we introduced both submersible and turbine pumps. Next, given the growth of the swimming pool market in Brazil, we began to manufacture a wide range of pool filters, fittings, and accessories. Eventually we also manufactured a line of vinyl-liner swimming pools.

To accommodate the production of the fiberglass swimming pool products, we decided to close our foundry and outsource our casting needs to others. We were then able to use the foundry building for the production of fiberglass diving boards and slides. The addition of swimming pool equipment to our product line was timely and profitable. In Brazil, the swimming pool market was new and growing, and Jacuzzi was the first full-line pool and pool equipment manufacturer. Virtually all of our swimming pool line was developed by Jacuzzi Canada and featured the latest equipment, allowing both our company and our resellers to share excellent growth and profitability.

Having our own fiberglass equipment to build swimming pool diving boards and slides also opened the doors for us to build whirlpool baths. Jacuzzi do Brasil was also the first manufacturer of whirlpool baths in Brazil. By the time of my return to the United States in 1980, we were manufacturing a complete line of modern whirlpool baths and outdoor spas for the Brazilian market and we sold the majority of all whirlpool baths in the country.

Our export business also was thriving with steadily increasing sales in Paraguay, Bolivia, and Uruguay. We did not sell into Argentina or Chile, as Jacuzzi had licensees in these countries.

Economy and Expansion

Though our company's financial position was solid, with sales and profits strong and growing, the Brazilian economy's high inflation and regulatory restraints affected costs of all our raw materials and labor. I had never encountered such challenges in the United States.

As the cost of living rapidly climbed, so did our payroll, which was closely regulated by the Brazilian government's Ministry of Labor. We significantly increased wages periodically, with each government-mandated raise in the 15 to 30 percent range. The high inflation rate required us to raise our own product pricing frequently. During periods of low to moderate inflation rates we raised prices by publishing new price lists. When the inflation rate became overly high we published elevated price lists and reduced the discount as needed to maintain profitability.

We also found it difficult to purchase the kind of machinery we needed, since much of it simply wasn't available in South America. The importation of machine tools and even components such as raw materials required a lengthy bureaucratic process and high duties.

Still, Jacuzzi do Brasil grew. We reported a loss in 1968, my first year there, but after that, each year was increasingly profitable. The Jacuzzi do Brasil management and sales teams were proud to send our yearly remittances to Jacuzzi Brothers, although the Brazilian government limited each year's remittance to 12 percent of our registered capital.

Gradually, we began to expand our operation throughout the country. We opened regional sales offices and/or warehouses in Belo Horizonte, Rio de Janeiro, Porto Alegre, Recife, and Brasilia.

Rapid inflation threatened us when we were in the market for land for a new factory. However, in 1978, after enlarging our São Bernardo do Campo facility three times with no more area to expand, we purchased land in the city of Itu, about seventy miles from São Paulo, where we built our new plant and relocated in 1979. I consider that factory one of the finest built by the Jacuzzi Brothers company.

Jacuzzi Chile

During most of my time in Brazil, Jacuzzi Brothers' products were manufactured under license in Argentina, Chile, and Venezuela. However, by early 1979, a sequence of events led to my helping to open a Jacuzzi subsidiary in Chile.

The economic instability in that country forced the licensee to stop remitting royalties. Since no remittances were being sent to our U.S. headquarters, I was sent to investigate. Once in Chile, I found the men who ran the franchise were very honest people. The money owed to Jacuzzi Brothers had not been permitted to leave the country. Many would have taken advantage of the precarious situation, but these men had instead set aside all the Jacuzzi Brothers' money in a reserve bank account.

While I was there, Fernando della Maza, the product manager of the Chilean licensee, requested a meeting. He believed the market potential for our jet pumps and whirlpool baths was very good, and he was interested in helping open a full Jacuzzi subsidiary in Chile. He and I met with attorneys, bankers, and all the proper government delegates, and we were able to make the necessary arrangements before I left. The new operation opened soon after and has always been a profitable venture. At the time of this writing, Fernando is still the manager of Jacuzzi Chile.

Our New Home and Friends

Living in Brazil was a great experience for our whole family and we loved our time there. The country is as beautiful as its people. Since I was fluent in Italian and Spanish before the move, it wasn't too difficult for me to learn how to speak, read and write Portuguese. The language was somewhat more difficult for Paula and the children to learn, but with time, they also were able to communicate quite well.

With our six growing children, our family soon outgrew the home we rented in the Cidade Jardim suburb of São Paulo. We didn't expect to live in São Paulo on a long-term or permanent basis and home rental was very expensive. So, in 1969 at a semi-annual Jacuzzi corporate advisory committee meeting, I recommended that Jacuzzi should undertake building a home in São Paulo for its resident manager. At the subsequent advisory committee meeting in April 1970, I was given the go-ahead on this project, and in November, we located a very nice, undeveloped one-acre lot in the gated Chacara Flora residential community. The location was excellent in many ways, not the least of which was that our children would have a ten-minute walk to the nearby school of Mary Immaculate. As the lot was covered with very dense, jungle-like growth, we hired a team of workers with machetes to open a path so we could inspect the property before its purchase by Jacuzzi do Brasil. The project became controversial, however, when some members of the Jacuzzi family heard of it. I then was encouraged by Ray Horan to personally assume the building of the home with the assistance of a loan from Jacuzzi do Brasil. A suitable agreement was worked out and approved by Jacuzzi's board of directors in July 1971.

We built a two-story, five-bedroom home with Spanish Colonial styling that was beautiful and functional. We moved in during August of 1972, just before our children's school year started. It was marvelous to own a larger home and yard. To assure a constant supply of water, I designed a modern pressure water system with a large underground reservoir supplemented by several reservoirs in the attic. Thank goodness, we never again went without water!

In 1973, we built a swimming pool with an adjoining spa in our back yard, along with a covered, open-sided patio area. Here we placed the large redwood table and benches that I made in California and brought to Brazil. Our backyard, pool, spa, and our open patio included a grill and was the setting for many good times and *churrascos* (barbecues) shared by our family and friends.

Our three-year Brazilian commitment passed quickly as I became engrossed in development of Jacuzzi do Brasil and as my family formed new friendships, and we gave almost no thought to returning home. Our years in São Paulo were not only a huge blessing for our family, but also a good investment, since we were able to pay off the home loan to Jacuzzi on an accelerated schedule in 1977, thanks to performance bonuses.

Many of our children's classmates were from the United States; their parents, like us, were working in Brazil. We became a very close-knit group of friends, and our collective family lives seemed to revolve around the school and its related functions. We spent many leisure hours at events like school soccer and basketball games, drama productions, barbecue fund-raisers, St. Patrick's Day dinner parties, and occasional weekend outings at the Oblate Fathers' Paiol Grande mountain retreat.

Through these school gatherings, Paula and I became close friends with many of these families. We regularly invited each other to our homes for dinners, as well as to other more casual gatherings.

During our years in Brazil, we were blessed to share many holidays, birthdays, and anniversaries with friends that included the Trevisons, Benadofs, Fersts, Barras, Presots, Dosmans, Gelenscars, Hargraves, Hinkleys, Sleys, Asplins, Landolts, DeBorbas, Lunds, Hylands, Sanchezs, Pullens, and many others. Our family was also fortunate to know a number of other families in Brazil during their shorter, two-to-five-year stays.

We were especially close to Vince and Anna Trevison, David and Sylvia Benadof, and Tony and Sandra Presot and their families, sharing many family holiday celebrations and other meals with them.

Not only were Tony and Sandra our good friends, but Tony also was our company's Santa Claus, for he was always eager to portray that jolly man at our corporate Christmas party. This lower hemisphere, summer Christmas party was held in one of the local parks or in a rented outdoor area. We always served barbecued beef cooked by employees, since a good meat meal was a great treat for many of our employees and their families, who typically dined on beans and rice and very little meat. We always were entertained by our employees who played wonderful Samba rhythms on drums, empty barrels, tin cans, and the like. A company soccer match was also a part of these Christmas parties.

Escola Maria Immaculata (School of Mary Immaculate)

The School of Mary Immaculate was excellent for our children. They received a good, broad education, an excellent background in Brazilian culture, fluency in Portuguese, and the school allowed them the opportunity to interact with children from all over the world. The main boys and girls sports played were track, kickball, basketball, tennis at private courts, and field and court soccer. The boys also played flag football. All of our children were active in the sports program. Loretta and Gretchen were also high school cheerleaders, as was their mother. Jennifer was on the yearbook staff and she, Remo V., and her sisters were also very active in the elaborate, very professionally staged yearly drama productions. These were produced and directed by James Colby, the school's highly talented teacher and drama director. Remo V. was lighting and stage manager, while Jennifer served as student director, in addition to their dramatic participation.

Our daughter Gretchen's involvement on school sports teams and as cheerleader eventually lead to her meeting her future husband, Tyson Roe. They had briefly met at a basketball game in which Tyson played for the American school in Campinas, a city located about seventy miles from São Paulo. In 1987, years after we left Brazil, she received a telephone call from Tyson when she was working as a schoolteacher in Dallas, where he was finishing dental school at Baylor University. He found her name in the Dallas phone book and called to find out if she once lived in São Paulo. Of course, she had, and after meeting for dinner and a period of courtship, they married in Little Rock on June 11, 1988. All the years since high school Tyson had been carrying a cheerleading picture of her in his wallet.

The School Board and Father Lindy

Within a couple of years of our arrival in Brazil, the Oblate Fathers of Mary Immaculate invited me and three other parents (Bob McKay, Tom Altaffer, and Allen Baker) to be financial advisors for our children's school. At our suggestion, the Fathers soon formed the first board of directors at the school, consisting of eight parents, three Oblate Fathers and one Felician nun. It was my honor to serve for a number of years as president of this board.

This involvement with the school was a challenge, for the school could have been operated more efficiently. Though we found the Oblate Fathers dealt effectively with educational issues, they had not kept careful track of the school's finances, so we hired a new administrator from the United States to overhaul several management practices.

Our dear friends Father William "Lindy" Lindekugal and Sister Carolyn Moritz always supported our reform efforts. Paula and I often hosted Father Lindy, Sister Carolyn, and a number of the other Oblate Fathers and Felician Sisters in our home. Meals would typically begin with a brief Mass, during which Paula, who was not Catholic, was unable to participate in receiving Holy communion with the rest of us.

However, after a couple of years of our hosting these events, we experienced a significant occurrence. One evening, as Father Lindy was preparing for Mass, he took me aside. He told me what a faithful Christian Paula was, how she never missed a morning chapel service at the school, and how she always supported the school's religious mission.

"Paula is a better Catholic than many of the other school's mothers. I want to make her officially one!" he said.

To Paula's and my surprise and delight, Father Lindy gave her an official blessing and "made her a Catholic." My children and I shared our first communion with her that night. Paula later received the Catholic Sacrament of Confirmation with our son Matthew at a church confirmation service.

As an aside to this, Paula, who was raised Presbyterian, long ago tried to convert to Catholicism. While in nursing school, she sought counseling in California from a Catholic priest prior to our marriage. However, things did not go well at this session. Paula confided in the priest that she felt a bit intimidated by the Catholic Church, and even somewhat fearful of some of its liturgies and traditions.

The priest flung a string of rosary beads on the table between them. "Are you afraid of these?" he asked.

Startled, Paula quickly ended the session and never pursued conversion again, although she always went to church with the children and me, and she thoroughly supported our children's Catholic upbringing. But finally, she was a Catholic, and we were all rejoiced at having her completely included by the church. Paula and I remained friends with Sister Carolyn and Father Lindy long after our return to the United States. In fact, each of them later visited us several times in our Little Rock home.

Timothy James DeShields

When my sister Teresa Jacuzzi DeShields's son Timothy was sixteen years old, he came to Curitiba Parana, Brazil, for the 1971–72 school year as a Rotary International exchange student.

Tim's father, Don DeShields, had been a Rotary Club member for many years and his club in Portland, Oregon, had a very active international student exchange program. Tim wanted to be an exchange student and he chose Brazil, since, at that time, we had lived there for three years. Since he was my godson, Tim had a special place in my heart and Paula and I were thrilled he would be a half day's drive away.

His Brazilian host family consisted of Ernani and Dixie Pereira and their three children—a boy, Johnny, who was about Tim's age, and two daughters. Ernani was a medical doctor and his wife, Dixie, was American, so the family spoke fluent English and Portuguese.

Tim flourished in Curitiba. He quickly gained fluency in Portuguese and he was very active and popular at his school, where he participated in basketball, swimming, and tennis. A strong leader, he took his Rotary exchange responsibilities seriously.

A few days before July 2, 1972, Tim's seventeenth birthday, Tim and Ernani traveled by car to the Pereiras' beach home to prepare it for a visit by Tim's parents, Don and Teresa. The DeShields were going to visit Tim on his birthday, and then the three of them were to come visit us in São Paulo, before returning home.

Tim's school was planning a going-away party for him on June 29, but tragically, as Tim and Ernani were returning that day from the beach, their car was hit head-on by a large truck.

My godson and his Brazilian father were killed instantly. I received a telephone call that evening from Ernani's brother-in-law, Dr. Jose, who lived in São Paulo, who notified us of the tragedy. He said he wanted to telephone Don and Teresa before we did. Paula and I immediately flew to Curitiba to do what we could, numbed though we were with grief.

The U.S. consulate officer and his wife, Mr. and Mrs. Henry Krausse, Jr., met us at the airport and graciously invited us to stay in their home.

Tim's school held a memorial service and we made arrangements for the transfer of his body to Portland, Oregon, and for our own travel arrangements, so we could accompany his body home. My parents, siblings and most of their children attended Tim's funeral.

Coping with this tragedy was one of the hardest things I've ever had to do. I prayed, and yet there seemed to be no easy answers. We still grieve for Tim and for his unrealized promise.

In the fall of 1972 Tim's older brother, Donald A. DeShields, his wife, Patti, and their one-year-old son, Shane, moved to São Paulo, when Don took a position with Jacuzzi do Brasil. He worked in purchasing and customer service and returned to the U.S. in 1974. We appreciated having them in São Paulo, and having Don working for the company.

Pa

Just as we had done with Tim's passing, we found ourselves drawing on the strength of our spiritual community of friends many more times during our life in Brazil.

On Saturday, March 11, 1973, I received word that my father had passed away. He was pruning a lemon tree when he died. As always, Pa had been wearing a suit while he worked at the ranch, dressed much like his father had typically dressed when working.

Although we had a difficult time obtaining a same-day exit visa, Paula, Matthew, Paulo, and I left that day for California.

Pa's requiem Mass was sung at St. Anthony's Catholic Church in Oakley and he was buried in the Holy Cross Cemetery at Antioch with a very large funeral. He was eighty-five.

Upon hearing news of his older brother's passing, Uncle Frank said: "Only two brothers remain, but it won't be too long before another is called to God."

This brother, who joined Pa for the family's first immigration quest in America, died six months later.

It was difficult to leave my mother after Pa's death and return to Brazil. But I knew she had the love and support of many family members who lived nearby. Later, Ma visited us in Brazil, which was a good reunion for all of us.

From Brazil to Italy

Paula and I tried to encourage our children to learn all they could of Brazil by taking them on family trips within the country whenever possible. However, it was very important to us that our family be aware of the cultures of their own country and of Europe, especially that of Italy. Therefore, we were fortunate to be able to take two landmark family journeys while we lived in Brazil.

The first was a trek through historical sites in America. We decided to do this in 1975, the year prior to the nation's 1976 bicentennial celebration. We began our journey in Toronto, where we visited my brother Virgil, sisters Flora and Rachel, and their families. We then visited by automobile many historic places, beginning with the Boston area, where we saw Plymouth Rock and a reconstruction of the *Mayflower*, the ship that brought the Pilgrims to this country. In New York we saw the Empire State Building, Ellis Island, and the Statue of Liberty. We also ended up driving into New York's Central Park—by accident—after making a wrong turn. The children were quite embarrassed by our predicament, but a helpful officer directed us to an exit. In Philadelphia we visited with Paula's brother Duane Putnam, who was on Ron Waller's coaching staff when he coached the Philadelphia Bells. He joined us during our visit to the Liberty Bell, Liberty Hall, and the Philadelphia Mint.

We then drove to western Pennsylvania and visited the Amish country, stopping for a great meal at the Good and Plenty restaurant in Lancaster. After visiting the White House and the Smithsonian Institution in Washington, D.C., we drove through the beautiful Smoky Mountains to Atlanta to visit our sister-in-law Patti Putnam, at her and Duane's home, and Beverly Algood, my brother Virgil's daughter. We ended our tour in Little Rock, where we visited with family and the Jacuzzi corporate office before returning home.

The second major journey began on June 11, 1977, nine days after the high school graduation of my oldest daughter, Jennifer. The seven of us first flew to Madrid, where we were met by Remo V., who had been studying in California. We all arrived on a Sunday morning and were looking forward to attending a bullfight that was to take place in the afternoon. We had made reservations for the event before leaving Brazil. Unfortunately, it was cancelled due to rain. Spain was in the middle of elections at the time and many red Communist Party flags were flying. My children were especially intrigued by wall signs that read, "A vote for Communism is a vote for Democracy." After visiting points of interest in Madrid and the city of Toledo, we embarked for Athens. While in Greece, we greatly enjoyed Athens, especially our tour of the Acropolis, and the many other fascinating ruins, particularly those in Corinth. After an island tour by ship, we traveled to Italy.

When we arrived in Rome, I tried to rent a large car or van. However, there were absolutely none to be found. I told the family we needed to pray for a car. We did, and fifteen minutes later, a vendor called to tell us he had a very large, four-seat diesel-engine station wagon available. I've always said that station wagon was a car brought to us by prayer.

After touring Rome, Assisi, Florence, Pisa, and Venice, we eagerly headed toward the Jacuzzi ancestral home in Casarsa. Being with my children in my father's boyhood home was a memorable experience even though the home was modernized by then.

We found Uncle Rachele's spike driven in an exterior rafter, which he used long ago for his experiments with pulleys. We visited the third-floor granary where the silk worms were raised. We examined the addition Pa worked on. We marveled at how close the soldiers were when they passed the house on the *Strada Maestra* and when they camped in the field across this road. I was grateful I was able to bring my family to this special place.

While in Casarsa we had dinner with my cousin Esther (Peruzzo) and her husband, George Regula. George was president of Jacuzzi Europe at the time. We also were able to meet with Ray Horan, Jacuzzi Brothers, Inc.'s president from Little Rock, who was visiting the Jacuzzi Europe facility in nearby Valvazone.

From Casarsa, we visited my mother's family in the small Alpine village of Soffranco, where she was born, and Longarone, where other relatives live. My cousins and other family members, whom I had met on an earlier trip to Italy, were very gracious and welcoming. My children say this was their favorite time during our entire journey.

After our visit with our relatives in the Italian Alps, we traveled to Switzerland, Germany, Holland, and Norway. In Norway we stayed a few days in Gjovick in comfortable accommodations arranged by our friends

Eirik and Nanni Asplin who lived in São Paulo and had recently returned to their native Norway. Our son Remo V. stayed on a few days after our departure, with the Asplins. After leaving the van we rented in Rome at the Oslo airport, we flew to Edinburgh, Scotland, where we stayed a few days before driving to London.

Immediately upon arriving in London, we tried to book hotel rooms only to find that, because of the Queen's Silver Jubilee celebration, none were available. After a several hours' search all I could arrange for Paula and I and our five children was one room with double beds at the Heathrow Airport. Certainly better than nothing, it did turn out to be a very memorable experience! We concluded our travels by visiting France, including Paris, through which the last of the Jacuzzi immigrants passed as they left Europe for America. While in that city, we visited with my mother's sister Giacomina Marcon and her two sons, my cousins Pietro and Bruno and their families, who lived just south of Paris. It was good to end our trip on the continent with another family reunion.

We were on the road for more than one month. It was a time for adventure, nostalgia, and learning. Most of all, it was a time for family.

Remo Valerian Jacuzzi

My oldest child and son, Remo Valerian Jacuzzi, was born twelve months after Paula and I wed. Quite early on, I noticed his aptitude for quickly learning how things work. He seemed to definitely have the Jacuzzi bent for needing to understand the inner workings of machines, motors, and electronic gadgets of all kinds.

On September 10, 1970, I was coming through customs in Belem, Brazil, with an electronic toy for Remo Valerian. I had endured an exhausting trip, having left Toronto and making stops in New York City; Port of Spain, Trinidad; Georgetown, Guyana; and Paramaribo, Surinam.

The Brazilian customs agent looked at the new toy and informed me there was a 100 percent duty on electronics. I argued, but finally paid the price of the toy, or about $35. To my dismay, when I arrived back at the hotel, I discovered I had left the gift back at the airport's custom office, so I went back to get it. By the time I returned to the airport and arrived back at the hotel, the roosters in the hotel's yard were crowing.

However, in the end, this toy proved to be worth all the trouble, for Remo V. was absolutely fascinated with the item. I credit it with further stimulating his lifelong interest in the marvels of electronics and machines and with his eventual mastering of almost everything related to computers.

In the summer before his senior year in high school, I took Remo on a trip through northern Brazil. In Recife, we rented a *jangada*, or wooden sail boat, used for fishing on the high seas. Its owner gave us an unforgettable, high-speed tour around the harbor. We have many fond memories of our time together, and I only wish I could have made such a journey with each of my children prior to his or her senior year.

At the time, Remo and I never knew how special that trip would seem in the months and years that followed.

My Family and Our God

In April 1976, our family again needed the support of our dear local friends and spiritual leaders during a time of great trial. Remo had just obtained his Brazilian driver's license at eighteen, the legal driving age there at the time. As he was driving home one night, he crashed head-on into a concrete pole. Paula and I received a phone call from a passer-by who had taken him to a first-aid-type hospital. We were told he was badly injured.

Our minds and hearts flashed back to our nephew Tim's accident. We jumped into our car and set out to find this remote hospital, which turned out to be scarcely more than a small clinic. Once we finally found it, a nurse informed us they had been unable to do anything for our son, and had transferred him to one of São Paulo's general hospitals.

We then rushed to that hospital, where a terrible sight greeted us! Everywhere we turned we saw injured people lying on stretchers, since this was the regional trauma hospital to which most accident victims were brought. When we finally found Remo, we discovered he had not yet received any attention. His knee was badly cut; he had glass in his face and bandages over both eyes, which seemed to have suffered the most serious injury.

We quickly arranged to have him moved to the Samaritano Hospital, where our son Paulo was born, so a specialist could perform eye surgery on him the next day. We were told Remo would probably lose the sight in one eye, and if his other one could not be saved, he could be left totally blind.

At that moment in my life, more than any previous time, I earnestly prayed, for I was powerless to help my son and I needed God's intervention. His friends and their parents from our school also held an around-the-clock prayer vigil for him.

The surgery seemed to go well. However, Remo's eyes had to remain bandaged for one week, and so we waited to know learn the real outcome and prognosis.

When the doctor removed the bandages, he asked Remo if he could see.

"Yes," Remo said, and went on to describe the red roses he saw sitting on the table in his room. What a relief!

However, Remo retained sight in only one eye. We learned of a specialist in Houston, Texas, and on April 15, Paula, Remo, and I left for an examination in Houston. Again, our circle of friends from work and school helped us by watching over our other children while we were gone.

After he put Remo through extensive testing and examinations in Houston, Dr. Girard informed us the eye could not be saved. So Remo lost one eye, but kept his life. We thank God for sparing him.

Although it was excruciatingly difficult to watch my son go through such trauma, the experience became a landmark event for me, a spiritual turning point.

Remo Jacuzzi with Jason International, Inc.'s first advertisement – 1982

Jason CA553P Carrera Bath – 2006

Jason MI635 Designer Bath – 2006

Chapter 17

Moving On

"Niente rimane per sempre."

"Nothing lasts forever."
—Valeriano Jacuzzi, my father

When Candido stepped down as president of Jacuzzi Brothers in 1969, a singular moment occurred in our company's history. The board of directors appointed the first nonfamily member to hold the chief executive office of Jacuzzi Brothers: Ray Horan was elected president and general manager of the company.

Initially, in 1967, upon Candido's recommendation, the board of directors appointed Ray Horan to replace him as the general manager and executive vice-president of the company to manage its day-to-day operations. With this appointment Ray Horan moved from California to Little Rock.

Prior to these promotions, Ray Horan with a degree in Mechanical Engineering from the University of California at Berkeley, served twenty years for Jacuzzi in the positions of engineer, chief engineer, vice-president of engineering, Western Region sales manager.

When Ray was appointed president, Uncle Frank was the company treasurer of Jacuzzi Brothers and my father, Valeriano, served as honorary chairman of the board of directors.

A Heritage Sold

While Ray Horan was a capable individual, I always felt this management position should have gone to my brother Virgil, based on

Virgil's proven sales ability and his many leadership accomplishments in founding and expanding Jacuzzi Canada.

Virgil had a track history of successful work, both before and after he obtained his Mechanical and Electrical Engineering degrees by attending night school. After being discharged from the Navy, he attended night school while he worked at Jacuzzi Brothers during the day. He later devoted many long and arduous years as Jacuzzi Brothers' national sales manager, often leaving his growing family in California for weeks at a time as he traveled by train, covering the nation on behalf of the company. Virgil was rightfully credited with fully developing Jacuzzi's national sales network.

Then in 1955, he founded and served as president of Jacuzzi Canada, opening up what became our most profitable subsidiary. Clearly, Virgil was the logical and best choice, or if not Virgil, my brother Dante, who very successfully managed Jacuzzi Brothers' manufacturing and sales operation in St. Louis, and who was instrumental in growing the company's Midwest and East Coast base. But family politics prevailed to designate a neutral leader. It was rumored no children of my father's would ever serve as president of Jacuzzi Brothers.

This resentment by some family members was based, in large part, on my father's supporting his brother, Rachele, when Uncle Rachele was deposed by some of the other brothers. It was also felt that some family members did not approve of us because we had been raised on a farm and weren't sufficiently "citified."

So, when Ray Horan took over, it goes without saying he was at the helm of a complex, troubled company. Adding to this difficult situation, he was at a disadvantage since he was not a family member. Although Ray's early intent was to grow the company through product development, acquisition, and/or a public stock offering, none of these alternatives came to fruition under his leadership.

In the beginning, Frank's son, Giocondo Jacuzzi, was assigned the responsibility of locating and initiating discussions with potential companies that Jacuzzi could acquire, but no serious opportunities materialized.

Much discussion within the family centered around the possibility of going public, but due to a less than favorable market condition, and less than favorable company financial results, this possibility did not materialize.

Since I had been working in Brazil for more than a decade by this time, I was not close to the discussions regarding the options of selling the company. I sensed Ray Horan cultivated and sold the desirability of this course of action to a number of family members as the solution to two issues.

First, he must have perceived a sale was in line with some but certainly not all of the family members' sentiments. Secondly, he had been unable to grow the company through product line expansion with products such as air compressors, gas grills, and marine jets, which were never very profitable and which drew the company's focus from its principal core product lines.

The disappointing profitability of the domestic Jacuzzi operations in the mid to late 1970s were the nub of this second problem. In addition, the Mexican subsidiary's profits were marginal, while the operation in Italy was losing money. The most profitable operations were the company's Brazilian and Canadian operations, with Canada leading the pack with the highest net income. Our Brazilian profit margin on the net sales, however, was the highest.

Both Beatrice Foods, Inc., and Textron, Inc., among others, expressed interest in acquiring the company, but both eventually withdrew from negotiations.

In 1979, however, after the board had undergone lengthy negotiations with Walter Kidde, Inc., the vast majority of Jacuzzi Brothers' shareholders voted to sell. The price was $73,000,000. Personally, I was against the sale, but being a minority shareholder, I felt I had no choice but to acquiesce and also sell my shares. Kidde bought all Jacuzzi shares.

Without question in my mind, I believe the core of the problem leading to the company's sale was leadership. First, Candido Jacuzzi's dictatorial, self-serving, and at times unethical leadership caused a split in the family's unity and led to the buyout of part of the family's ownership. Second, the remaining family leadership did not place Virgil—who had proven himself highly capable and ethical—in charge.

In retrospect, I feel strongly that the family made a mistake in selling our inheritance, produced through so much work and sacrifice by our forefathers. I also doubt very seriously that the sale benefited the Jacuzzi family in the long term, and the majority of family members I have spoken to agree, adding that the acrimonious Jacbros lawsuit signaled the end of family ownership of the business. While it is true several of my cousins were able to sell and realize sizable nest eggs, in some cases the next generation of children suffered by getting too much too early, and lost much if not all of their inheritance through bad investments or misuse of funds. The verse in Holy Scripture "Wealth does not last to all generations" has certainly proven true for some of the Jacuzzis.

Certainly, the sale of Jacuzzi Brothers by the family put a close to the dreams of the original Jacuzzi brothers and sisters. They had built a solid family enterprise, after undergoing much heartache. The family company, which was the focal point of the family's aspiration and unity, was now in the hands of others.

I always remember the adage, "The first generation of a family starts a business; the second expands it, and the third sells or destroys it." In the case of our family, both the founding and the second generations allowed the occurrences that led to the sale of our company.

What the family and company did not recognize was the name "Jacuzzi" was becoming synonymous with whirlpool therapy baths. Interestingly, at that time, our whirlpool bath operation was our company's smallest division. However, this universal linking of the family name with hydrotherapy products was making the company much more valuable than the sale price. We sold not only our company, but also our name, for Jacuzzi was quickly becoming one of the world's most identifiable brands.

Back to America

In 1980, I was asked to become president of the Jacuzzi Brothers division in Little Rock. Although my family was very happy living in Brazil, in 1980, our fourth child, Gretchen, was leaving home to attend college in the United States. Gretchen was enrolling at Hendrix College in Arkansas, where her two sisters, Jennifer and Loretta, were attending college. At the time, their brother, Remo V., was studying at the University of California at Berkeley.

Gretchen's departure would leave only our two youngest children, Matthew and Paulo, at home in Brazil. As our family has always been close, Paula and I felt I should accept the transfer back to the United States. During the first six months in my new post, I commuted between Little Rock and Brazil about every two or three weeks, both to assist Valentin Duarte, who was Jacuzzi do Brazil's sales manager and whom I recommended to replace me, assume his new position as president, and to make the transition to my new position in Little Rock. By the start of the 1980 school year, we had completed our move to Little Rock.

In 1979, my brother Dante's son, Dante Paul Jacuzzi II, came to visit our Brazilian operation. Then in late 1980, after my return to the United States, he moved to Brazil with his wife, Susan, and served as Jacuzzi Brazil's vice-president of planning and manager of export sales. He returned to Little Rock in 1983.

Home in Little Rock

With some sadness about leaving our home and friends in São Paulo, we made arrangements for our move to Little Rock, Arkansas. Since at the time it was difficult to convert Brazilian *cruzeiros* into U.S. dollars, we decided to lease rather than sell our house in the Chacara Flora until conditions changed. We had no problem in leasing it to a Ford executive. We packed our belongings for the ocean voyage, but before leaving Brazil, we made stops in Salvador, Recife, and Manaus to give our children the opportunity to visit these beautiful and colorful northern cities and their surrounding areas.

Upon arrival in Little Rock we stayed at the Hilton Hotel while we looked for a home, which, due to the size of our family needed to be fairly large. After several weeks, we found a beautiful and spacious house that overlooked the Arkansas River, with the added attractions of a swimming pool and tennis court. Since it was located on the same street and about ten houses away from my brother Dante and his family, we made certain they were pleased having us live near them, and they were, so we purchased the home. My aunt Rena Jacuzzi, who moved to Little Rock after her husband, Uncle Joseph, died on January 5, 1965, and her son Aldo and his family also lived on our street.

Though our family visited the United States over the years, returning home was somewhat of a culture shock for all of us. We missed our life in Brazil and our circle of friends. While America offered more conveniences than we had in São Paulo, life in the USA was much faster paced and less friendly. The transition was less difficult and hectic for me than for Paula, since she had to set up our household and mother our children.

Our daughters all attended Hendrix College in Conway, Arkansas, and enjoyed their school, but it was a different story for our two youngest sons, Matthew and Paulo, who were fifteen and eleven years old, respectively, at the time. They both missed their friends and school in São Paulo. We placed Paulo in a parochial grade school and Matt in the all-boys Catholic High School, from which they both graduated. Matt, who is very musically inclined, played in the school band, but not in the sports that he had played in São Paulo. Paulo, who is very outgoing, was one of the school cheerleaders. Looking back, I wish I had worked harder to make the transition easier for them. They probably were thinking our life in Little Rock would be more like California, where we spent most of our summer home leaves.

Jacuzzi, Inc.

The new owner, Walter Kidde, Inc., had reorganized Jacuzzi Brothers, Inc., into several subsidiaries, with all reporting to the parent, Jacuzzi, Inc. Jacuzzi Brothers Division in Little Rock was the largest of the subsidiaries and was primarily a manufacturer of water pumps, swimming pool equipment, marine jet propulsion units, air compressors, and gas barbecue grills. Another U.S. division, Jacuzzi Whirlpool Bath, in Walnut Creek, California, produced the whirlpool baths and spas. All foreign subsidiaries also reported to the corporate office Jacuzzi, Inc., located in a west Little Rock office building.

I found that working for Jacuzzi Brothers in Little Rock, now no longer a family business, just wasn't the same and I began to consider starting my own company. It seemed to me I had essentially built a profitable company in Brazil. If I could do it there, why not in America?

I resigned from Jacuzzi Brothers, effective the end of 1981, and took a few months to ponder my options. I was sure I wanted to start my own company, but I was not fully settled on what product or products I should manufacture, nor did I know where I should locate my new business. From my days in São Paulo, a city with a surrounding population of about 12 million, I had learned the advantages of starting up a business in a large city, where you can begin finding a customer base at the new company's door.

I gave serious consideration to Dallas, Texas, and went there on several scouting trips to check out possible manufacturing locations. However, we had only recently moved to Little Rock and really liked the area and our new home. It's a relatively small, but centrally located city and ideal for national distribution of product. It seemed to offer much of what we wanted and needed, both as a family and for a company, so we decided to stay there.

Jason International, Inc.

In May 1982, along with some family members, I founded Jason International, Inc., with my immediate family owning the majority of the company's shares.

Much thought went into naming our new company. Drawing on our heritage, we selected Jason International, Inc., a contraction of JAcuzzi<u>SON</u>, including "international" in our name to affirm that we intended to be global.

As I considered possible products to manufacture and market, water therapy devices seemed a natural choice, since, except for the period of my youthful ranch days, I had spent my entire working life in and around water products. From my earliest days with Jacuzzi Brothers, I worked with many different types of pumps and my work in sales sparked my interest in everything about how these pumps worked, and how they were designed, manufactured, and applied. It was this curiosity that brought me to back to Berkeley to get a second degree in Mechanical Engineering.

My career included work with domestic water systems, industrial and agricultural industry's water needs, with swimming pools and related equipment, and with marine jet and air compressors. Then, during my years in Brazil, I also developed an expertise in the development, manufacturing, and marketing of hydrotherapy bathing products for home use.

Relying on my knowledge and background in water products, and aware that the water pump industry was mature and very competitive, I decided water therapy spas would be Jason's initial products.

At the time of our incorporation, and while I was considering the best initial product choice, I was the only employee. My morning commute to work consisted of walking down to the basement of our home. Traffic was light!

My daughters Loretta and Gretchen; Richard Jacuzzi, one of my cousin Tullio's sons; Phil Adamo; my cousin Doris Tunesi Adamo's son; and Victor Jacuzzi, my cousin Aldo Jacuzzi's son joined me a few months later. Our first plant location was a rented facility off Colonel Glenn Road in southwest Little Rock. We bought office furniture and production equipment, and started production in September 1982, when our first Jason Spa was built. We introduced our spa product line that fall at the National Swimming Pool and Spa Institute show in Dallas.

Shortly afterward, my daughter Jennifer, with a degree in Accounting, and my son Remo V., with a degree in Mechanical Engineering, joined our company. During the summer school vacation months, my sons Matthew and Paulo, along with some of their school-age cousins, worked for us as well.

Behind every Jason Spa stands a Jacuzzi. I wish I could put my name on it.

One of Jason International's first trade ads was an advertisement of a picture of me that was titled "Behind every Jason Spa stands a Jacuzzi. I wish I could put my name on it." This advertisement, which appeared in a number of trade journals, was widely acclaimed for introducing our new company. It made our Jacuzzi background clear; it also made clear the fact that we were not affiliated with the original Jacuzzi Brothers,

Inc. It helped thrust Jason International into the marketplace and is remembered still. Several years later we introduced a special Signature Series of whirlpool baths that was identified with a Jason logo, reflecting "Signature Series," with my signature in script.

We were cautious in all of our advertisements not to infringe upon the original Jacuzzi Brothers name, and when any question arose, we always consulted with legal counsel. Nonetheless, in early 1991, we received a series of letters from Jacuzzi Whirlpool Bath, whose then-president was Roy Jacuzzi, claiming that we improperly used and infringed on the Jacuzzi name, and to cease and desist. After several exchanges of letters between our companies that were not resolving the issue, it was decided that we should file suit in Arkansas against Jacuzzi, claiming our rights to use Jason's founder's name as we had, that the Jacuzzi name was generic, and that Roy Jacuzzi was misrepresenting Jacuzzi's history in making various claims that he was the inventor of the modern-day whirlpool bath system for the home.

Soon after the filing, on December 29, 1992, I received a telephone call from Roy asking that we settle the lawsuit between our companies, which we did. The terms of our Settlement Agreement set out certain nondisclosure obligations which required that we not divulge the specific terms of our 1992 settlement. It is, nevertheless, obvious from Jason's advertising since our settlement that we agreed on how Jason could use our Jacuzzi name in our advertisements and logos. Further, our Joint Stipulation and Order of Dismissal stated that the Jacuzzi name was not generic.

We agreed to settle leaving the question of Roy's role in the development of the modern Jacuzzi bath line open and dismissed the cause of action "without prejudice," meaning it was left undecided and that the issue could be reopened at a future date. Though the question of Roy's role in the development of the modern Jacuzzi bath line was left unresolved, we thought he would desist from his claims, but he did not, to the continuing dismay of the Jacuzzi family. However, with much work ahead in developing our Jason International company, we never felt it worthwhile to pursue the matter.

Re-writing of Jacuzzi Whirlpool Bath History

Soon after Walter Kidde, Inc., acquired Jacuzzi Brothers, Inc., in 1979, they reorganized its various entities. Roy Jacuzzi, a grandson of Uncle Joseph Jacuzzi, was named president of the Jacuzzi Whirlpool Bath Division, where he had been working a few years under Pete Kosta, Candido's son-in-law. Pete Kosta had been earlier terminated from his management position at Jacuzzi Research when revelations of improprieties surfaced. The name Jacuzzi Research, Inc., used for the company's whirlpool subsidiary, was subsequently changed to Jacuzzi Whirlpool, Inc.

Several years after Roy became the company's president, the Jacuzzi Whirlpool Bath division started a marketing campaign crediting him as the inventor of modern whirlpool bathing for the home, much to the consternation of most of the Jacuzzi family. While Roy is rightly credited for several patents, much of the legend he is given credit for is fabricated marketing hype.

It is somewhat comical to read some of this reconstructed history such as Roy selling whirlpool baths in his early days with the company out of the back of a pickup truck. The basis of this story was taken from true Jacuzzi Brothers history, but the real version was the story of Candido Jacuzzi selling injector pumps out of a pickup truck in the 1920s.

Roy takes much credit for being the inventor of modern built-in whirlpool baths for the home, while in fact Jacuzzi's much earlier J-500 and J-600 baths were also built-in. While he did introduce the Roman whirlpool bath, for which he had a patent, it included the old technology of drawing the water into the recirculating pump through the bath drain opening rather than using Candido Jacuzzi's earlier patented design principle and of the even earlier Family Spa, both of which utilized a plumbing system that is now universally employed.

Growth

Since Jason's founding almost twenty-five years ago and the production of our first hydrotherapy spa, we have become a comprehensive producer of a large line of hydrotherapy products. This includes whirlpool baths that we ship throughout the United States and to many international markets, including the Southeast Asia territory that we recently established with a product launch.

Since our inception our company has stressed innovation and the premise that "success is the detail" of what we do. This emphasis, along with our concentration on design, quality, and customer service, has served us well, and we have enjoyed steady, profitable growth.

In 1989, we bought a larger facility across the Arkansas River, on MacArthur Drive in North Little Rock, where we remain today. We made several plant additions and purchased adjoining property for future growth. We now have more than two hundred people working for us, including employees and sales agents.

Our products target the middle to high end of the market and, in keeping with our business goals, Jason hydrotherapy products are distinctive and are available with an assortment of options and in a number of sizes, shapes, and design styles. They are also ergonomically comfortable and known for their quiet design. As with many of Uncle Rachele's experiments, our Quiet Design™ feature resulted from perceiving a need and was accomplished by thinking through the problem, tinkering some, and testing a great deal.

The need was suggested by a Korean distributor, who felt our whirlpool baths were too noisy. At first we were surprised by his comment, but we knew noise level is an industry-wide concern, especially in marketplaces where many people live in close quarters, such as multistory apartment complexes.

I was reminded of the problems my father and uncles had with pump competitors in the late 1920s, when these companies attempted to undermine the new Jacuzzi pump by spreading unfounded rumors. It seems one of our competitors attempted to convince our Korean friend that Jason's whirlpools had a noise problem. Our distributor decided to run some tests, found the claim to be false, and apologized for his error. We also lab tested our baths against competition models and found ours to be among the quietest.

However, this incident made me think more about noise prevention and abatement. I was determined to lead the way in finding a solution, which we did with our engineering staff. Now our trademarked Quiet Design™ is a key component of all our bath products.

We produced other industry "firsts." In 1999, we were the first manufacturer in the United States to produce an air bath, which we designate as the AirMasseur™. These therapy baths use heated air bubbles that are released from the bottom radius of the bath, providing a gentle, full body massage.

In 2001, we were one of the first in the nation to introduce the combination Air-Whirlpool therapy baths. These offer the option of either air therapy, which provides a gentle massage of the outer body, or whirlpool jet therapy needed for deep tissue massage of sore muscles, and bruises, or a combination of the two.

There are certainly whirlpool bath brands that are less expensive than ours, but our hallmark is quality and quality costs a little more. Many manufacturers please a customer for ninety days, but our goal is to provide a product that our consumers will enjoy for a lifetime. More information on our company can be reviewed on our www.jasoninternational.com website.

I am very proud that three of my children, Remo V., Jennifer Jacuzzi Peregrin, and Paulo, today work alongside me at our plant. Remo serves as vice president of manufacturing. He has a B.S. degree in Mechanical Engineering from the University of Arkansas at Fayetteville. Jennifer is our vice president of operations and has a B.S. in Business Administration and Economics from Hendrix College in Conway, Arkansas. My son Paulo, who has a B.S. in Business Administration from the University of Arkansas at Little Rock recently returned to work for us as a sales manager. He had gained valuable marketing and management experience by working several years in Dallas as the admissions director for a treatment facility.

We also are pleased that my nephew Dante Jacuzzi II, my brother's son, with a B.S. in Business from the University of Missouri at Columbia, serves as our business development manager.

Brazil Revisited

Since returning to the United States in 1980, Paula and I, our children, and their spouses and two of our grandchildren have had the good fortune to visit São Paulo and Rio de Janeiro several times together. We returned three separate times for a week or so visit during the Christmas to New Year periods in 1983, 1985, and 1987, when it was winter at home but summer in Brazil. We rented homes with pools during these visits from Americans who were spending this time for their own visits to their families in the USA.

These were wonderful and memorable family get-togethers, when time was spent with Brazilian friends, sightseeing, taking trips to the beach, and just relaxing. At the time of our last family trip to Brazil in 1987, three of our children, Remo V., Jennifer, and Loretta were married. Our first two grandchildren, Nina born to Remo V. and his wife, Lynn, and Jacqueline born to Jennifer and her husband, Dan Peregrin, also accompanied us on this trip. Our home in Chacara Flora was not leased during the time of our visit so it gave our family the opportunity to visit it for what turned out to be the last time. We still reminisce about these trips and would like to return, but today the logistics would be more difficult with five of our children married, fourteen grandchildren, and some grandchildren in college.

When we left São Paulo in 1980, we left the responsibility of leasing our home with a friend who very capably handled our affairs. We used the lease income to fund our wonderful family trips to Brazil. While we never had a problem in leasing our home, in 1988 we decided to sell it when it became too difficult to manage our affairs there from so far away. In 1988, I took a rather pensive trip to São Paulo to handle its sale to the Mercedes Benz Company for their executive housing. Our thoughts of possibly returning to live in our São Paulo home were not to be.

While we still owned the home there, we maintained our Brazilian residency as well as a banking account and safety deposit box there. Interestingly, when I closed the account and attempted to open the box, I found it was rusted shut thanks to its lack of use and the high humidity of São Paulo. A specialist was brought in to open it. In addition to our family trips to São Paulo, Paula and I also returned to Brazil several times to visit friends and for business.

Brazilian Relatives

When we initially moved to Brazil, my mother told me that she had an uncle, her father's brother, who moved to Brazil with his family around 1900 but that her family, due to lack of communication, lost track of them.

Therefore, while living and traveling in Brazil I searched without success, in phone books and other directories for anyone living there with my mother's maiden name, Piucco. However, on one visit to my mother's family in Soffranco, Italy, I was told that a young man named Rogue Piuco from Brazil came to Soffranco looking for his roots. It turned out that his great-grandfather Valentin Piucco, born in the same house in Soffranco as my mother, was my long-lost mother's uncle. His family name, however, was incorrectly transcribed upon arrival in Brazil, without the second c, so it became Piuco.

Rogue, who was working in Milan, came to meet us in Soffranco during our visit the following year. He was a nice young man and I made the necessary legal arrangements for him to work for Jason International as a trainee for a one-year period, which we extended for a second year. I then tried to legally sponsor him to become a U.S. resident but was not successful. This was very disappointing seeing how many illegal immigrants eventually gain residency. After he returned to Brazil, Paula and I traveled to meet him and his family in Rio Grande del Sul. We were amazed at the family resemblance between my family and his. Rogue and his wife, Sandra, now live near Recife in northern Brazil with their young child.

Pa's Legacy

Just as we watch the professionalism and talent Remo V., Jennifer, and Paulo bring to work every day, Paula and I are delighted to know our other children lead productive and fulfilling lives in their various endeavors and that our fourteen grandchildren are growing up in their footsteps.

Remo V. and his wife, Lynn, have three children, Nina now in college at the University of Arkansas at Little Rock, Remo Alexander "Alex," and Emily. Jennifer and her husband, Daniel Peregrin, have four children. Their two oldest children, Jacqueline and Daniel O., are both studying at Rollins College in Winter Park, Florida, and their younger daughters are Madison and Anastasia. Paulo and his wife, Jennifer, also live in Little Rock and have a teenage daughter, Mallory.

Loretta and her husband, Rev. Scott Stewart, pastor a nondenominational evangelical church they founded in Stirling, Scotland. They have three children, a son Ethan, daughter McKenzie, and their son Seth, who is now attending Oklahoma Christian University. Gretchen and her husband, Dr. Tyson Roe, D.D.S., and their children Addison, Asher, and Hannah live in Raleigh, North Carolina. Our son, Matthew, lives and works in Little Rock.

Jacuzzi family reunion, December 28, 1949, Bellini's Restaurant, Oakland, CA

Jacuzzi family reunion, August 16, 1958, Colombo Club, Oakland, CA

Jacuzzi family reunion, September 6, 2003, Cline Cellars, Sonoma, CA

Epilogue

"Scrivendo questo libro, divenni il co-ordinatore di memorie."
"As I wrote this book, I became the coordinator of remembrances."
—Remo Jacuzzi

The early 1980s were a time of tremendous change for me and for my family. We returned to the United States and made Little Rock our home. After leading the nonfamily version of Jacuzzi Brothers, for several years, I left to begin my own company. Since its inception, Jason International certainly consumed most of my waking hours, but family continued to be most important.

I talked with many family members as I gathered research for this book. I knew that their memories, their interpretations, and their written records would all be critical to my telling of what is really their story. All of them were deeply interested in my telling the Jacuzzi story as accurately and as fairly as I possibly could. Many of my closest family members now have passed away. Each one of them played an important role in the Jacuzzi family's saga.

Certainly, the spirit and memory of my father and my mother inspired me to complete this project.

Giuseppina and the Ranch

A day of enormous sorrow occurred on February 2, 1984, when my mother, Giuseppina, died. She was eighty-five and revered by both her immediate and the greater Jacuzzi family. Ma had suffered from some health problems in her later years, although she continued to live at our ranch, where she spent most of her life. Though she was diagnosed as having "hardening of the arteries," we now believe she suffered from Alzheimer's disease.

In the last years of Ma's life, Thelma Lund was her caregiver and a godsend. My sister, Jaconda Jacuzzi Hawkins, learned of Thelma's availability and secured her services for Ma. Thelma was a religious person who loved my mother and family. She also greatly enjoyed living at the ranch with Ma. Without Thelma, and another caregiver, Maria, who also assisted Ma in the last years of her life, it would have been difficult for my mother to spend her later years at her beloved ranch home. Ma lived for eleven years after Pa died and, with the help of Thelma and Maria, she spent most of this time at the ranch.

Inez Marchetti, my mother's close friend, summed up in a sympathy note how we all felt when Ma passed away:

> I know we are never ready for the departure of our dear ones, but I am sure all of you will find comfort in the thought that something of her will always be with you. The wisdom and the love she gave all of you will never fade away.

Today, our family ranch home and surrounding gardens, where my parents taught their children so much about the simple joy and satisfaction found in hard work, are still basically the same. It is, of course, filled with memories of all the times shared there with family and friends. As Mrs. Marchetti said, the wisdom and love our mother gave to us can never fade away.

Six years after Ma's passing, our sister, Flora Jacuzzi Nicoletti, died of leukemia on February 6, 1990, at the age of fifty-nine. Although Flora lived in Canada, Paula and I and our children stayed in regular touch with her, and we felt very close to her, her husband, Joe, and their children. Flora was a very joyful, happy, kindhearted, and devout person— a role model for all of us. Sadly, Flora's son, Joseph, or Joey, died two months after his mother's death, due to heart problems, on April 8, 1990. Joey left a wife and three young sons.

Two years later, in October 1992, since my brothers and sisters and I were living away from northern California, we felt the need to reunite the Bay Area Jacuzzi family at our ranch home. So, together with our spouses, we sponsored a lively Jacuzzi family reunion at the ranch. This included many of our immediate family, plus cousins and our surviving aunts and uncles. With almost one hundred of us in attendance, we had a grand time catching up on recent developments and remembering old times.

One topic we discussed was the eventual development of our ranch property for home sites and related infrastructures. This development of the site had been in the making since the 1980s when my family engaged Richard Loewke, a land planner, to represent us in the local land use planning process.

In 1994, Paula and I, along with three of my sisters and their spouses, bought the ownership that my other siblings held in the ranch, as the latter group wanted to liquidate their ownership. When we made this purchase, we divided the property into two parcels. The first we designated the Delizia Ranch, which consisted of approximately ten acres zoned for commercial use. This property included the ranch home and all improvements. The name Delizia Ranch was chosen in honor of the name my father called our original ranch property. The approximately 150-acre balance, designated as Rolling Hills Ranch, was zoned for residential development.

In 1995, we donated approximately thirty acres of the Rolling Hills Ranch's choicest hilltops to the city of Antioch for an open space in memory of our mother and father. This parcel of connected knolls is called the Valeriano and Giuseppina Jacuzzi Knolls Open Space. It offers a sweeping view of the San Joaquin River, portions of Mount Diablo, Oakley, Brentwood, and Antioch, and on a clear day, a visitor to the hilltops can see the Sierra Nevada range.

Two years after this public space was created in honor of our parents, my family suffered another sad loss. My brother Dante died at age seventy-six on May 17, 1997—also the birthday of his wife, Rosalyn. He succumbed to heart failure after a series of coronary surgeries.

Dante and Rosalyn made their home near us in Little Rock, where Rosalyn still resides. Dante was a patient, kindhearted, smart businessman. He experienced an impressive career, having served as a Navy pilot during World War II, and, later, as the general manager of the Jacuzzi Brothers' St. Louis plant, which was instrumental in greatly expanding the sales of Jacuzzi products in the central and eastern part of the United Sates. Dante became the company's executive vice-president in charge of Sales and Marketing after Jacuzzi Brothers consolidated its major manufacturing operations in Little Rock.

On Saturday, July 28, 2001, approximately 145 of the 240 descendants of Valeriano and Giuseppina Jacuzzi gathered at the Delizia Ranch. Although Ma, Pa, Flora and Dante, as well as my brothers-in-law, Jim Cline and Bob Hawkins, and three nephews were no longer with us, their spirits were present at our weekend reunion.

A special Mass in honor of my parents was said at our family's long-time church, St. Anthony's Catholic Church in Oakley. We made a commemorative donation to the capital campaign for the church's new youth center. Afterwards, we all visited the Holy Cross Cemetery in Antioch for a special floral tribute and memorial service. We returned to the ranch for lunch, a day of Italian music, reminiscing, partying, games, wine tasting, and also dinner. While the main reunion day was on July 28, most of the participants gathered for a prereunion reception at St. Anthony's Church Hall on Friday evening and a further day of visiting and final good-byes at the ranch on Sunday.

My brother Virgil greatly anticipated and enjoyed this family reunion. Unfortunately, we lost both Virgil and his wife, Beulah, shortly afterwards. Beulah passed away in September 2002, and Virgil died in April 2003.

Virgil was sixteen years my senior, and like my other older brother, Dante, he was a major influence in my life. Since we both became engineers, we were bonded by our fascination with how everything in the world worked. Virgil shared my interest in the Jacuzzi family's history, and his thoughts and memories were vital contributions to the telling of our tale.

With the inevitable development of our ranch property into a residential neighborhood, we sold the residentially zoned Rolling Hills Ranch portion, on October 1, 2002.

This was a moment of sadness, since most of the farmland that meant so much to our family was now gone. However, we were relieved, not only because the sales price was fair, but the burden of planning for the land use was now lifted. I regretted, though, that my brothers and sisters, who sold their land portions in 1994, did not wait a few more years to sell, so they and their families could have realized some of the property's appreciation in value since the mid-1990s. I used my share of the sale to buy a farm in central Arkansas, where I hope someday to build a home. I want my grandchildren—and hopefully even their children—to visit and learn about life spent on the land. As a start on my development of this Arkansas farm, I plan to install a windmill that once pumped water on our California ranch.

During the summer of 2005 the California State Highway 4 By-Pass Authority began construction of an extension of their new four-lane highway that will cut diagonally across the northeast corner of our Delizia Ranch property. Scheduled for completion by the end of 2007, this project has cut off utility and road access to our ranch home and when completed will pass within fifty yards from the main house. Since our loss of access, we made valiant attempts to secure our family home and yards with security fencing and electrical generators, but nevertheless our property was broken into, vandalized, and robbed several times.

In August 2006, the owners of Delizia Ranch LLC resolved, through a mediated settlement, an eminent domain litigation process with the Highway By-Pass Authority regarding the valuation of the land being acquired for the highway.

Yes, as my father would often say, "Nothing lasts forever." We are thankful for the many years we had to enjoy our family ranch and for the many wonderful memories we take with us. A special thanks is extended to Juan Ramos, our loyal employee and friend since he first came to work for us in the 1950s, for helping maintain our ranch property over the years.

Jacuzzi, Inc.

Since the 1979 sale the original Jacuzzi Brothers, Inc., has undergone enormous changes under several different owners. Kidde, Inc., the conglomerate that originally purchased Jacuzzi Brothers, was itself acquired in 1987, by Hansen PLC Trust, a British mega-company. In 1995, Hansen PLC Trust formed a separate, publicly traded company, U.S. Industries, as owner of its North American companies. Most recently in 2004, U.S. Industries, after selling a number of its companies, reorganized itself as Jacuzzi Brands, a publicly traded company on the New York Stock Exchange. Jacuzzi Brands is owner of the

SPIRIT, WIND & WATER

worldwide Jacuzzi, Inc., operation and other, principally plumbing-related companies.

The current product lines of the Jacuzzi company are very different from those produced by the family company at the time of its sale. Through the years, the marine jet, gas grill, swimming pool, as well as all injector, centrifugal, turbine, and submersible pump lines were sold to other companies. However, the Jacuzzi company remains one of the world's most recognized manufacturers of whirlpool baths and therapy spas.

Our Jacuzzi Entrepreneurial Spirit

I'm proud that even though the company started by the Jacuzzi brothers is no longer in the family, a number of descendants of the original Jacuzzi brothers and sisters have kept up the entrepreneurial spirit by starting their own businesses.

Within my father Valeriano's branch of the family, Paul Jacuzzi, my brother Virgil's son, owns and operates WATERITE Technologies, Inc., a company in Winnipeg, Manitoba, Canada. Pat Hawkins, a son of my sister Jaconda, is a partner in the sales representative firm, Hawkins and Janke of Minneapolis, Minnesota, which was started by his father. Pat also developed and patented a product line that he produces and sells under the name of Pipe Pier™Support Systems.

Shawn-Ian Bruce, the son of my sister Rachel, is an established designer with an excellent reputation. Shawn designs and manufactures postmodern furniture. Although he is relatively young, he is widely acclaimed and has shown his furniture in design shows in many countries. Additionally, he has been featured in museums and galleries internationally. Shawn is currently designing some bath products for Jason International.

In addition to the wineries owned by my sister Mary's sons, Fred and Matthew Cline, their brother Mike Cline owns a landscaping business. Fred is also building a farm animal petting zoo on one of his produce farms. This will have a display of old farm equipment, so "city kids" can experience farm life close up. We gave him many of our antique Jacuzzi ranch implements and pieces of equipment to use in this enterprise.

Examples of Jacuzzi entrepreneurial spirit abound in the other branches of the original Jacuzzi family, including the founding of manufacturing and construction companies, real estate businesses, and automobile dealerships. Other members have become physicians, teachers, attorneys, or have entered other professional careers.

Jacuzzi Family Reunion

The latest reunion of the Jacuzzi family, a very large one indeed, including descendants of all thirteen original brothers and sisters, was held on September 6, 2003, at the Cline Cellars winery in Sonoma, California. At that time, we counted almost 700 living descendants and their spouses, with approximately 350 of us in attendance.

It was a beautifully sunny day in Sonoma and the grounds of Cline Cellars winery were immaculate for the reunion. The day was filled with visiting among relatives, many of whom had not seen one another for some years, and with talks given by representatives of all thirteen families. The last surviving members of the original Jacuzzi siblings, Aunt Stella and Aunt Gilia, had prime spots on the program.

The day was capped off with a joyful dinner under tents decorated with green, white, and red Italian flags and white chrysanthemums. Excellent Cline Cellars and Trinitas wine, provided by Fred and Matthew Cline, flowed freely.

During the 2003 reunion, Fred Cline shared his plans to build a second winery and olive oil operation in Sonoma. As he showed artist's renderings, Fred announced the new venture's name—the Jacuzzi Family Vineyards.

Today the Jacuzzi Family Vineyards' beautiful two-story wine tasting and winery building is under construction and is scheduled to be completed in the spring of 2007. The building features Italian country villa architecture with a stone façade, terra-cotta roof tiles imported from northern Italy, as well as design elements of the Jacuzzi family ancestral home in San Vito al Tagliamento. Plans are being made to hold a combination Jacuzzi Family Vineyards dedication of its new facility along with another Jacuzzi family reunion commemorating the one-hundred-year anniversary of my father and Uncle Frank's immigration to the United States in 1907.

Blessings and Curses

Over the years I often wondered why the Jacuzzi family enjoyed the success that life had brought us. Certainly we have had our share of tragedy, sorrow, and shortcomings, but overall, we have enjoyed many successes and victories along with times of prosperity. Since turning to spiritual matters at the time of my son Remo V.'s automobile accident in Brazil, I have studied and also reread the Holy Bible a number of times, and I have observed that as promised in scripture there are consequences for the way one leads his or her life. On the other hand, children whose parents are ungodly and lead dishonest, unfaithful lives most often follow the same pathway.

After studying the scriptures and observing life, I had a feeling that my grandparents Giovanni and Teresa must have been God-fearing people to have had a family with many more successes, victories, and healthy lives than many others. This belief was overwhelmingly strengthened by my aunts Cirilla, Stella, and Gilia when I interviewed them. They told me that my grandmother Teresa, who was especially devout, was raised in a religious home with a grandfather who led daily prayer and that she herself was a dedicated Christian and for a time wanted to be a nun. She also taught her own children right from wrong and the need to stay close to God. While some of her children strayed from this teaching and suffered the consequences, most held to these truths.

Spirit, Wind & Water

When I started to work for Jacuzzi Brothers in the 1950s, I wanted to learn the business from the ground up. My first job was masking pumps before they were painted with their "Jacuzzi Blue" paint. From there I worked in every production department, which gave me the opportunity to learn not only how each product was made, but just as importantly, it gave me the opportunity to get to know the people who worked for us, to learn how they lived and what was important in their lives.

I believe, due to the influence and teachings of my parents, my grandparents, and my extended family, I have been privileged to observe and learn about many things in life, again, often from the ground up. I was taught to have a keen eye, a questioning mind, a sensitive ear, and, I trust, a caring heart.

Although my many hundreds of Jacuzzi relatives now live all over the world, and physical reunions are not as easily organized, nor as frequent as they used to be, we forever will all be bound by spirit, wind and water. The same glorious stars and moon that grandparents Giovanni and Teresa used to inspire the earliest dreams of Uncle Rachele, my father, and their brothers and sisters still illuminate our sky, no matter where we may live.

I still follow those stars. I am blessed to be a Jacuzzi.

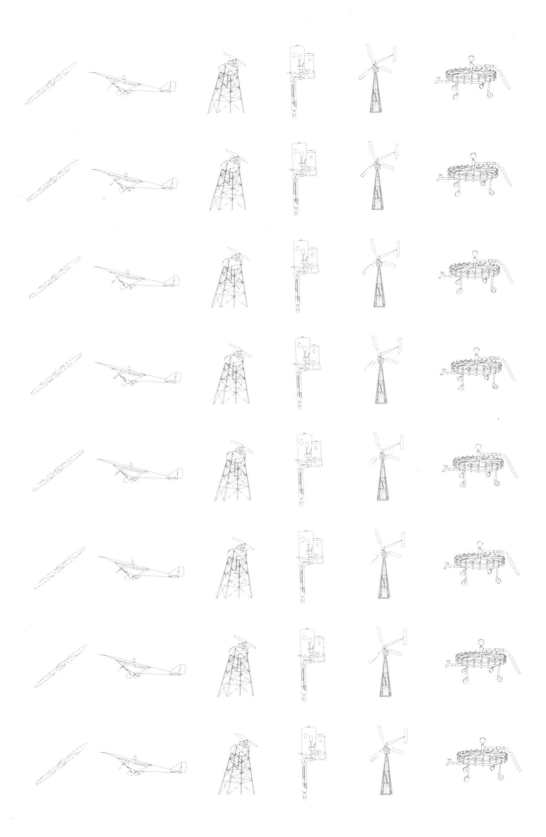